E-Privacy and Online
Data Protection

E-Privacy and Online Data Protection

Peter Carey LLB, LLM

Solicitor, Charles Russell

Precedents by Eduardo Ustaran of Berwin Leighton Paisner

Butterworths
LexisNexis™

Members of the LexisNexis Group worldwide

United Kingdom	Butterworths Tolley, a Division of Reed Elsevier (UK) Ltd, Halsbury House, 35 Chancery Lane, LONDON, WC2A 1EL, and 4 Hill Street, EDINBURGH EH2 3JZ
Argentina	Abeledo Perrot, Jurisprudencia Argentina and Depalma, BUENOS AIRES
Australia	Butterworths, a Division of Reed International Books Australia Pty Ltd, CHATSWOOD, New South Wales
Austria	ARD Betriebsdienst and Verlag Orac, VIENNA
Canada	Butterworths Canada Ltd, MARKHAM, Ontario
Chile	Publitecsa and Conosur Ltda, SANTIAGO DE CHILE
Czech Republic	Orac sro, PRAGUE
France	Editions du Juris-Classeur SA, PARIS
Hong Kong	Butterworths Asia (Hong Kong), HONG KONG
Hungary	Hvg Orac, BUDAPEST
India	Butterworths India, NEW DELHI
Ireland	Butterworths (Ireland) Ltd, DUBLIN
Italy	Giuffré, MILAN
Malaysia	Malayan Law Journal Sdn Bhd, KUALA LUMPUR
New Zealand	NexisLexis Butterworths, WELLINGTON
Poland	Wydawnictwa Prawnicze PWN, WARSAW
Singapore	Butterworths Asia, SINGAPORE
South Africa	Butterworths Publishers (Pty) Ltd, DURBAN
Switzerland	Stämpfli Verlag AG, BERNE
USA	LexisNexis, DAYTON, Ohio

A CIP Catalogue record for this book is available from the British Library.

ISBN 0 406 94588 8

Typeset by Doyle & Co, Colchester
Printed and bound in Great Britain by The Cromwell Press, Trowbridge, Wilts

Visit Butterworths LexisNexis *direct* at www.butterworths.com

Preface

This book is a specialist work for practitioners, particularly those who advise e-commerce businesses. It should be stated, at the outset, that this book does not seek to inform its readers about the entire range of legal considerations relating to the electronic communications by businesses with individuals. Rather, it is confined to those aspects of such communication that have an impact on the privacy rights of individuals. Nor does the book deal generally with communications by telephone – despite the fact that many online transactions can seem as if they use the telephone, the distinction is that such transactions merely use telephone lines rather than telephone apparatus per se. Further, this work is not concerned with the media, in the general sense of that word – press freedom and the wealth of 'privacy law' generated by disputes concerning media intrusions into private lives is beyond the scope of this book.

I would like to first thank my friend and colleague, Eduardo Ustaran of Berwin Leighton Paisner. Not only has he provided a set of excellent precedents (set out at the back of this book and on the accompanying CD-ROM); he has also been centrally involved in every step of its production. I am indebted to him for his patience and expertise.

Thanks are also due to Cindy Burnes of Privacy & Data Protection, for her invaluable advice on United States privacy law and the Safe Harbor Privacy Principles; to Gabriella Wright, of Charles Russell, for her advice on data protection in the field of employment law; and to Jo Sanders, for her incredible attention to detail in legal research, advising on content and providing other assistance.

Peter Carey
May 2002

Contents

Contents

Glossary

Automated decision   A decision taken by or on behalf of a data controller which significantly affects that individual and which is based solely on the processing by automatic means of personal data in respect of which that individual is the data subject for the purpose of evaluating matters relating to him such as, for example, his performance at work, his creditworthiness, his reliability or his conduct.

Banner advertisement   A combination of text and graphics taking up a section of a web page that promotes a product or service and, usually, incorporates a link to that product or service.

Billing data   *Data that comprise information in respect of all or any of the following matters:*

(a)   the number or other identification of the subscriber's station;

(b)   the subscriber's address and the type of the station;

(c)   the total number of units of use by reference to which the sum payable in respect of any accounting period is calculated;

(d)   the type, date, starting time and duration of calls and the volume of data transmissions in respect of which sums are payable by the subscriber and the numbers or other identification of the stations to which they were made;

(e)   the date of the provision of any service not falling within sub-paragraph (d); and

(f)   other matters concerning payments including, in particular, advance payments, payments by instalments, reminders and disconnections.

(The Telecommunications (Data Protection and Privacy) Regulations 1999, SI 1999/2093, Schedule 1.)

Browser   Software that allows the user to view websites; common examples are Microsoft's Internet Explorer and Netscape's Navigator.

Communications data — *Means any of the following:*

(a) *any traffic data comprised in or attached to a communication (whether by the sender or otherwise) for the purposes of any postal service or telecommunications system by means of which it is being or may be transmitted;*

(b) *any information which includes none of the contents of a communication (apart from any information falling within paragraph (a)) and is about the use made by any person—*

    (i) *of any postal service or telecommunications service; or*

    (ii) *in connection with the provision to or use by any person of any telecommunications service, of any part of a telecommunications system;*

(c) *any information not falling within paragraph (a) or (b) that is held or obtained, in relation to persons to whom he provides the service, by a person providing a postal service or telecommunications service.*

(Regulation of Investigatory Powers Act 2000, section 21(4).)

Cookie — A text file placed on the hard drive of the user's computer by the operators of websites. Usually used for saving settings on the user's system and for sending those settings back to the server that originally created them, thus allowing a website to 'recognise' a revisiting user. Cookies may be temporary (session) or permanent. Temporary cookies are used to pass information between web pages in a single visit (for example, for use with an online shopping cart) and the user's browser will delete temporary cookies when it is shut down. Permanent cookies are stored on the user's hard drive for a finite period, commonly one year, and can be used to save a user's personal choices and preferences between visits. More controversially, cookies can be used to transmit information about a user's activities online to the website that placed the cookie on the user's hard drive – profiles on surfing habits can thus be accumulated for marketing purposes.

Data — *Information which—*

(a) *is being processed by means of equipment operating automatically in response to instructions given for that purpose,*

(b) *is recorded with the intention that it should be processed by means of such equipment,*

(c) *is recorded as part of a relevant filing system or with the intention that it should form part of a relevant filing system,*

(d) *does not fall within paragraph (a), (b) or (c) but forms part of a accessible record, or*

(e) *is recorded information held by a public authority and does not fall within any of paragraphs (a) to (d).*

(Data Protection Act 1998, section 1(1).)

Glossary

Data controller   *A person who (either alone or jointly or in common with other persons) determines the purposes for which and the manner in which any personal data are, or are to be, processed.*

(Data Protection Act 1998, section 1(1).)

Data matching   The electronic comparison of two or more sets of personal information which have been collected for separate purposes, in order to identify any information which is inconsistent or overlapping. Some jurisdictions seek to restrict the use of data matching technologies – see, for example, the Australian Data Matching Program (Assistance and Tax) Act 1990.

Data mining   The use of automated tools to examine and analyse data that have been stored in a database in order to find new, previously unknown relationships.

Data processor   *Any person (other than an employee of the data controller) who processes personal data on behalf of the data controller.*

(Data Protection Act 1998, section 1(1).)

Data Protection Principles

1. *Personal data shall be processed fairly and lawfully and, in particular, shall not be processed unless—*

   (a) *at least one of a set of the conditions in Schedule 2 is met, and*

   (b) *in the case of sensitive personal data, at least one of the conditions in Schedule 3 is also met.*

2. *Personal data shall be obtained only for one or more specified and lawful purposes, and shall not be further processed in any manner incompatible with that purpose or those purposes.*

3. *Personal data shall be adequate, relevant and not excessive in relation to the purpose or purposes for which they are processed.*

4. *Personal data processed shall be accurate and, where necessary, kept up to date.*

5. *Personal data processed for any purpose or purposes shall not be kept for longer than is necessary for that purpose or those purposes.*

6. *Personal data shall be processed in accordance with the rights of data subjects under this Act.*

7. *Appropriate technical and organisational measures shall be taken against unauthorised or unlawful processing of personal data and against accidental loss or destruction of, or damage to, personal data.*

8. *Personal data shall not be transferred to a country or territory outside the European Economic Areas unless that country or territory ensures an adequate level of protection for the rights and freedoms of data subjects in relation to the processing of personal data.*

(Data Protection Act 1998, Schedule 1.)

Data Subject	*An individual who is the subject of personal data.*
	(Data Protection Act 1998, section 1(1).)
Data warehousing	Copying and storing data specifically structured for querying and reporting – thus creating a historic database from an operational one. Information stored in data warehouses may be used for data mining.
Direct marketing	*The communication of any advertising or marketing material which is directed to particular individuals.*
	(Data Protection Act 1998, section 11(1).)
Distance contract	*Any contract concerning goods or services concluded between a supplier and a consumer under an organised distance sales or service provision scheme run by the supplier who, for the purpose of the contract, makes exclusive use of one or more means of distance communication up to and including the moment at which the contract is concluded.*
	(Consumer Protection (Distance Selling) Regulations 2000, SI 2000/2334, paragraph 3(1).)
European Economic Area	The 15 member states of the European Union, plus Iceland, Liechtenstein and Norway.
Encryption	The process by which information is encoded prior to some usage, for example, transmission over the Internet, with the intention that only a person using an appropriate key will be able to decrypt it.
E-signature	*Data in electronic form which are attached to or logically associated with other electronic data and which serve as a method of authentication*
	(The Electronic Signatures Regulations 2002, SI 2002/318.)
Information requirements	*Information that must be supplied to the data subject upon the first obtaining of that information by the data controller, consisting of:*
	(a) the identity of the data controller,
	(b) if he has nominated a representative for the purposes of this Act, the identity of that representative,
	(c) the purpose or purposes for which the data are intended to be processed, and
	(d) any further information which is necessary, having regard to the specific circumstances in which the data are or are to be processed, to enable processing in respect of the data subject to be fair.
	(Data Protection Act, Schedule 1, Part II, paragraph 2(3).)
Information Society Services	*Any service normally provided for remuneration, at a distance, by electronic means and at the individual request of a recipient of services.*
	(Council Directive 98/34/EC.)

iTV   Interactive television.

Location tracking   The technological capability to locate the geographical whereabouts of a mobile telephone, such an ability being an essential prerequisite to some m-commerce applications.

M-commerce   Electronic commerce using mobile cellular technology.

Means of distance communication   *Any means which, without the simultaneous physical presence of the supplier and the consumer, may be used for the conclusion of a contract between those parties.*

                                       (Consumer Protection (Distance Selling) Regulations 2000, SI 2000/2334, paragraph 3(1).)

Notification   The process by which data controllers register their personal data processing activities with the Office of the Information Commissioner.

Opt-in   A device used to obtain consent from an individual to a usage by an organisation of his data, usually consisting of a statement about the proposed uses for data and a box allowing the individual to indicate his consent by ticking.

Opt-out   A similar device to an opt-in, but incorporating a box that allows a user to object to certain proposed data usage.

P3P   'Platform for privacy preferences'. An industry standard providing an automated method for users to gain greater control over the use of their personal data online. P3P is a standard set of multiple-choice questions that cover most aspects of a websites' privacy policies. P3P websites make this information available to the user's computer in machine-readable format. A P3P-enabled browser can 'read' this information and compare it with the privacy preferences that have been set (if any) by the user. Users can then be informed of any proposed uses for their data that do not match their own preferences and make an informed choice.

Personal data   *Means data which relate to a living individual who can be identified—*

                                       (a)   from those data, or

                                       (b)   from those data and other information which is in the possession of, or likely to come into the possession of, the data controller,

                                       and includes any expressions of opinion about the individual.

                                       (Data Protection Act 1998, section 1(1).)

PET   'Privacy enhancing technology'. A coherent system of information and communications technologies that protects privacy by eliminating or reducing personal data or by preventing unnecessary and/or undesired processing of personal data.

Private telecommunications system	*Any telecommunication system which, without itself being a public telecommunication system, is a system in relation to which the following conditions are satisfied—*

(a)   it is attached, directly or indirectly and whether or not for the purposes of the communication in question, to a public telecommunication system; and

(b)   there is apparatus comprised in the system which is both located in the United Kingdom and used (with or without other apparatus) for making the attachment to the public telecommunication system.

(Regulation of Investigatory Powers Act 2000, section 2.)

Processing	*Obtaining, recording or holding the information or data or carrying out any operation or set of operations on the information or data, including—*

(a)   organisation, adaptation or alteration of the information or data,

(b)   retrieval, consultation or use of the information or data,

(c)   disclosure of the information or data by transmission, dissemination or otherwise making available, or

alignment, combination, blocking, erasure or destruction of the information or data.

(Data Protection Act 1998, section 1(1).)

Profiling	The use of various bits of information, possibly sourced separately, to build up a picture about a person, especially in relation to purchasing habits.

Public telecommunications network	*any transmission system, and any associated switching equipment and other resources, which (in either case) –*

(a)   permit the conveyance of signals between defined communication points by wire, by radio, by optical or by other electro-magnetic means, and

(b)   are used, in whole or in part, for the provision of publicly available telecommunications services.

(The Telecommunications (Data Protection and Privacy) Regulations 1999, SI 1999/2093, section 2.)

Public telecommunication system	*Any such parts of a telecommunication system by means of which any public telecommunications service is provided as are located in the United Kingdom.*

(Regulation of Investigatory Powers Act 2000, section 2.)

Relevant filing system	*Any set of information relating to individuals to the extent that, although the information is not processed by means of equipment operating automatically in response to instructions given for that purpose, the set is structured, either by reference to individuals or by reference to criteria relating to individuals, in such a way that specific information relating to a particular individual is readily accessible.*

(Data Protection Act 1998, section 1(1).)

Sensitive personal data

Those data that consist of information as to—

(a) the racial or ethnic origin of the data subject,

(b) his political opinions,

(c) his religious beliefs or other beliefs of a similar nature,

(d) whether he is a member of a trade union,

(e) his physical or mental health or condition,

(f) his sexual life,

(g) the commission or alleged commission by him of any offence, or

(h) any proceedings for any offence committed or alleged to have been committed by him, the disposal of any such proceedings or the sentence of any court in such proceedings.

(Data Protection Act 1998, section 2.)

SMS

'Short message service' or 'text message'. A messaging service available using mobile telephones and consisting of a maximum of 160 characters.

Spam

'junk' email, usually unsolicited.

Stealth viral marketing

Viral marketing which purports or appears to be from someone other than the provider of the product or service which is being marketed.

Telecommunications services

Services, the provision of which consists, in whole or in part, of the transmission and routing of signals on telecommunications networks, not being services by way of radio or television broadcasting.

(The Telecommunications (Data Protection and Privacy) Regulations 1999, SI 1999/2093, section 2.)

Traffic data

Means, in relation to any communication,

(a) any data identifying, or purporting to identify, any person, apparatus or location to or from which the communication is or may be transmitted,

(b) any data identifying or selecting, or purporting to identify or select, apparatus through which, or by means of which, the communication is or may be transmitted,

(c) any data comprising signals for the actuation of apparatus used for the purposes of a telecommunication system for effecting (in whole or in part) the transmission of any communication, and

(d) any data identifying the data or other data as data comprised in or attached to a particular communication.

(Regulation of Investigatory Powers Act 2000, section 21(6).)

URL

'Uniform resource locator'.

Viral marketing

The process of sending one or more emails that contain some form of marketing communication that is designed with the intention that the recipient of the communication will forward the communication to one or more third parties.

Webcast

The making available, to one or more persons simultaneously, of information such as moving pictures and sound transmitted via the Internet.

Table of legislation

Table of cases

1

Introduction to privacy law

1.1 ■ WHAT IS PRIVACY?

A satisfactory definition of 'privacy' is almost as elusive as a determination of whether the right exists in United Kingdom law. Privacy may be defined as 'a right to be let alone'.[1] More specifically, the European Convention on Human Rights and Fundamental Freedoms talks about 'respect for private and family life, home and correspondence'.[2]

Whatever the definition, it is probably true to say that, in the United Kingdom, there is no law of privacy as such. Instead, there are a number of legal provisions that outlaw certain types of behaviour that we might collectively describe as 'privacy protection'. Those legal provisions may be subdivided into aspects of the law that protect interests in the following categories:

- rights to the security and integrity of one's physical person;

- rights to security and integrity of one's home and possessions; and

- rights over one's personal information.

This book considers those rights in the latter category. It does so from the point of view of an e-commerce business or other organisation with a presence on-line.

---

1 See 'The End of Privacy' by Charles J Sykes, 1999.
2 Article 8.

1.2 ■ SIGNIFICANT PRIVACY CASE LAW

1.2.1 Introduction

There has been a variety of cases in English law that have been seized upon by privacy proponents as heralding the beginnings of a new law of privacy in the United Kingdom. The first was probably *Prince Albert v Strange*,[3] which concerned the alleged misuse of a catalogue of etchings by Queen Victoria and Prince Albert. The catalogue was claimed to be 'private' and an order was granted by the court preventing the defendant from publishing the catalogue. Although the decision was said to have been made to protect the Queen's 'privacy', the foundation of the judgment lay in the property right in the etchings. In the *Duchess of Argyll*[4] case, it was held that communications passing between a husband and wife were subject to an obligation of confidence – the Duchess obtained an injunction preventing a newspaper from publishing information she had passed to her husband during the course of their marriage. The case was based in the law of confidentiality, rather than any pervasive right protecting personal information per se.

In *Kaye v Robertson*,[5] the claimant was a well-known actor and star of a television series called *'Allo 'Allo*. He had undergone extensive surgery on his head after part of an advertisement hoarding had fallen through his car windscreen in a storm. Whilst in a semi-conscious state in hospital, some reporters gained access to his room and purported to conduct an 'interview' with him. His attempt to restrain publication on the grounds of privacy infringement failed, although he succeeded in obtaining an interim injunction for malicious falsehood.

1.2.2 The *Douglas* case

Various other cases throughout the 1990s tipped the scales this way and that in an inconclusive manner – the one constant feature was that the law of confidence was being slowly expanded to serve as a vehicle for privacy-type actions. Then, in December 2000, another case involving attempted media restraint came before the courts. This time it involved the celebrity wedding of Catherine Zeta-Jones and Michael Douglas. The Douglases had entered into an exclusive arrangement with *OK!* magazine whereby *OK!* was to obtain the rights to the publication of the wedding photographs during the week following the wedding. Despite the considerable security measures that had been implemented at the wedding, someone was able to surreptitiously take some photographs that were sold to *Hello!*

---

3   (1849) 18 LJ Ch 120, 1 H & Tw 1, 13 Jur 109, 1 Mac & G 25, 41 ER 1171.
4   *Duchess of Argyll v Duke of Argyll* [1967] Ch 302, [1965] 1 All ER 611, [1965] 22 WLR 790.
5   [1991] FSR 62.

magazine. The Douglases and *OK!* were able to obtain an interim injunction in the High Court preventing the publication of the photographs. In lifting the interim injunction, the Court of Appeal recognised, for the first time, that a legal right of privacy is *capable* of existing in English law independently from the law of confidential information. The court also stated that it had taken into account the provisions of the Human Rights Act 1998 and, in particular, article 8 of the European Convention on Human Rights and Fundamental Freedoms concerning an individual's right to privacy – this latter aspect was controversial due to the fact that the action was brought against neither the state nor a 'public authority'. At the time of going to press the *Douglas*[6] case has yet to come to trial, but unless it is settled, is expected to do so in early 2003.

1.2.3 The *Wainwright* case

In *Home Office v Wainwright,*[7] the Court of Appeal was again asked to consider whether a privacy right exists in English law. This case involved a mother and son who were strip-searched when they went to visit another of the mother's sons, Patrick, in Armley prison in Leeds. They had been informed that the strip search was necessary in the search for drugs, and that they would be refused entry to the prison to see Patrick if they did not consent to the search. The search was 'not conducted in as seemly a manner as was consistent with discovering anything concealed'. The trial judge was of the view that consent to the strip-search, although forthcoming from the mother and son, was not real due to the pressure they were under to give that consent. He found that trespass to the person had been committed consisting of wilfully causing a person to do something to himself which infringes his right to privacy – this was the first case where recovery of damages was achieved simply for breach of the right to privacy (ie in absence of any duty of confidence). The appeal was allowed by the Court of Appeal – Mummery LJ stated that:[8]

'there is no tort of invasion of privacy. Instead there are torts protecting a person's interests in the privacy of his body, his home and his personal property. There is also the equitable doctrine of breach of confidence for the protection of personal information, private communications and correspondence.'

Although the strip-search had taken place in January 1997, and thus had to be decided on the law as it stood prior to the coming into force of the Human Rights Act 1998, it is clear from the

---

6   *Douglas v Hello! Ltd* [2001] QB 967, [2001] 2 All ER 289, [2001] 2 WLR 992, [2002] 1 FCR 289, [2001] 1 FLR 982, CA.

7   *R (on the application of Wainwright) v Richmond upon Thames London Borough Council* [2001] EWCA Civ 2062, CA.

8   [2001] EWCA Civ 2062 at paragraph 57.

Court of Appeal judgments that the judges were not of the view that a right to privacy exists per se. Instead, as Mummery LJ stated:[9]

> 'I see serious definitional difficulties and conceptual problems in the judicial development of a "blockbuster" tort vaguely embracing such a potentially wide range of situations. I am not even sure that anybody – the public, Parliament, the press – really wants the creation of a new tort, which could give rise to as many problems as it is sought to solve. A more promising and well trod path is that of incremental evolution, both at common law and by statute ..., of traditional nominate torts pragmatically crafted as to conditions of liability, specific defences and appropriate remedies, and tailored to suit significantly different privacy interests and infringement situations.'

1.2.4 The *Campbell* case

As the first substantive judicial interpretation of the Data Protection Act 1998,[10] the case of *Campbell v Mirror Group Newspapers* is of significant importance to data protection lawyers and privacy lawyers alike. It concerned an application under section 13 of the Data Protection Act 1998 for compensation for distress caused by unlawful processing of personal data.

Following the *Mirror*'s publication, in February 2001, of the first of two sets of articles, Naomi Campbell sued the paper for breach of confidentiality and for compensation for distress due to breaches of the Data Protection Act 1998. The articles stated that Ms Campbell was a drug addict (something she had publicly and, as it turned out, falsely, denied) and that she was attending Narcotics Anonymous (NA) meetings in London. Also published were details of the NA meetings, the 'fragility' of Naomi Campbell's state of health and a photograph of her leaving a meeting in Chelsea dressed 'ordinarily' in jeans and a baseball cap. The first article, which reportedly left Ms Campbell feeling 'shocked, angry, violated and betrayed', acknowledged that her attendance at NA meetings was low key and as an ordinary, private person.

Four days after the first article, and after proceedings had been brought, the *Mirror* published further, less complimentary articles. These included a photograph of the model captioned 'pathetic' and the statement 'after years of self-publicity and illegal drug abuse, Naomi Campbell whinges about privacy'.

9   [2002] EWCA Civ 2062 at [60].
10   See section 1.3.4.

There was agreement that Naomi Campbell's name and picture were personal data and that their obtaining, preparation and publication was processing by the data controller (the *Mirror*). It was also agreed by the parties that the processing was for the 'special purposes'[11] of journalism and that there had been no consent given by Ms Campbell. Sensitive personal data[12] include personal data relating to a data subject's racial or ethnic origin or her physical or mental health or condition. Mr Justice Morland confirmed that the type and details of the therapy Ms Campbell was receiving (including the photograph and caption) were sensitive personal (health) data. The judge noted that, although photographs of Ms Campbell used by the *Mirror* inevitably revealed information as to her racial/ethnic origin, this had no bearing on the case, as Ms Campbell had obviously suffered no distress due to the photographs revealing that she was black.

Section 32 provides an exemption from certain provisions of the Act, including the broad First Data Protection Principle.[13] The exemption applies where data are being processed *only* for the special purposes (which include journalism) provided that certain other conditions are met.[14] Mr Justice Morland ruled that this exemption did not apply and that section 32 had no application post-publication. He also dismissed the *Mirror's* assertion that the Act offended Article 10, pointing out that the Data Protection Directive required articles 8 and 10 of the Convention to 'march in step'.

The First Data Protection Principle consists of three requirements: (1) the personal data processing must be fair and lawful in general terms; (2) at least one condition in Schedule 2 to the Data Protection Act 1998 must be met; and (3) where sensitive personal data are involved, at least one Schedule 3 condition must also be met. The court found none of the three necessary elements was present and held that the *Mirror* had therefore breached the First Principle. The court awarded damages of £3,500 under both section 13 of the Act and for breach of confidence. The *Mirror* was also ordered to pay Ms Campbell's costs.[15]

At the time of going to press there was a strong likelihood that the High Court decision in *Campbell* would be appealed.

For an analysis on the effect of the 'September 11' tragedy in the United States in 2001 on United Kingdom privacy law, see Peter Grundberg 'The Right to Privacy', *Privacy & Data Protection* volume 2, issue 3, page 9.

---

11 See section 3.4.15.
12 See section 3.2.
13 See section 3.1.1.
14 See section 3.4.15.
15 For further detailed analysis of the Naomi Campbell case, see Kate Brimsted's article in *Privacy & Data Protection*, volume 2, issue 6, page 8.

1.3 ■ STATUTORY FRAMEWORK

It can be seen from section 1.2 that there is no all-encompassing tort of invasion of privacy in English law. Instead there is a hotchpotch of legal provisions that protect interests that we may collectively call a right to privacy. This section provides an introduction to those statutory provisions that regulate the use of personal information.

1.3.1   Computer Misuse Act 1990

The Computer Misuse Act 1990 created criminal offences for persons engaging in those activities that we may generically describe as 'hacking'.

By section 1, a person is guilty of an offence if:

(a)   he causes a computer to perform any function with intent to secure access to any program or data held in any computer;

(b)   the access he intends to secure is unauthorised; and

(c)   he knows at the time when he causes the computer to perform the function that that is the case.

The offence is one where the mens rea is 'intention', but the intent a person has to have to commit an offence under this section need not be directed at:

(a)   any particular program or data;

(b)   a program or data of any particular kind; or

(c)   a program or data held in any particular computer.

A person guilty of an offence under section 1 is liable on summary conviction to imprisonment for a term not exceeding six months or to a fine.

Sections 2 and 3 of the Computer Misuse Act 1990 create further offences where the section 1 offence ('the unauthorised access offence') is committed with intention to commit a serious offence and where a person causes unauthorised 'modification of the contents of any computer'. In each case the maximum punishment is six months' imprisonment on summary conviction and five years' on indictment.

Generally, in determining day-to-day data processing operations, procedures and policies, e-businesses will not be concerned with the Computer Misuse Act 1990. However, its provisions may serve to protect the information held by an e-business.

1.3.2 European Data Protection Directive (Council Directive 95/46/EC)

The European Directive on the Protection of Individuals with Regard to the Processing of Personal Data and on the Free Movement of such Data[16] (the 'Data Protection Directive') was adopted in October 1995. Its implementation date, 24 October 1998, was not met by any of the member states. At the time of going to press, however, only Ireland and France had yet to implement the Data Protection Directive fully.

The Data Protection Directive is a general framework legislative provision, which has as its aims:

(a) the protection of an individual's privacy in relation to the processing of personal data; and

(b) the harmonisation of the data protection laws of member states.

It sets out the conditions under which the processing of personal data by European organisations is lawful, the rights of individuals in relation to that processing and the minimum standards of personal data 'quality' that must be met. The Data Protection Directive seeks to establish an equivalent level of protection for personal data in all member states to facilitate the transfer of personal data across national boundaries within the European Union.

The Data Protection Directive applies to personal data processed wholly or partly by automatic means, and to manual data held in filing systems that are structured by reference to individuals, but it does not apply to activities which fall outside the scope of European Union law.

Article 6 of the Data Protection Directive establishes fundamental principles that should be followed during all instances of personal data processing (the data protection principles). Article 7 sets out a number of conditions, one of which must be satisfied before personal data can be legally processed (the legitimising conditions). Article 8 bans the processing of personal data revealing racial or ethnic origin, political opinions, religious or philosophical beliefs, trade-union membership, offences or convictions and health or sex life (sensitive personal data) unless one of a set of exemptions exist. Member states are given the right to create further such exemptions from the sensitive data processing ban as they see fit.

Each relevant data subject has the right to be informed, where his personal data are first collected by a business, of the identity of that business, the purposes for which the data are to be used and of any further information that would enable the processing to be fair. Other rights of individuals include:

16   Council Directive 95/46/EC.

(a) the right of access to personal data without constraint, at reasonable intervals and without excessive delays or expense;[17]

(b) the right to have incomplete or inaccurate data rectified, erased or blocked;[18]

(c) the right to object to processing of personal data, and where there is a justified objection, to have the processing stopped;[19]

(d) the right to object to personal data being used for direct marketing;[20] and

(e) the right not to be subject to a decision that has legal effects and which is based solely on automated processing of data.[21]

Data security must be such as to ensure that personal data are protected against accidental or unlawful destruction or accidental loss. Data must also be protected against unauthorised alteration, disclosure or access and all other forms of unlawful processing. The level of security must be appropriate to the risks associated with the processing and the nature of the data to be protected, having regard to the state of technology and the cost from time to time.

The Data Protection Directive sets out the conditions under which personal data that are being processed in the European Union may be transferred to countries outside the European Economic Area.[22]

1.3.3 The Telecommunications Data Protection Directive (Council Directive 97/66/EC)

The European Directive concerning the Processing of Personal Data and the Protection of Privacy in the Telecommunications Sector[23] (the 'Telecommunications Data Protection Directive') arose from a concern about 'new advanced digital technologies', particularly the Integrated Services Digital Network (ISDN) and digital mobile networks. Whilst the Data Protection Directive[24] regulates the use of personal data in the European Union generally, the Telecommunications Data Protection Directive takes the law into two principal areas of regulation not covered by the Data Protection Directive:

17   Council Directive 95/46/EC, article 12(a).
18   Council Directive 95/46/EC, article 12(b).
19   Council Directive 95/46/EC, article 14(a).
20   Council Directive 95/46/EC, article 14(b).
21   Council Directive 95/46/EC, article 15.
22   Ie the member states of the European Union plus Norway, Iceland and Liechtenstein.
23   Council Directive 97/66/EC.
24   Council Directive 95/46/EC.

(a) the use of information, such as telephone numbers, that does not necessarily amount to 'personal data'; and

(b) the application of the law to all legal persons, as opposed to merely natural persons.

The Telecommunications Data Protection Directive has the stated objective of providing for the:

'harmonisation of the provisions of the Member States required to ensure an equivalent level of protection of fundamental rights and freedoms, and in particular the right to privacy, with respect to the processing of personal data in the telecommunications sector and to ensure the free movement of such data and of telecommunications equipment and services.'

and introduced the following new measures:

(a) providers of publicly available telecommunications services must take appropriate measures to ensure the security of such services;

(b) member states must ensure the confidentiality of communications, in particular prohibiting 'listening, tapping, storage or other kinds of interception or surveillance of communications' without the consent of users;

(c) restrictions on the processing of traffic and billing data;

(d) the right for users to receive non-itemised bills;

(e) rights of subscribers in relation to the presentation and restriction of calling and connected line identification;

(f) a right for subscribers to stop automatic call forwarding by a third party to the subscriber's terminal;

(g) a limit, without the consent of the subscriber, to the content of publicly available telephone directories; and

(h) a ban on the use of automated calling systems.

Member states were required to implement the Telecommunications Data Protection Directive by 24 October 1998. The United Kingdom's implementing legislation is the Telecommunications (Data Protection and Privacy) Regulations 1999[25] (see section 1.3.6). The Telecommunications Data Protection Directive is due to be replaced by the Directive on Data Protection in the Electronic Communications Sector (see 1.3.13).

1.3.4 Data Protection Act 1998

The Data Protection Act 1998 implements Council Directive 95/46/EC on the processing of personal data by 'data controllers'. The 1998 Act repealed the Data Protection Act 1984, and set up,

25 SI 1999/2093.

in the United Kingdom, a new and more complicated data protection regime.

There are essentially two obligations on data controllers (defined as persons that *determine the purposes for the processing of personal data* – thus including the vast majority of e-businesses). The first is to notify, to the Office of the Information Commissioner, the fact that personal data are processed by the business and the purposes for such processing – the notification system is discussed in more detail in Chapter 3. The second is to comply with a set of eight principles concerning the processing of personal data. Unless a relevant exemption applies, all processing of personal data must comply with the eight Data Protection Principles, as specified in Schedule 1 to the Data Protection Act 1998 – a substantially similar set of rules applies, by virtue of Council Directive 95/46/EC, to all personal data processing carried out in all member states of the European Union. The Principles are set out in the Glossary and referred to, where appropriate, throughout this book.

Transitional periods in the legislation meant that certain established businesses did not have to comply with the new legislation until 24 October 2001 for certain aspects of their processing. The remaining transitional provision, relating solely to certain archived manual records, expires on 24 October 2007.

1.3.5 Human Rights Act 1998

The Human Rights Act 1998 came into force on 2 October 2000. The Act gives the European Convention for the Protection of Fundamental Rights and Freedoms ('the Human Rights Convention') the force of United Kingdom law. As far as this work is concerned, the relevant articles of the Convention are 8 and 10 – the right to respect for private and family life and the right to freedom of expression. These articles are set out below.

Article 8

1. Everyone has the right to respect for his private and family life, his home and his correspondence.

2. There shall be no interference by a public authority with the exercise of this right except such as is in accordance with the law and is necessary in a democratic society in the interests of national security, public safety or the economic well-being of the country, for the prevention of disorder or crime, for the protection of health or morals, or for the protection of the rights and freedoms of others.

> **Article 10**
>
> 1. Everyone has the right to freedom of expression. This right shall include freedom to hold opinions and to receive and impart information and ideas without interference by public authority and regardless of frontiers. This Article shall not prevent States from requiring the licensing of broadcasting, television or cinema enterprises.
>
> 2. The exercise of these freedoms, since it carries with it duties and responsibilities, may be subject to such formalities, conditions, restrictions or penalties as are prescribed by law and are necessary in a democratic society, in the interests of national security, territorial integrity or public safety, for the prevention of disorder or crime, for the protection of health or morals, for the protection of the reputation or rights of others, for preventing the disclosure of information received in confidence, or for maintaining the authority and impartiality of the judiciary.

A court or tribunal determining a question which has arisen in connection with a Human Rights Convention right must take into account any judgment, decision, declaration or advisory opinion of the European Court of Human Rights. This provision opens up a raft of 'foreign' case law that must be considered by e-businesses when determining business operations, for example, policies on e-mail usage and monitoring.

Considerable controversy exists over whether the Human Rights Act 1998 applies to private bodies and persons – such as most e-businesses. The Act is expressly applicable only to 'public authorities' – defined as including:[26]

(a) a court or tribunal, and

(b) any person certain of whose functions are functions of a public nature.

However, there have been several notable judicial pronouncements (see, for example, the judgment of Sedley LJ in the *Douglas*[27] case) to the effect that the court will be obliged to interpret English law in the light of Human Rights Convention rights, even where neither party to the litigation in question is a public authority, due to the fact that the court itself is a public authority.

1.3.6 Telecommunications (Data Protection and Privacy) Regulations 1999[28]

The Telecommunications (Data Protection and Privacy) Regulations 1999 were produced in the United Kingdom to give effect to Council Directive 97/66/EC[29] on the Processing of

---

26 Inserted by the Freedom of Information Act 2000, section 68(1), (2)(b).
27 *Douglas v Hello! Ltd* [2001] QB 967, [2001] 2 All ER 289, [2001] 2 WLR 992, [2002] 1 FCR 289, [2001] 1 FLR 982, CA.
28 SI 1999/2093.
29 See section 1.3.3.

Personal Data and the Protection of Privacy in the Telecommunications Sector. They repeal and replace the Telecommunications (Data Protection and Privacy) (Direct Marketing) Regulations 1998.[30] The 1999 Regulations came into force on 1 March 2000.

The 1999 Regulations create rights for individuals and companies over and above those under the Data Protection Act 1998. The key provisions of the Regulations are the following:

(a) restrictions on the processing of traffic data and billing data;

(b) obligations on telecommunications companies to allow subscribers certain powers over calling and called line identification;

(c) rights of subscribers in relation to entries in publicly available telephone directories;

(d) restrictions on direct marketing by telephone and fax;

(e) technical and organisational security obligations; and

(f) rights of subscribers to receive non-itemised bills.

The 1999 Regulations are due to be replaced by a new directive on data protection in the electric communications sector, which is designed to be 'technologically neutral' – see section 1.3.13.

1.3.7 Freedom of Information Act 2000

The Freedom of Information Act 2000 received Royal Assent on 30 November 2000 and applies to information kept by 'public authorities'. Only a few of its provisions came into force on the day of Royal Assent and a further small number came into effect two months later. The remaining provisions, including the 'right to know', which are at the heart of the Act, will be implemented in phases according to the type of public authority concerned. The 'public authorities' affected are listed in Schedule 1 to the Act, and may be amended from time to time.

The Freedom of Information Act 2000 has to be in full force by 30 November 2005 at the latest, although doubt has been expressed as to whether this will be practicable. The implementation timetable is yet to be finalised and approved by the government, but it is assumed that central government and those bodies that work to the Open Government Code will be amongst the first to have to comply, ie by Summer 2002. The first step to compliance is the establishment of Publication Schemes (see section 19). The view of the Information Commissioner (who is to enforce the Act) is that all public authorities should immediately focus on records management, as there is much to do in preparation for the full force of the Act.

30   SI 1998/3170.

The aim of the Freedom of Information Act 2000 is to encourage openness by allowing access to information held by public authorities, resulting in greater public accountability. Information held by a third party on behalf of a public authority will be caught. It is important to note that the information sought may be of a personal or non-personal nature and hence the legislation is, in this sense, wider than the Data Protection Act 1998.

The rights given to any person (legal or natural) in Part I of the Freedom of Information Act 2000 are (a) to know whether information, either about oneself or a third party, of a particular kind is held by a public authority and (b) to have this information communicated. There is not an immediate right to the documents themselves although an applicant may state that they prefer the information to be in copy document format and the public authority would, as far as is reasonably practicable, be required to accommodate the applicant. The reasonableness test includes consideration of the costs involved.

There are, of course, conditions to be met before an authority is required to perform these duties: a request must be in writing (although it need not expressly refer to the Freedom of Information Act 2000); the applicant must provide details reasonably required by the authority to be able to identify the applicant and locate the information sought; and the relevant fees (if any) must be paid. Fees will be addressed in more detail in Regulations to be issued under the Act. The general rule is that a request must be effected within 20 working days, a shorter period than under the Data Protection Act 1998.

Exemptions to the rights to know come in two categories: absolute exemptions and those that require an evaluation of the public interest. An example of information subject to an absolute exemption is information that is otherwise reasonably accessible (whether at a price or not) to the applicant. The Publication Schemes are the ideal way to satisfy this exemption that was, no doubt, an intention behind this provision.

The effect of the Freedom of Information Act 2000 is expected to reach beyond public authorities. Private sector organisations doing business with public authorities need to take the Act into consideration. They also need to take steps to protect against disclosure of their own information in response to a Freedom of Information Act 2000 request made on the relevant public authority. Sensitive commercial information, such as pricing details, require special consideration. One solution is to ensure that there are contractual provisions placing watertight confidentiality provisions on the authority, breach of which will be actionable by the other party. This will trigger an absolute exemption to the rights to know.[31]

---

31   Freedom of Information Act 2000, section 41.

Once in force, there will be consequences for non-compliance. The Information Commissioner's enforcement powers are set out in Part IV and Schedule 3 to the Freedom of Information Act 2000. The Commissioner can issue Decision Notices (for example, overriding an authority's decision not to disclose information), Information Notices (requiring the authority to provide whatever information is requested) and Enforcement Notices (for example, requiring the authority to change its systems so as to achieve compliance). These have the force of an order of the court and transgression will be a contempt of court. Rights of appeal are available to both the authority and applicant, depending on the type of notice issued. The Information Commissioner also has a right of entry to premises and inspection of records, although a warrant is needed. Unlike the Data Protection Act 1998, the 2000 Act does not confer any right of civil proceedings in respect of any failure to comply with any duty imposed by or under it.

All public authorities must comply with the Freedom of Information Act 2000, so they need to have the necessary systems and procedures in place to meet their statutory duties. If possible, these systems should be amalgamated with those dealing with data protection, so that a co-ordinated approach to both regimes exists.

There is an overlap between the Freedom of Information Act 2000 and the Data Protection Act 1998. Under the 2000 Act a request can be made by any person, legal or natural, from anywhere in the world about information relating to themselves and/or third parties. This is a much wider right than that given to data subjects under the 1998 Act. There is a proviso – where an individual wants a copy of their own personal data (as defined in the Data Protection Act 1998), then the access request must be made under the 1998 Act. However, where non-personal data are sought, the 2000 Act can be used. This means that commercial data can be sought as can data (personal or otherwise) that is not in electronic form nor held in a structured manual system.

The right to obtain data about third parties is, however, tempered by the Data Protection Act 1998. A public authority must apply the tenets of the Data Protection Principles when deciding on disclosure of a third party's personal data. While an authority must comply with the Freedom of Information Act 2000, it must equally ensure not to expose itself to the consequences (such as the statutory right to damages and/or compensation for a data subject) for breaching the 1998 Act. Where the risks are high, a safe solution would be to seek a court ruling on the disclosure.

> For further information on the attitude of the Information Commissioner to 'publications schemes' and recommendations to public authorities for compliance procedures, see Cinzia Biondi 'Freedom of Information', *Privacy & Data Protection* volume 2, issue 1, page 8.

1.3.8   Regulation of Investigatory Powers Act 2000

The Regulation of Investigatory Powers Act 2000 repealed the Interception of Communications Act 1985 and set up the regulatory regime in the United Kingdom governing the interception of communications. It creates both criminal offences and torts concerned with unlawful interception. In order to understand the legislation it is useful to note that Chapter I of the Act deals with interception and permits interception of the *content* of a communication. Chapter II deals with *use* of the service only, and not content.

By virtue of section 1, it is an offence intentionally, and without lawful authority, to intercept in the United Kingdom any communication in the course of transmission by (a) public post or (b) a public telecommunications system. It is also a criminal offence intentionally, and without lawful authority, to intercept at any place in the United Kingdom any communication in transmission by a private telecommunications system unless the interception is carried out by a person who has:

(i)   a right to control the operation or use of the system; or

(ii)   the express or implied consent of such a person to make the interception.

Further, it is a tort under section 1(3), unlawfully to incept a communication that uses a private telecommunications system. Such activity is actionable at the instance of the sender or recipient of the communication.

According to the Home Office guidance notes to the Act, a communication is considered to be in the course of its transmission at any time while it is stored awaiting receipt by the intended recipient, for example, an e-mail stored on a web-based service provider or a pager message waiting to be collected. Thus the contents of such an e-mail or pager message being made available to someone other than sender or intended recipient may constitute interception.

Conduct will be rendered lawful, for both the criminal and civil actions above, where:

(a)   both the sender and recipient have consented to the interception;

(b)   either the sender or the recipient has consented and the surveillance is authorised under Part II of the Act (Part II deals with 'intrusive' surveillance and use of covert human intelligence);

(c)   it is undertaken by a person who provides the telecommunications system and is for the provision or operation of that service;

(d)   it is undertaken within the provisions of the Wireless Telegraphy Act 1949;

(e) it is for the purpose of obtaining information on a person thought to be outside the United Kingdom and relates to the use of a public telecommunications system and the service provider has been required by the law of another country to carry out the interception;

(f) it is authorised by regulations made by the Secretary of State for Trade and Industry for the purpose of carrying on business; or

(g) it is undertaken under statutory power for the purpose of obtaining a document or other property.

Further, the Secretary of State for Trade and Industry may authorise an interception warrant if it is both necessary and proportionate for:

- national security;

- preventing or detecting serious crime;

- safeguarding the economic well-being of the United Kingdom; or

- an international mutual assistance agreement.[32]

By section 2(5) of the Act, conduct that takes place only in relation to traffic data does not fall within the definition of an 'interception of a communication'. However, Chapter II of Part I of the Act is concerned with the provision of 'communications data', which in essence is data which comprise information about the use of a communication service but not the contents of the communication itself (see below).

To aid the Secretary of State for Trade and Industry in his surveillance aspirations, public telecommunications services providers can be required to take certain specified action to facilitate interception. This may include the installation of certain electronic surveillance equipment at the premises or connected to the infrastructure of the telecommunications service provider – although the expense of such installation is to be met by the telecommunications company in question, there is power in the legislation for the Secretary of State for Trade and Industry to pay a contribution to the cost.[33]

Section 21(2) provides that conduct in relation to a postal service or telecommunication system for obtaining communications data shall be lawful where the conduct of the person is authorised by an authorisation or notice under Chapter II.

---

32 Regulation of Investigatory Powers Act 2000, section 5.
33 Regulation of Investigatory Powers Act 2000, section 14.

Communications data[34] may be intercepted by any 'relevant public authority' where it is necessary:

(a)   in the interests of national security;

(b)   for the purpose of preventing or detecting crime or of preventing disorder;

(c)   in the interests of the economic well-being of the United Kingdom;

(d)   in the interests of public safety;

(e)   for the purpose of protecting public health;

(f)   for the purpose of assessing or collecting any tax, duty, levy or other imposition, contribution or charge payable to a government department;

(g)   for the purpose, in an emergency, of preventing death or injury or any damage to a person's physical or mental health, or of mitigating any injury or damage to a person's physical or mental health; or

(h)   for any purpose (not falling within paragraphs (a) to (g)) which is specified for the purposes of this subsection by an order made by the Secretary of State.

A relevant public authority, for the purposes of access to communications data, is any one of the following bodies:

(a)   a police force;

(b)   the National Criminal Intelligence Service;

(c)   the National Crime Squad;

(d)   the Commissioners of Customs and Excise;

(e)   the Commissioners of Inland Revenue; or

(f)   any of the intelligence services.

Part III of the Act deals with investigation of data protected by encryption. By section 49, where information protected by

34   By virtue of any of section 21(4) of the Regulation of Investigatory Powers Act 2000, 'communications data' means any of the following:
(a)   any traffic data comprised in or attached to a communication (whether by the sender or otherwise) for the purposes of any postal service or telecommunication system by means of which it is being or may be transmitted;
(b)   any information which includes none of the contents of a communication (apart from any information falling within paragraph (a)) and is about the use made by any person—
(i)   of any postal service or telecommunications service; or
(ii)   in connection with the provision to or use by any person of any telecommunications service, of any part of a telecommunication system;
(c)   any information not falling within paragraph (a) or (b) that is held or obtained, in relation to persons to whom he provides the service, by a person providing a postal service or telecommunications service.

encryption has come into the possession of a person with appropriate statutory power (as specified in subsection (1)) then that person may serve notice on the person he believes to have possession of the key to the encryption to disclose it. To serve such notice the person must reasonably believe:

(a) that a key to the protected information is in the possession of any person,

(b) that the imposition of a disclosure requirement in respect of the protected information is-

    (i) necessary on grounds falling within subsection (3) (the interests of national security; for the purpose of preventing or detecting crime; or in the interests of the economic well-being of the United Kingdom), or

    (ii) necessary for the purpose of securing the effective exercise or proper performance by any public authority of any statutory power or statutory duty,

(c) that the imposition of such a requirement is proportionate to what is sought to be achieved by its imposition, and

(d) that it is not reasonably practicable for the person with the appropriate permission to obtain possession of the protected information in an intelligible form without the giving of a notice under this section.

Under section 71 of the Act, the Secretary of State is under a duty to prepare a code of practice in respect of interception powers. The Regulation of Investigatory Powers (Interception of Communications: Code of Practice) Order 2002[35] came into force on 1 July 2002. That Order brought into being the 'Interception of Communications Code', under which various government and quasi-government bodies are able to gain access to various communications, including e-mails, SMS messages and mobile telephone location data. The Interception Code is set out at Appendix V.

To oversee the exercise and performance of powers and obligation conferred by the Act, it also provides for the appointment of an Interception of Communications Commissioner (section 57).

1.3.9 Consumer Protection (Distance Selling) Regulations 2000[36]

The Consumer Protection (Distance Selling) Regulations 2000 oblige those businesses that trade with consumers on-line or electronically, inter alia, to:

1. make certain information available to consumers; and

2. provide a 'cooling off' period.

---

35 SI 2002/1693.
36 SI 2000/2334.

Consumer information

Prior to the conclusion of a distance contract,[37] regulation 7 of the Consumer Protection (Distance Selling) Regulations 2000 obliges a distance seller (such as an e-commerce business) to provide a consumer with the following information:

(i)   the identity of the supplier and, where the contract requires payment in advance, the supplier's address;

(ii) a description of the main characteristics of the goods or services;

(iii) the price of the goods or services including all taxes;

(iv) delivery costs where appropriate;

(v)   the arrangements for payment, delivery or performance;

(vi) the existence of a right of cancellation (except in certain exempted cases);

(vii) the cost of using the means of distance communication where it is calculated other than at the basic rate;

(viii) the period for which the offer or the price remains valid; and

(ix) where appropriate, the minimum duration of the contract, in the case of contracts for the supply of goods or services to be performed permanently or recurrently.

The distance supplier must ensure that the information above is provided in a clear and comprehensible manner appropriate to the means of distance communication[38] used, with due regard in particular to the principles of good faith in commercial

37   Any contract concerning goods or services concluded between a supplier and a consumer under an organised distance sales or service provision scheme run by the supplier who, for the purpose of the contract, makes exclusive use of one or more means of distance communication up to and including the moment at which the contract is concluded.

38   Any means which, without the simultaneous physical presence of the supplier and the consumer, may be used for the conclusion of a contract between those parties; an indicative (but not exhaustive) list is:
  1   unaddressed printed matter;
  2   addressed printed matter;
  3   letter;
  4   press advertising with order form;
  5   catalogue;
  6   telephone with human intervention;
  7   telephone without human intervention (automatic calling machine, audiotext);
  8   radio;
  9   videophone (telephone with screen);
  10 videotext (microcomputer and television screen) with keyboard or touch screen;
  11 electronic mail;
  12 facsimile machine (fax); and
  13 television (teleshopping).

transactions and the principles governing the protection of those who are unable to give their consent, such as minors.

Except in the case of telephone communications, the supplier must ensure that his commercial purpose is made clear when providing the information required.

The cooling-off period

Consumers who purchase products on-line are entitled to return the goods to the on-line retailer within seven working days for a full refund.[39] This so-called 'cooling-off' period applies whether or not the goods are defective. Where the on-line retailer fails to inform its customers of their right of return under the Consumer Protection (Distance Selling) Regulations 2000,[40] the period is deemed to be extended to three months plus seven working days or seven working days from when the consumer is informed of the right by the on-line business (whichever comes first).[41]

1.3.10 E-Commerce Directive (Council Directive 2000/31/EC)

The European Directive on certain legal aspects of information society services, in particular electronic commerce, in the Internal Market (the 'E-Commerce Directive') has a limited impact on e-privacy and on-line data protection issues generally. In recital 14, the Directive makes it clear that,

'The protection of individuals with regard to the processing of personal data is solely governed by Directive 95/46/EC [the Data Protection Directive] ... and by Directive 97/66/EC [the Telecommunications Directive] ... this Directive should be made in full compliance with the principles relating to the protection of personal data, in particular as regards unsolicited commercial communication and the liability of intermediaries; this Directive cannot prevent the anonymous use of open networks such as the Internet.'

Article 1(5)(b) goes on to state that:

'This Directive shall not apply to questions relating to information society services covered by Directives 95/46/EC and 97/66/EC.'

However, there are two aspects of the E-Commerce Directive that merit closer examination, as regards the remit of this book. It applies in general to 'information society services'. The meaning of 'information society services' is crucial to the

---

39   Regulation 10.
40   SI 2000/2334.
41   SI 2000/2334, regulations 11 and 12.

operation of the Directive and the question of whether it will apply to any particular e-business. Article 2 provides that the meaning of 'information society services' in the E-Commerce Directive is to have the same meaning as Council Directive 98/34 EC, as amended by Council Directive 98/48 EC. An information society service is therefore 'any service normally provided for remuneration, at a distance, by electronic means and at the individual request of a recipient of services'. E-businesses operating on-line will of course be operating 'at a distance' and 'by electronic means'. As far as the phrase 'at the individual request of a recipient of services' is concerned, the E-Commerce Directive states that the service must be 'provided through the transmission of data on individual request'. This further clarification may be important when considering whether, to be an 'information society service', the service must be provided at the request of the individual recipient of the service. The definition, on the face it, suggests it must be the service recipient who makes the request, but the subsequent interpretation indicates it will not be prevented from being an information society service if another individual *other than the person using or receiving the service* has made the request for the service. The E-Commerce Directive further goes on to state explicitly that radio broadcasting services, and television broadcasting services are not included within the definition.

Annex V to Council Directive 98/34/EC provides an indicative list of services that are not to be considered as information society services. These include:

(a)   Services 'not at a distance', ie any service provided in the physical presence of the provider and recipient, even if an electronic device is used, such as, consultation of an electronic catalogue in-store; airline ticket reservations at a travel agents using computer; electronic games in a video arcade.

(b)   Services 'not by electronic means', ie

  (i)   any service which has a 'material content' even though is provided via an electronic device, such as automatic cash machines, ticket machines, or road toll or car park machines;

  (ii)   offline services, such as the distribution of CD-ROMs or disks;

  (iii)   services which are not provided via electronic processing/inventory systems:

   •   voice telephony services;

   •   telefax/telex services;

   •   services provided via voice telephony or fax;

   •   telephone/telefax consultation of a doctor or lawyer;

   •   telephone/telefax direct marketing.

(c)   Services 'not supplied at the individual request of recipient of services' provided by transmitting data without individual demand for simultaneous reception by an unlimited number of individual receivers (point-to-multipoint transmission):

(i)   television broadcasting services (including near-video on-demand services);

(ii)   radio broadcasting services;

(iii)   teletext.

Recital 18 to the E-Commerce Directive discusses the intended scope of information society services and suggests that an 'economic activity' is also a relevant factor. Services that are not remunerated by those who receive them, such as search tools or services offering on-line information or commercial communication, will be an information society service *in so far as they represent an economic activity*. The use of e-mail or equivalent by natural persons acting outside of their trade, business or profession will not constitute an 'information society service'. The E-Commerce Directive also explicitly states that services transmitted point-to-point, such as video on-demand or commercial communications by e-mail, are information society services.

Without further clarification, it is not clear what services may be caught by the definition of information society services. Further, with many developing technologies, there will be applications that do not fit easily within the definition. The definition when applied to specific services raises the following considerations:

•   SMS: Services provided via SMS will be caught. They are provided at a distance by electronic means and at the request of the individual recipient. It is arguable whether unsolicited services provided via SMS would therefore not be information society services as they would not be at the request of the recipient of the service. However, they would be caught by article 7 of Council Directive 2000/31 EC on unsolicited commercial communication which does not rely on the definition of information society services.

•   iTV: As with SMS, services via iTV will be caught by the definition.

•   Webcast: Whether a webcast it is caught by the definition would depend on the interpretation of whether the webcast is provided at the individual request of a recipient of the services. In some senses it is akin to a television broadcast in that it is the transmission of data available for simultaneous reception by an unlimited number of receivers. However, it is received only when a user visits a particular site to receive it and therefore may be seen as being supplied only on individual demand. It is not specifically excluded by Annex V of Council Directive 98/48/EC.

•   Video on demand: The position appears unclear from the definition although the recital to the E-Commerce Directive indicates it is intended to be within the definition of information society services.

The E-Commerce Directive regulates certain aspects of commercial e-mails and imposes an obligation on businesses to consult opt-out registers. These aspects of the Directive will be discussed where relevant throughout this book.

Council Directive 2000/31 should have been implemented by member states on or before 17 January 2002. Draft implementing regulations were published on 7 March 2002 and subsequently entered an eight-week consultation period. Implementation was expected, at the time of going to press, in late Summer 2002.

1.3.11 The Anti-Terrorism, Crime and Security Act 2001

The Anti-Terrorism, Crime and Security Act 2001 deals specifically with the retention by communications providers[42] of communications data.[43] The Secretary of State for Trade and the Internet Service Providers Association are expected to work together, in co-operation with the government, the Information Commissioner and law enforcement agencies, to develop and maintain a voluntary code of practice[44] on the issue of data retention that appears necessary:

(a)   for the purpose of safeguarding national security; or

(b)   for the purposes of prevention or detection of crime or the prosecution of offenders which may relate directly or indirectly to national security.

The Act will enable certain law enforcement agencies to access logs of traffic data,[45] not content data, retained by

---

42   A person who provides a postal service or a telecommunications service (Anti-Terrorism, Crime and Security Act 2001, section 107(1)).

43   See note 35 above.

44   A failure by any person to comply with a code of practice or agreement under the part of the Act that deals with retention of communications data shall not of itself render him liable to any criminal or civil proceedings (Anti-Terrorism, Crime and Security Act 2001, section 102(4)). However, such code of practice or agreement shall be admissible in evidence in any legal proceedings in which the question arises whether or not the retention of any communications data is justified on the grounds that a failure to retain the data would be likely to prejudice national security, the prevention or detection of crime or the prosecution of offenders (Anti-Terrorism, Crime and Security Act 2001, section 102(5)).

45   Ie, in relation to any communication:
    (a)   any data identifying, or purporting to identify, any person, apparatus or location to or from which the communication is or may be transmitted,
    (b)   any data identifying or selecting, or purporting to identify or select, apparatus through which, or by means of which, the communication is or may be transmitted,
    (c)   any data comprising signals for the actuation of apparatus used for the purposes of a telecommunication system for effecting (in whole or in part) the transmission of any communication, and
    (d)   any data identifying the data or other data as data comprised in or attached to a particular communication.
    (Regulation of Investigatory Powers Act 2000, section 21(6).)

communications service providers who have signed up to the voluntary Code of Practice, for the prevention and detection of crime. It will also compel service providers to retain data for a specified period. The Code of Practice had yet to be drafted at the time of going to press.

The Act also empowers the Secretary of State, after reviewing the operation of any requirements contained in the code of practice and where it appears necessary to him to do so, to by order made by statutory instrument authorise the giving of directions[46] for the retention of communications data for the purposes described above. Such directions may be given to:

(a)   communications providers generally;

(b)   communications providers of a description specified in the direction; or

(c)   any particular communications providers or provider.

Certain provisions exist to allow the Secretary of State to make a financial contribution to the cost to a communications provider of retaining the relevant data – for further detail see section 106 of the Act.

1.3.12   Electronic Signatures Regulations 2002[47]

The Electronic Signatures Regulations, which came into force in the United Kingdom on 8 March 2002, implement the provisions of the E-Signatures Directive.[48] The purpose of that Directive is to facilitate the use of electronic signatures by ensuring that such signatures are not denied legal admissibility under conflicting rules in different jurisdictions – in other words that e-businesses can rely on an e-signature to be a binding contractual promise for legal purposes.

In the United Kingdom, the Electronic Communications Act 2000 gave e-signatures legal recognition under United Kingdom law and removed legal obstacles to their use by giving

---

46   Such an order must specify the maximum period for which a communications provider may be required to retain communications data by any direction given while the order is in force. Before giving a direction the Secretary of State shall consult–
(a)   with the communications provider or providers to whom it will apply; or
(b)   except in the case of a direction confined to a particular provider, with the persons appearing to the Secretary of State to represent the providers to whom it will apply.
Such direction must be given or published in such manner as the Secretary of State considers appropriate for bringing it to the attention of the communications providers or provider to whom it applies. It shall be the duty (enforceable by civil proceedings) of a communications provider to comply with any direction under this section that applies to him (Anti-Terrorism, Crime and Security Act 2001, section 104(3)–(6)).
47   SI 2002/318.
48   Council Directive 99/93/EC.

government ministers power to remove specific statutory requirements for communications to be on paper. The 2002 Regulations addressed the remaining issues under the E-Signatures Directive by establishing benchmarks for signature creation devices and for supporting digital certificates. The main provisions deal with the supervisory regime for providers of digital certificates, liability for loss suffered as a result of reliance on a certificate and data protection issues relating to the issue of such certificates.

The Regulations oblige the Secretary of State for Trade and Industry to supervise certification service providers ('persons who issue certificates or provide other services related to electronic signatures') in the United Kingdom, to maintain a register of such providers and to publicise instances of providers being guilty of 'detrimental conduct'. The certification service provider has a duty of care to the person relying on an e-signature and the Regulations set out the criteria for liability (the Regulations reverse the burden of proof so that provided the criteria are met, the service provider will be liable for any loss suffered unless it can prove that it was not negligent).

The Regulations also impose stringent data protection constraints on certification service providers. They may, for example, only obtain personal data for the purposes of issuing or maintaining the certificate directly from the data subject or with the data subject's explicit consent, and such data may only be processed for the purposes of, and to the extent necessary for, the issue or maintenance of the certificate (or any other purpose to which the data subject has given explicit consent).

1.3.13 Directive on Data Protection in the Electronic Communications Sector (2002/58/EC)

The Directive on the Processing of Personal Data and the Protection of Privacy in the Electronic Communications Sector (in this section, known as 'the Directive') applies 'to the processing of personal data in connection with the provision of publicly available electronic communications services in public communications networks in the Community' and is designed to replace the Telecoms Data Protection Directive of 1997[49] (implemented in the United Kingdom by the Telecommunications (Data Protection and Privacy) Regulations 1999[50]). As mentioned in the explanatory memorandum of the European Commission's document, the Directive is primarily aimed at adapting and updating the existing provisions to new and foreseeable developments in electronic communications services and technologies. In other words, it is designed to be

49　Council Directive 97/66/EC.
50　SI 1999/2093.

(no)

technologically neutral and hence to apply to transactions over the Internet in the same way as to transactions using telephone or fax. In furthering its objectives, the Directive uses much of the terminology from the Data Protection Directive.[51]

The preamble to the Directive states that:

'The Internet is overturning traditional market structures by providing a common, global infrastructure for the delivery of a wide range of electronic communications services. Publicly available electronic communications services over the Internet open new possibilities for users but also new risks for their personal data and privacy.'

The 1997 Telecommunications Directive included the definitions of *public telecommunications networks* (transmission systems permitting the conveyance of signals) and *telecommunications services* (services which consist of the transmission of voice or data over public telecommunications networks). These definitions are to be replaced by the concepts of *electronic communications networks* and *services* to ensure that all types of transmission services are covered regardless of the technology used.

In amending the existing legislative framework, the Directive includes some new definitions:

- **Communication**: any information exchanged or conveyed between a finite number of parties by means of a publicly available electronic communications service. This does not include any information conveyed as part of a broadcasting service to the public over an electronic communications network except to the extent that the information can be related to the identifiable subscriber or user receiving the information.

- **Electronic mail**: any text, voice, sound or image message sent over a public communications network which can be stored in the network or in the recipient's terminal equipment until it is collected by the recipient

- **Location data**: any data processed in an electronic communications network, indicating the geographic position of the terminal equipment of a user of a publicly available electronic communications service.

- **Traffic data**: means any data processed for the purpose of the conveyance of a communication on an electronic communications network or for the billing thereof.

- **User**: any natural person using a publicly available electronic communications service, for private or business purposes, without necessarily having subscribed to this service.

---

51   Council Directive 95/46/EC.

- **Value added service**: any service which requires the processing of traffic data or location data other than traffic data beyond that which is necessary for the transmission of a communication or the billing thereof.

The Directive:

- limits the ability of member states to intercept electronic communications by prohibiting any form of wide-scale, general or exploratory electronic surveillance other than where necessary to safeguard national security, defence, public security or the prevention, investigation, detection and prosecution of criminal offences. For these purposes member states may provide for the retention of data for a 'limited period';

- requires the facilitation of cryptography and anonymisation or pseudonymisation tools as a way of protecting the confidentiality of communications;

- approves the recording of communications, where necessary and legally authorised, for the purpose of providing evidence of commercial transactions;

- gives a right to subscribers to receive non-itemised bills;

- introduces the ability of member states to introduce certain privacy enhancing techniques in relation to itemised billing, such as requiring the deletion of a certain number of digits from the called numbers mentioned in itemised bills, in order to preserve the privacy of individuals;

- introduces an obligation to impose specific data protection requirements on sub-contractors that provide electronic communications services and value added services on behalf of service providers;

- introduces an obligation to inform individuals of any disclosures of traffic or location data from a provider of electronic communications services to a provider of value added services;

- amends the term 'traffic data' to refer only to what is generally necessary to ensure communication over an electronic communications network;

- introduces the concepts of value added service and electronic mail (see above for the definitions of these terms) as defined terms;

- introduces a requirement to inform users of the use of devices to store information, or gain access to information stored, in the terminal equipment of a user (for example, via cookies, web bugs, hidden identifiers and similar devices);

- gives users and subscribers the right to object to the use of the devices specified above;

- introduces a right to withdraw the consent for the processing of location data (other than traffic data) at any time except where necessary to safeguard national security, defence, public security or the prevention, investigation, detection and prosecution of criminal offences. For these purposes member states may provide for the retention of data for a 'limited period';

- introduces a right to opt-out free of charge of the publication of personal data in publicly available directories prior to such publication;

- limits the way in which data transmitted to third parties for the purposes of operating public directory services may be used;

- introduces an obligation to limit the information available via public directories to what is necessary to identify a particular subscriber (unless the subscriber has given his consent to the publication of additional personal data);

- introduces a specific obligation to seek individuals' consent, prior to the sending of SMS messages for marketing purposes;

- requires member states to make unsolicited commercial e-mails subject to opt-in consent;

- prohibits the practice of sending unsolicited commercial e-mails disguising or concealing the identity of the sender, or without a valid address to which the recipient may send a request that such e-mails cease;

- prohibits the development of technical equipment that would infringe users' data protection rights and requires standardisation of equipment such that it can be used in all member states;

- extends the remit of the Article 29 Working Party and requires it to take into account the views of all interested parties (including industry and consumers) when carrying out its advisory role;

- establishes a new period for implementation of the Directive – 15 months from its adoption; and

- requires the European Commission to submit to the Parliament and to the Council a report on the effects of the Directive (particularly in connection with unsolicited communications) within three years of its implementation.

For an informed opinion on the effects of the Directive on commercial organisations, see 'European facelift for E-Communications Data Privacy' by Rowan Middleton and Dominic Callaghan in *Privacy & Data Protection*, volume 2, issue 7, page 3.

1.4 ■ UNITED STATES PRIVACY LAW

In the United States, there is no overall data protection legislation as such. However, there is a right to privacy protected by the Fourth Amendment to the United States Constitution, which provides: 'The right of the people to be secure in their persons, houses, papers, and effects, against unreasonable searches and seizures ...' That right extends only to the right of a person to be free from *governmental* intrusion. There is no constitutional right to privacy from other individuals or companies.

There are, however, a variety of state and federal laws regarding privacy. These privacy laws are not comprehensive, and they cover only limited areas or activities. There is no all-encompassing legislation dealing with the collection, handling, and management of people's data, as there is in Europe. Commonly in United States law, federal laws regulate a particular area, and the states are prohibited from making additional requirements. In respect of the federal privacy legislation currently in force, the states are free to require greater privacy protection. Therefore, United States law requires a person or company to comply with the laws of the federal government, as well as the law of all of the states in which they do business which could easily be all 50 states! Some lawmakers are calling for the federal government to pass more comprehensive privacy laws and pre-empt the states from legislating in this area – until then, the piecemeal approach will continue.

1.4.1 Federal law

One of the main laws that regulates e-privacy at the federal level is the Electronic Communications Privacy Act 1986, 18 USC, section 2510ff, as amended by the Uniting and Strengthening America by Providing Appropriate Tools Required to Intercept and Obstruct Terrorism Act 2001 (the 'USA PATRIOT Act'). The 1986 Act was adopted to address the legal privacy issues that were evolving with the growing use of computers and other innovations in electronic communications and updated legislation passed in 1968 that had been designed to clarify what constitutes invasion of privacy when electronic surveillance is involved. The Act extended privacy protection outlined in the earlier legislation to apply to radio paging devices, electronic mail, cellular telephones, private communication carriers, and computer transmissions.

The Electronic Communications Privacy Act 1986 makes the knowing 'disclosure of contents', of any transmitted or stored contents of a communication illegal. As far as e-mail, in general, is concerned, it is illegal for an Internet Service Provider to release a person's e-mail communications to a third party. Section 2702 of the 1986 Act lists the exceptions to this rule, the four most relevant of which are where:

- the person consents to the disclosure (which could be obtained at the time that the terms of use are agreed);

- the provider of the service needs to protect its rights;

- an employer owns the e-mail system used by the employee – then the employer may inspect the contents of the employee e-mail on the system; and

- there is an emergency situation.

In addition to the Electronic Communications Privacy Act 1986, there are additional federal laws regarding on-line privacy matters which deal with a specific area.

Children's On-line Privacy Protection Act 1998

Title XIII, section 1301ff of the Children's On-line Privacy Protection Act 1998 requires certain commercial websites to obtain permission from parents before collecting, using, or disclosing personal information from children under the age of 13. This requirement applies to websites and on-line services that are targeted to, or know they are collecting data from, children under 13.

Websites must also post a privacy policy describing what personal information they collect from children, how it is to be used, and whether it is given to third parties. A link to the privacy policy must be prominently displayed or accessible on the website's home page and on any other area where personal information can be collected from children.

Health Insurance Portability and Accountability Act 1996

The Health Insurance Portability and Accountability Act 1996 contains standards requiring safeguards for the physical storage, maintenance, transmission and access to individual health information. These standards must be followed by all healthcare providers, healthcare clearing-houses and health plans that electronically maintain or transmit health information pertaining to an individual. By 14 April 2003, doctors, hospitals and insurance companies must be in compliance with the Act.

For a detailed analysis of the effects of the USA PATRIOT Act, see *Privacy & Data Protection* volume 2, issue 4, page 12.

1.4.2 Federal regulators

Much of the current on-line privacy enforcement regime is undertaken by the Federal Trade Commission, an independent agency of the United States government, created by the Federal Trade Commission Act 1914, 15 USC §41ff. The Commission is charged with enforcing section 5(a) of the Federal Trade Commission Act 1914, 15 USC §45(a), which prohibits unfair or deceptive acts or practices in or affecting commerce. 'Commerce' is broadly defined in section 4 of the 1914 Act, 15 USC §44.

The typical scenario involving Federal Trade Commission enforcement in the arena of privacy occurs in this type of situation:

> John Doe has a website selling goods on the Internet. In the process of selling goods, he collects people's data. On his site, he posts a privacy policy saying that he will not share his customers' information with any outside parties, but he will use their details for his own marketing purposes. At this point, he has made promises to his customers in respect of their data. Then, if he later divulges his customers' details to a third party, the Federal Trade Commission can start an enforcement action against him seeking an injunction and/or damages for breach of his own policy. The rational here is that he has acted deceptively by promising his customers one thing, but doing something different. It is because of this deceptive nature of his acts that the Commission can intervene. If, for example, Fred had clearly stated that he would sell his customers' details to the highest bidder, then the Federal Trade Commission would not intervene, for there would not have been any deceptive act on his part.

1.4.3 State laws

In order to comply fully with United States law on privacy, it would be necessary to comply with the laws of every state in which there would be any relevant transaction. The common law tort of privacy was first adopted in 1892, and all but two states recognise a civil right of action for invasion of privacy in their laws. In addition to the common law of each state, certain states have statutory provisions which impact on on-line privacy issues and each state's Attorney-General may investigate privacy violations, in the same way as the Federal Trade Commission. The details of the individual states' laws are beyond the scope of this book, but one should keep in mind that it will be necessary to comply with those laws and that local advice may be needed, as appropriate. Merely complying with the federal laws will not guarantee safety from legal enforcement.

The acquisition of customer information

The point at which an individual's information is acquired by an organisation is the most crucial moment in the lifetime of that organisation's personal data usage. The way that an organisation goes about obtaining data will dictate all activities that can lawfully be undertaken with the information from that moment, and into the future. It is vital that all relevant permissions are taken from an individual at an early stage in the relationship between the individual and the organisation – the value of each appropriately 'permissioned' customer may be counted in the hundreds of pounds and this will inevitably have a substantial impact on the valuation of any company.

In order to assist e-commerce companies in understanding their obligations under the European Directive on the 'protection of individuals with regard to the processing of personal data and on the free movement of such data'[1] (the 'Data Protection Directive'), the Article 29 Working Party (the independent body set up under article 30 of the Directive to advise on the application of data protection legislation to the member states) produced, in May 2001, a 'Recommendation on certain minimum requirements for collecting personal data on-line in the European Union'.[2] In this document the Working party made reference to the:

1   Council Directive 95/46/EC.
2   'Recommendation on certain minimum requirements for collecting personal data on-line in the European Union', Recommendation 2/2001.

'importance of ensuring that adequate means are put in place to guarantee that individual Internet users get all the information they need to place their trust, in full knowledge of the facts, in the sites with which they enter into contract, and if need be, to exercise certain choices in accordance with their rights under European legislation. This is particularly important given that Internet use multiplies the opportunities for collecting personal data and consequently the risks to the fundamental rights and liberties of individuals, in particular their private life.'

It is likely that the national data protection authorities will take considerable notice of the view of the Working Party's Recommendation when taking enforcement action against e-commerce businesses – the view of commerce, on the other hand, is that many of the opinions of the Working Party on the application of the Directive are commercially unrealistic. This chapter considers the various methods of obtaining data on-line and those aspects of data protection law that are relevant to that activity – in doing so, reference will be made to the Working Party's views where appropriate.

The topic of obtaining consent for 'marketing' purposes is dealt with more fully in Chapter 4.

2.1 ■ FIRST CONTACT

Customer information may be obtained in a number of ways, the most common of which in the e-commerce context is via the website user registration page – commonly the point of first contact with a new customer. Frequently, a user will be asked to supply some or all of the following information as a prerequisite for 'registration' on a site:

- name;
- address;
- e-mail address;
- date of birth;
- credit card information.

Additionally, security information may be requested from a user, such as:

- password;
- mother's maiden name;
- town of birth.

Sometimes additional 'marketing' data are requested from a user. Common examples include:

- number of children;

- newspaper commonly read;

- type of car;

- annual household income.

The content of the user registration page will be crucial in determining how this information may be used by the e-business and whether that business will be able to transfer the data to third parties.[3]

2.2 ■ FAIR AND LAWFUL PROCESSING – THE 'FAIR COLLECTION' NOTICE

One of the fair and lawful processing obligations in the First Data Protection Principle[4] (see Chapter 3) requires that certain information – the so-called fair collection information – be made 'readily available' to the data subject at the point that data are first obtained. In the context of on-line activities, the point of first obtaining will usually be the clicking of a 'submit' or similar button by the user following his completion of the user registration page. At that moment the user's personal data will be stored on the server of the relevant website, which will be under the control of the e-business.

The information with which the data subject must be provided is shown below.

Fair collection information

(a) the identity of the data controller;

(b) the identity of any representative of the data controller;

(c) the purpose or purposes for which the data are intended to be processed; and

(d) any other information which is necessary to enable the particular processing to be fair.

(a) Identity of the data controller

In most cases, this will be the name of the e-business responsible for collecting the data. Particular care should be taken where the website is jointly operated (such as a co-branded or framed site) to ensure that both businesses are identified. In its

---

3   On this latter point, see the need for an appropriate opt-out / opt-in clause at section 2.3.1.
4   Data Protection Act 1998, Schedule 1, Part I, paragraph 1.

Recommendation on minimum standards for on-line data collection,[5] the Article 29 Working Party stated that an on-line business should also give:

- its physical address (ie street address); and

- its electronic address (ie website homepage and e-mail address).

(b) Identity of representative

This will be applicable only where the data controller is located outside the European Economic Area[6] and uses equipment in the United Kingdom for processing personal data (see Chapter 6).

(c) Purposes for processing

The e-business will be required to state the purposes for which it intends to use the data collected. There is no guidance in the legislation on how this should be done. The Article 29 Working Party states that an on-line business must:

 'state clearly the purpose(s) of the processing for which the controller is collecting data via the site. For example, when data are collected both to execute a contract (Internet subscription, ordering a product, etc) and also for direct marketing, the controller must clearly state these two purposes.'[7]

For further detail on the information to be provided where data are to be used for direct marketing, see Chapter 4.

The requirement to state the purposes for processing is separate from, and should not be confused with, the need to provide the user with a method of opting-out of certain kinds of processing.[8] Prior to the drafting of the relevant notice, an e-business should ascertain all the purposes for which it will use the personal data that will be collected from users. Some uses will be inherently obvious from the nature of the relevant site – for example, a site that asks users to sign up to receive daily e-mail updates will request the user to give his or her e-mail address and the 'obvious' purpose for processing is to use the e-mail address to send daily e-mails. Where the e-business was to also transmit the e-mail addresses to a third party for marketing purposes, such use would not be obvious and would need to be the subject of an appropriate notice provision on the site.

---

5   Recommendation 2/2001.
6   Ie the member states of the European Union plus Norway, Iceland and Liechtenstein.
7   Recommendation 2/2001.
8   See section 2.3.

(d) Information enabling the processing to be 'fair'

There is little legislative guidance on what may or may not constitute fairness in this regard, but it is made clear[9] that regard must be had to 'the specific circumstances in which the data are or are to be processed'. Some therefore regard this provision as requiring the data controller to provide information on any non-obvious data processing activities.

In respect of 'fairness', it is likely that data will not be treated as having been obtained fairly on a website unless users of the site have been informed of, inter alia, the operation of cookies on the site and of the potential use of the user's information for marketing purposes (if relevant). The Article 29 Working Party recommends that e-commerce businesses should provide certain additional information to enable the processing to be fair.[10] That information, which should be shown 'directly on the screen before the [data] collection', includes the following:

- the obligatory or optional nature of the information requested (some sites use optional fields to request, for example, data that may be used for future marketing activities);

- the recipients or categories of recipients of the collected data;

- the existence of the right of access and rectification;

- the existence of the right to oppose any disclosure of the data to third parties for purposes other than the provision of the requested service and the way to do so;

- the information which must be supplied when using automatic collection procedures; and

- the level of security during all processing stages including transmission, for example, over networks.

The fair collection notice provisions apply *whether or not* the data were obtained from the data subject him or herself. However, where the data were obtained from someone *other than* the data subject, for example, by way of list rental, there is an exemption from the need to provide the above information where to do so would constitute 'disproportionate effort'. The Information Commissioner has indicated that all circumstances will be taken into account in determining what is 'disproportionate' in this context, including the nature of the personal data, the likely duration of their retention and the cost to the data controller involved in making the information available.

Further, the fair collection notice provisions will not apply where the data controller received personal data from another data

9   Data Protection Act 1998, Schedule 1, Part II, paragraph 2(3)(d).
10   Recommendation 2/2001.

controller, and that other data controller had informed the data subject of the transfer and of all the relevant information about the new data controller before the transfer took place.

There is no prescribed form for the provision of the above fair collection notice. Indeed, many websites achieve compliance by using an appropriately worded privacy policy (see section 2.7). The only requirement of the legislation is that the information must be 'readily available' to the data subject at the point of data collection.[11] Best practice would, however, dictate that the fair collection notice should appear on the user registration (data collection) page.

2.3 ■ USER REGISTRATION PAGE – OBTAINING CONSENT

At the heart of data protection legislation is the concept that it is possible to do almost anything with personal data if the relevant consent to the relevant purpose has been obtained from the relevant individual – consent is one of the six preconditions for the lawful processing of personal data.[12] It is thus desirable to obtain consent for all desired purposes (other than those for which another legitimising condition can be established – see section 3.2) for data at the time they are collected. Consent may be needed not only for future direct marketing,[13] but also to legitimise data exports where the server of the e-business is located outside the European Economic Area and for other purposes. It should be remembered that consent may also be used to legitimise the processing of sensitive personal data – however in such a case, the consent must be 'explicit'.[14]

Consent is not defined in the Data Protection Act 1998, but the Data Protection Directive[15] states that it means:

---

11 Data Protection Act 1998, Schedule 1, Part II, paragraph 2(1)(a). This rule is modified in the case of personal data which have been obtained from someone other than the data subject – in this instance, the data controller must make the information readily available to the relevant data subject before the 'relevant time' or as soon as practicable after that time. Relevant time in this context means:
  (a) the time when the data controller first processes the data, or
  (b) in a case where at that time disclosure to a third party within a reasonable period is envisaged—
    (i) if the data are in fact disclosed to such a person within that period, the time when the data are first disclosed,
    (ii) if within that period the data controller becomes, or ought to become, aware that the data are unlikely to be disclosed to such a person within that period, the time when the data controller does become, or ought to become, so aware, or
    (iii) in any other case, the end of that period.
12 Data Protection Act 1998, Schedule 2, paragraph 1.
13 See Chapter 4.
14 Data Protection Act 1998, Schedule 3, paragraph 1.
15 Council Directive 95/46/EC, article 2(h).

'... any freely given specific and informed indication of his wishes by which the data subject signifies his agreement to personal data relating to him being processed.'

The word 'signify' indicates the need for some active communication between the parties and almost certainly leads to the conclusion that the non-response by a data subject to a communication from a data controller cannot constitute consent. Thus the sending of a circular or other communication to the data subject which states that consent will be *assumed* 'unless we hear from you to the contrary' would be ineffective in obtaining consent.

Nevertheless, consent may be obtained by a number of methods. Use of an opt-out clause is particularly popular with commercial organisations – see section 2.3.1 and **Precedent 2**. It is important that such a clause is drafted to take account of all the anticipated uses of the personal data by the organisation concerned. It may be, for example, that an organisation wishes only to send marketing information concerning its own products or services to its customers. On the other hand, the organisation may wish to transfer copies of its customer database to 'carefully chosen' third parties. It should be remembered that opt-out consent will not be acceptable for certain types of processing activity – see further section 4.5 – and that, from September 2003, only opt-in consent will legitimise most forms of direct marketing using electronic media.[16]

Consent should generally be viewed as a last resort, not least because the present Information Commissioner has indicated dissatisfaction with consent being relied on generally by organisations. Further, it must be borne in mind that it is inherent in the nature of consent that it can usually be withdrawn by the data subject at any time – and thus it is an inherently dangerous method of legitimising personal data processing, particularly for commercial purposes. However, as is discussed further in Chapter 4, consent may be the only method of legitimising certain types of processing, for example future direct marketing – something that most e-businesses that collect personal data on-line will wish to engage in.

Where a business is processing customer data that do not benefit from current consent, it may be necessary to obtain consent before marketing activities commence – see below.

2.3.1 Opt-out/opt-in

Probably the best method of obtaining consent on a website (or indeed in offline documentation) is by use of an opt-out or opt-in clause. Such a clause consists of a statement of the intended

16 See further sections 1.3.13 and 2.3.3.

uses for data together with a box that allows a user to indicate, by ticking, that he does not wish his data to be used for a particular specified purpose (opt-out) or a box that allows a user to indicate that he assents to particular specified processing (opt-in).

Example of opt-out

> The Company will occasionally send you e-mails containing information that it considers to be of use to you. Please tick the box if you do not wish to be contacted in this way.

Example of opt-in

> The Company would like to make your data available to other partnership organisations so that special offers can be made to you from time to time. Please tick the box if you are happy with this arrangement.

In each case, a box that the user can tick should accompany the appropriate clause. Some websites use pre-ticked boxes, which allow the user to un-tick as appropriate. Whilst such pre-ticked boxes may be a legitimate method of obtaining consent to the processing of ordinary personal data, they will be insufficient to obtain explicit consent for sensitive personal data processing purposes.

2.3.2 Drafting an opt-out/opt-in clause

In guidance, drafted in response to the *Linguaphone* case[17] (see section 4.4.2), the Information Commissioner stated that the wording of opt-out or opt-in clauses will be crucial in determining whether appropriate consent has in fact been taken to the processing in question. The Commissioner has provided the following questions as constituting guidelines on the wording of clauses:

> 1. Do the words used convey all the likely non-obvious uses and disclosures of the customer's information?
>
> 2. Do the words properly convey the fact that information about the customer will be passed on to others?
>
> 3. Do the words convey the full implications for the customer of the use or disclosure, for example that he might receive telephone marketing calls?
>
> 4. Do the words explain the above in a way that would be understood by the great majority of likely data subjects?

---

17   *Linguaphone Institute Ltd v Data Protection Registrar* 14 July 1995, unreported.

It seems clear, therefore, that the Information Commissioner will consider that phraseology used to mask non-obvious uses or disclosures of personal data will not be operative in obtaining consent to such uses or disclosures.

On the question of the size and positioning of the wording, the Commissioner has offered the following questions by way of guidance on whether the text used will satisfy the requirement in the legislation to notify data subjects of the proposed uses of their personal data:

1.	Is the type in the notification of at least an equivalent size to the type used in the rest of the form?
2.	If not, is the print nevertheless of sufficient size for the customer's eye to be drawn to it?
3.	Is the layout and print size such that the notification is easy to read and does not appear cramped?
4.	Is the notification placed at or very close to the place where the customer supplies his details or signs the form?
5.	If not, is it placed in such a way that the customer will inevitably see it in the course of filling in the form?
6.	If not, is it nevertheless placed where the customer's eye will be drawn to it?
7.	Is the general nature and presentation of the form such that it conveys to the customer the need to read carefully all the details including the notification clause?

The guidelines that these questions represent apply to both on-line and offline opt-out clauses.

2.3.3 Effect of the Directive on the Processing of Personal Data and the Protection of Privacy in the Electronic Communications Sector[18]

In the Summer of 2002, Europe introduced a legislative measure that regulates the use of personal data in the electronic communications sector.[19]

The most significant aspect of the new legislation is that it requires opt-in consent to be obtained from users for all electronic direct marketing – this measure is intended to prevent unsolicited commercial e-mails ('spam'). This aspect of the legislation is likely

18   See section 1.3.13.
19   Council Directive 2002/58/EC.

to have a dramatic effect on e-commerce businesses – these organisations must alter existing opt-out clauses on their websites to take opt-in consent from users from September 2003. In respect of their existing customers, e-businesses will be permitted to target them with marketing communications where the products or services offered are not dissimilar to those for which the recipient is already a customer and where, in each communication, the recipient has been given an opportunity to opt-out of receiving direct marketing communications.

Although the wording of the Directive is not clear on the point, it is unlikely that the Directive will have retrospective effect – consents validly obtained on websites by way of opt-out clause should still be valid to legitimise relevant processing after the effective commencement of the legislation in October 2003.

2.3.4 Linking Arrangements

It may be that a user has come to the user registration page of a website having been referred to the page from another website. Where such a referral takes place, the referring site will often wish to gain access to the data of users who register on the referred-to site. Generally, such a sharing arrangement will fall foul of the Data Protection Act 1998 unless the referred-to site obtains consent from users to make such a transfer. Such consent should usually be obtained by appropriate opt-out clause[20] on the referred-to site, although it would also be possible to obtain the users' consent on the referring site prior to the referral.

2.4 ■ USER REGISTRATION PAGE – REQUESTING EXCESSIVE DATA

Care should be taken to ensure that the quantity of data requested from a user does not breach the Third Data Protection Principle, which provides as follows:

'Personal data shall be adequate, relevant and not excessive in relation to the purpose or purposes for which they are processed.'[21]

The legislation effectively obliges a business to consider first, what its purposes are for the processing of personal data, and second, what information is actually needed from a user for those purposes. Any information that is excessive for the purpose or purposes must not be requested from the user. That is not to

---

20 See section 2.3.1.
21 Data Protection Act 1998, Schedule 1, Part I, paragraph 3.

say that large quantities of personal data may not be collected by e-businesses, but more that the collection process is regulated. As long as a website clearly states its purposes for personal data processing (see section 2.2), then any information relevant to those purposes may be collected and stored without breaching the Third Data Protection Principle. If no purposes are stated then the purposes will be deemed to be those that are obvious from the nature of the transaction – data collected for non-obvious purposes will therefore be unlawfully collected.

Example

A website offers to supply daily news bulletins by e-mail to those that sign up for the service. The user registration page requests the user to supply his name, e-mail address and street address. The request by the website operator for name and street address breaches the Third Data Protection Principle's excessive data prohibition, unless the user is given clear information as to why those data are being requested.

Use of non-compulsory fields will not obviate the data controller's obligation to comply with the Third Data Protection Principle. In other words, the mere fact that a user is not *forced* to supply the information in order to use the service will not, of itself, satisfy the Principle's requirements. The reason for this is that consent is irrelevant to the operation of the Third Data Protection Principle. Where non-compulsory (optional) fields are to be used on a user registration page, those fields should be clearly identified as such. In its Recommendation on the collection of data on-line[22] (see section 2.2 and Appendix II), the Article 29 Working Party states that:

'The obligatory or optional nature [of the information to be provided] could be indicated, for example, by a star referring to the obligatory nature of the information, or alternatively, by adding "optional" besides non-obligatory information. The fact that the data subject does not supply optional information cannot count against him/her in any way.'

2.5 ■ SENSITIVE PERSONAL DATA

As with non-sensitive personal data, organisations should try to find a legitimising condition other than consent. If explicit consent is the only likely candidate, then it must be borne in mind that 'explicit' in this context means fully informed and

---

22 'Recommendation on certain minimum requirements for collecting personal data on-line in the European Union', Recommendation 2/2001.

freely given consent. This will require specific detail being given to the data subject on the precise uses for the data and any disclosures of the data that may be made by the data controller. Once this information has been imparted in an appropriate location on the website, an opt-in clause (an opt-out clause will not be sufficient for explicit consent) could be devised to take the consent – see section 2.3 and **Precedent 2**.

2.6 ■ M-COMMERCE AND LOCATION DATA

Mobile telecommunications technology makes it possible for the network provider to ascertain the geographical position of each mobile telephone on its network. The police already use this technology to ascertain the location of emergency callers and to provide evidence in criminal trials, such as information tending to disprove an alibi pleaded by a defendant. The commercial significance of the ability to pinpoint someone's location has not been lost on the mobile network operators, who paid over £21 billion for Third Generation ('3G') mobile telecommunications licenses in the government auction in 2000. It is expected that information will soon be delivered to users based on their location, thus enabling, for example, a user to receive an on-screen version of the menus of the two nearest Italian restaurants, plus directions on how to get to each.

The question that arises, however, is to what extent a mobile telephone user may be sent information on products or services based on his location *that he has not specifically requested*. To take the above example of the Italian restaurant, this might occur where the restaurant routinely sent a half-price offer on its steamed mussels to all mobile telephone users that entered within 200 metres of the restaurant.

The use of a mobile subscriber's telephone number, coupled with the telephone's geographical location, will not necessarily amount to the processing of personal data – and thus the restrictions in the Data Protection Act 1998 may not apply. However, under the Telecommunications (Data Protection and Privacy) Regulations 1999[23] (see section 1.3.6), the use of telecommunications data for marketing purposes is prohibited, subject to the limited exception that telecommunications companies are able to use their customers' data to send them marketing information on their own products and services with the consent of the customer.

The Directive on Data Protection in the Electronic Communications Sector (see section 1.3.13), expected to be effective in the United Kingdom by October 2003, includes provisions that modify the total ban on the processing of location data for marketing purposes. The new Directive

23   SI 1999/2093.

anticipates the use of location data by commercial organisations and introduces an obligation to inform individuals of any disclosures of traffic or location data from a provider of electronic communications services to a provider of 'value added services'. The ban on the use of location data for marketing purposes will be replaced by a requirement to obtain the consent of the mobile telephone user as a prerequisite to such use. Further, individuals must be provided with a simple means to temporarily suppress the processing of their location data, except for emergency services, public and national security, and criminal investigations.

2.7 ■ PRIVACY POLICIES

A 'privacy policy' is an increasingly common feature of websites. Although the presence of a privacy policy is not a legal requirement in the European Union per se (compare United States law and the requirements of the Federal Trade Commission, and in particular the need to impart certain information in order to obtain Safe Harbor[24] certification), a policy can perform a number of useful functions, including:

- complying with the fair obtaining notice requirements in the First Data Protection Principle[25] (see section 2.2 and the Explanatory Notes to **Precedent 1**);

- providing users with information on how to obtain subject access (see section 3.4); and

- providing the staff of the e-business with information on how the business uses personal data.

In its Recommendation on the collection of personal data by e-commerce companies (see section 2.2 and Appendix II),[26] the Article 29 Working Party makes it clear that all European Union-based e-commerce companies should have a clearly accessible privacy policy on their websites. The UMIST Compliance Check

---

24 The Safe Harbor regime (see Chapter 6) requires those United States companies that certify adherence to the scheme to impart a considerable quantity of information to users on their websites, including the purposes for which they collect and use information about users, how to contact the organisation with any inquiries or complaints, the types of third parties to which they disclose the information and the choices and means the organisation offers individuals for limiting its use and disclosure. Many Safe Harbor companies choose to provide the bulk of this information in a privacy policy – it must however be realised that the information 'must be provided in clear and conspicuous language when individuals are first asked to provide personal information to the organisation or as soon thereafter as is practicable, but in any event before the organisation uses such information for a purpose other than that for which it was originally collected' (see section 6.7.4).
25 Data Protection Act 1998, Schedule 1, Part I, paragraph 1.
26 'Recommendation on certain minimum requirements for collecting personal data on-line in the European Union', Recommendation 2/2001.

Project[27] found that 42% of United Kingdom sites surveyed did not contain any form of privacy statement.[28]

2.7.1 Obtaining consent in a privacy policy

Most websites provide their privacy policies on a non-compulsory click-through basis. It should be remembered that a non-compulsory click-through privacy policy should never be used to obtain data protection consent (for example, for direct marketing) from users by way of opt-out, as such an attempt will fail to be effective for the purposes of the Directive[29] and will be regarded as inadequate by the Information Commissioner. Although the legal position is not entirely clear, it is likely that an opt-in consent provision in a non-compulsory click-through privacy policy and an opt-out in a compulsory privacy policy will be effective methods of obtaining consent – but neither of these approaches should be regarded as 'best practice'.

2.7.2 Drafting a privacy policy

Website privacy policies are commonly criticised for their obscurity of language, assumption of user knowledge or misleading content. In its Compliance Check Project,[30] UMIST observed that:

'Privacy notices and explanations may be written in such a way as to be misleading or unclear to the ordinary visitor who may not be familiar with the exact terms of the law. Alternatively, the position on the website may be such that it is effectively unavailable, whether intentionally or unintentionally. Only about 5% of privacy statements reached the recommended level for intelligibility to the average reader when assessed using the Flesch Reading Ease[31] score. Financial and Insurance sites faired worse while children's sites, travel and retail sites scored better.'

Before drafting a privacy policy, care should be taken to research all the functions (or proposed functions) of the website, particularly regarding the usage of personal data collected on the site. Initially, a list should be collated of all the personal

27 'Study of Compliance with the Data Protection Act 1998 by UK Based Websites', May 2002, available on the Commissioner's website (see Appendix IV).
28 See section 3.14.
29 Council Directive 95/46/EC.
30 See section 3.14.
31 The Flesch Reading Ease score rates text on a 100-point scale; the higher the score, the easier it is to understand the document. For most standard documents, the aim is to score between 60 and 70. The Privacy Statement for sites surveyed scored an average of around 45.

data that are collected from individuals on the site – this will mainly be on the user registration page but data may be taken elsewhere, such as in the 'contact us' page or, on an 'e-mail updates' page or by the use of cookies.

The following questions[32] should then be asked to determine precisely the ambit of data collection and usage. By doing so, the likely content of the privacy policy will become clear.

Questions *about* data collection

1.	What are the purposes for the data that are collected on the site?
2.	Will any sensitive personal data be collected on the site?
3.	Will children's data be collected?
4.	Are cookies used, and, if so, what is their function?

Questions *on* accuracy and security *of information*

1.	Are there any procedures for verifying the accuracy of information provided by individuals on the site?
2.	Is there a procedure for the regular purging of old information?
3.	Are there procedures in place to ensure the integrity of information collected on the site?
4.	Is it possible for a user to obtain access to his 'file' on-line for the purposes of making alterations?
5.	Who has access to the information collected on the site?
6.	Are third parties that may have access to the information bound by appropriate contractual provisions?
7.	Is training provided to employees of the e-business in appropriate data handling techniques and procedures?

Questions *on the use of the information*

1.	Is all the information collected on the site processed by the e-business itself, or do others process data on behalf of the e-business?
2.	Will the information be provided to third parties for their own use?

32   Adapted from an article, 'Privacy Policies' by Cindy Burnes in *Privacy & Data Protection* volume 1, issue 4, page 10.

> 3. Can a user opt-out of future usage of his information, if so how?
>
> 4. Will the e-business need to pass personal data to a third party debt-collector?
>
> 5. Is the server for the website, on which personal data will be stored, located outside the European Economic Area?

Questions on user access to information

> 1. Does the e-business provide ready access, for data subjects, to their information?
>
> 2. If so, is there a fee involved?
>
> 3. If so, how is the fee payable?
>
> 4. How long will it usually take for a user to obtain access to his information?
>
> 5. In what form will the information be provided?
>
> 6. If a user feels that information processed by the e-business is inaccurate, is there a method by which he can request rectification?

See **Precedent 1** for an example of a privacy policy.

2.7.3 Location and accessibility of the privacy policy

Privacy policies should be clearly accessible from the website of all e-commerce businesses. It is most likely that the policy will be located at:

> www.website.com/privacypolicy

In its Recommendation on the acquisition of personal data on-line,[33] the Article 29 Working Party stated that:

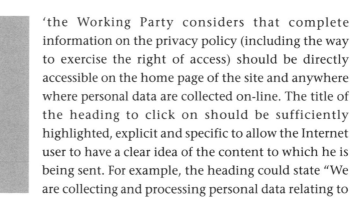

'the Working Party considers that complete information on the privacy policy (including the way to exercise the right of access) should be directly accessible on the home page of the site and anywhere where personal data are collected on-line. The title of the heading to click on should be sufficiently highlighted, explicit and specific to allow the Internet user to have a clear idea of the content to which he is being sent. For example, the heading could state "We are collecting and processing personal data relating to

---

33 'Recommendation on certain minimum requirements for collecting personal data on-line in the European Union', Recommendation 2/2001.

you. For further information, click here" or "Personal Data or Privacy Protection". The content of the information to which the user is directed should also be sufficiently specific.'

It seems then, at least as far as the Article 29 Working Party is concerned, that all privacy policies must be accessible from both the homepage of the website and each and every user registration or data collection page on the site. Further, the link itself must make it clear what information the user is being directed to – merely wording the link 'privacy policy' seems unlikely, at least in the eyes of the Working Party, to be sufficient.

2.7.4 Privacy policies and children

Although there are no specific provisions in the Data Protection Act 1998 regarding children, common sense dictates that a privacy policy on a website which is aimed at, or has a substantial audience of, children should be written with that particular audience in mind. The terminology and language used should be clear enough to be comprehensible by a normal child of the age of those children that commonly visit the site. The present Information Commissioner has indicated that she will pay particular attention to websites aimed at children when targeting any relevant enforcement action – indeed, children's sites were amongst the categories of websites investigated by UMIST on behalf of the Commissioner in early 2002.[34]

2.7.5 Privacy policies and subject access

The Directive[35] makes it clear that information about the right of subject access[36] must be imparted to users at the point of data collection. This aspect of the European legislation is not repeated in the 1998 Act – this latter point provides small comfort to those businesses who do not wish to suffer the inevitable increased administrative burden that informing individuals of their access rights would undoubtedly bring. If it is necessary to inform users of their rights of subject access, then the privacy policy may be an appropriate location for such information. The name of a contact at the organisation together with an e-mail address and/or telephone number can also be supplied for best practice.

The UMIST Compliance Check Project criticised United Kingdom websites for failing to supply information on subject access rights:

---

34   See the Compliance Check Project, available on the Commissioner's website (for the URL, see Appendix VI). See also section 3.14.
35   Council Directive 95/46/EC.
36   See section 3.4.

'Although 43% of those with Privacy Statements tell users how to gain access to data held about them, only around a third of notices mention it is a user right to see data.'[37]

2.7.6 Privacy policies and the use of cookies

If one or more cookies are to be placed on the hard drive of the user, this fact should be stated in the privacy policy. Similarly, where third party cookies may be placed on the user's hard drive when a user visits the site,[38] this fact should also be made clear to the user.

2.7.7 Privacy policies and third party data transfers

It should be remembered that part of the fair processing provisions in the Data Protection Act 1998[39] require information to be made available to the user on the purposes for the processing of personal data. Information concerning any proposed transfers of data from the e-business to a third party (including inter-group transfers) should ideally be stated in the privacy policy. Where consent is to be relied on to legitimise such third party transfers, the statement in the privacy policy will not necessarily[40] constitute such consent.

2.8 ■ ACQUIRING CUSTOMER DATABASES

In the era of consolidation of e-commerce businesses, the acquisition of customer databases is an increasingly common feature of commercial life. It has only recently been realised that the impact of data protection law on this activity may not only be substantial, but may also render the acquired database commercially valueless.

The effect of data protection law on the sale and acquisition of customer databases depends, in large part, on whether the business is being acquired as a whole, or whether parts only are being bought. In the case of an asset sale, the legal position is somewhat more complicated than that of a share sale or takeover – in the latter case there should be no particular data protection consequences unless the acquiring business wishes to use the database for its own purposes. The difficulty in acquiring

---

37 'Study of Compliance with the Data Protection Act 1998 by UK Based Websites', May 2002, page 14.
38 This may be done, for example, by a third party advertiser or advertising agent.
39 See Data Protection Act 1998, Schedule 1, Part II.
40 See section 2.7.1.

customer databases without the remainder of the business of the transferor lies in the need to comply with one of the conditions of Schedule 2 to the Data Protection Act 1998 (see Chapter 3) for all personal data processing. The transfer of a customer database from the transferor and the acquisition of the database by the transferee will both amount to 'data processing' by the two relevant data controllers.

The condition in Schedule 2 that is often seized upon by practitioners wishing to facilitate transfers of customer databases is the so-called 'legitimate interests' condition.[41] However, this condition requires a hypothetical balancing exercise to be carried out between, on the one hand, the necessary and legitimate interests of the data controller and, on the other, the privacy interests of the customers. As Jason Chess and Jamie Radford point out:[42]

'It is impossible to reconcile the inspiring philosophy of the DPA (which is to protect data subjects from abuse of their personal data), with a disclosure of data which will result in the processing of that data by a person to whom the data subject has given no consent, and with whom the data subject has had no dealings; and from whom the data subject has requested no goods or services. To transfer customer data to third parties, without restriction, is to do what is prohibited by the central tenets of the DPA; it is arguably also a breach of the human right to privacy. If this is not true, then consider the consequences of the contrary: the "legitimate interests" condition could be used to sanction any use of data otherwise prohibited by the DPA merely by virtue of the fact that it would be commercially advantageous to, and hence a "legitimate interest" of the companies concerned.'

If the 'legitimate interests' condition is indeed unavailable then the remaining condition in Schedule 2 that is most likely to be relevant is the consent of the data subject. Essentially, the acquiring e-business will (probably) not be in a position, at the moment of acquisition, to benefit from the consent (the first condition of Schedule 2) of the customers to its processing of their personal data because it will not have been in contact with them. However, it may be that the transferor of the database obtained consent from its customers for their data transfer at the point of their data collection – assuming that both the transfer and the proposed use for the data are covered by such consent then those activities will be effectively legitimised. If such consent has not been taken in advance, then the

41   Data Protection Act 1998, Schedule 2, paragraph 6.
42   'The Sale and Transfer of Customer Databases', *Privacy & Data Protection* volume 2, issue 5, page 3.

transferring business would have to revert to its customers to obtain their consent for the proposed transfer. Bearing this potential difficulty in mind, the advice for any new business should be specifically to refer to the disclosure of customer data to potential future successors in title at the point of data collection.

On a strict construction of the legislation, the acquiring business would not, unless the consent to do so had been taken from the customers, be able to use the customer database for its own marketing purposes – and this is probably the main reason for acquiring the database. However, it may be possible to send information to the customer base, informing individuals of the change and of the nature of the business of the new data controller and inviting customers to consent, by virtue of an appropriate opt-out or opt-in clause, to future marketing use.

Where the acquiring business has taken not only the customer database, but also the assignment of contracts with persons on the database, the situation is eased by the existence of the second paragraph of Schedule 2, which provides that the processing of personal data will be legitimised where:

 'the processing is necessary for the performance of a contract to which the data subject is a party.'

It should also be remembered that, upon obtaining personal data for the first time, a business must comply with the 'fair processing' requirements (see section 2.2). This will require, inter alia, the acquiring business to inform the customer database of the transfer to itself unless:

(i)   to do so would constitute disproportionate effort, or

(ii)   the customers have already been informed of the transfer.

It is likely, unless sensitive personal data on customers are to be processed by the acquiring organisation, that the Commissioner would approve the reality of the commercial view of the situation, which is that to inform all customers within the statutory timeframe[43] would involve disproportionate effort.

2.8.1   Foreign acquisitions

Where the acquiring company is based outside the European Economic Area, the data export ban[44] will be an additional hurdle to overcome where the acquiring company wants to gain access to the data in its own territory – see Chapter 6.

---

43   See note 12 above.
44   See the Eighth Data Protection Principle contained in the Data Protection Act 1998, Schedule 1.

2.9 ■ JURISDICTIONAL ISSUES

A brief reference should be made at this point in this book to the potential challenges that may arise where there is a collection of data that involves international data transfers. For example, a United Kingdom company may collect data on a website that is hosted on a server that is located in Germany. These issues are dealt with more fully in Chapter 6.

3

Managing privacy on-line

Privacy and data protection law are of fundamental importance to any e-commerce business. What e-businesses may and may not do with personal information governs, in large part, how the business functions on a day-to-day basis. This chapter considers those aspects of the law that regulate the way we do business on-line and the rights of individuals that give rise to specific business obligations.

3.1 ■ THE DATA PROTECTION PRINCIPLES

The eight Data Protection Principles, set out in Schedule 1 to the Data Protection Act 1998, form the backbone of European data protection legislation. Every e-commerce business in the European Union should ensure that, unless it is able to use a relevant exemption, all of its personal data processing complies with all eight of the Principles.

3.1.1 First Data Protection Principle – fair and lawful processing

> Personal data shall be processed fairly and lawfully and, in particular, shall not be processed unless—
>
> (a)   at least one of the conditions in Schedule 2 is met, and
>
> (b)   in the case of sensitive personal data, at least one of the conditions in Schedule 3 is also met.[1]

1   Data Protection Act 1998, Schedule 1, Part I, paragraph 1.

The First Principle therefore requires that:

- personal data be processed fairly;

- personal data be processed lawfully; and

- at least one of a set of conditions is applicable to all personal data processing carried out by an organisation.

When processing sensitive personal data (see below), an organisation must additionally be able to show that it benefits from one of a set of further legitimising conditions.

Fair processing

In determining whether any processing of personal data is 'fair', the Data Protection Act 1998 requires that particular regard must be paid to the method by which the data were obtained. Part II of Schedule 1 to the Act indicates that it is likely that processing will not be fair where the person from whom data are obtained is 'deceived or misled' as to the purposes of processing. Thus, personal data will be obtained unfairly where, for example, a person is misled into thinking that he will not receive marketing e-mails that he does in fact receive.

Further, personal data are not to be regarded as having been obtained fairly unless, at the time of the obtaining, or very soon afterwards, the relevant data subject is provided with certain information ('the information requirements'). See section 3.2 for further detail on the 'information requirements'.

Lawful processing

To process personal data in compliance with the First Data Protection Principle, the e-business must process the data 'lawfully'. This means that an e-business must observe general legal obligations – both statutory and common law.

Of particular relevance will be the laws of *confidence* (especially that arising between the data subject and the e-business), ultra vires (where an action is taken which is outside the scope of the e-business's powers) and article 8 of the European Convention on Human Rights (the requirement for respect for the private life of the individual).

Exemptions to the First Data Protection Principle

Although none are of general applicability to commercial organisations per se, there are a number of exemptions from the need to comply with some or all of the First Data Protection Principle.

The exemptions that remove the need for relevant personal data processing to comply with the First Data Protection Principle in its *entirety* are as follows:

- national security;
- crime and taxation;
- journalism, literature and art; and
- domestic purposes.

An exemption from the 'fair' and 'lawful' processing requirements in the First Data Protection Principle exists where the processing is for the purposes of any of the following:

- public inspection;
- disclosures required by law; and
- legal proceedings.

Exemptions from the 'information requirements' (see section 3.2) contained in the First Data Protection Principle are available for the following types of processing:

- health;
- education;
- social work;
- regulatory activity;
- public inspection;
- corporate finance;
- armed forces;
- judicial appointments and honours;
- Crown or ministerial appointments;
- management forecasts;
- negotiations; and
- legal professional privilege.

The detailed provisions concerning these exemptions are beyond the scope of this work as they are not of general applicability to e-businesses; this section therefore merely lists the exemptions. Those requiring the detail of the exemptions are referred to sections 27–39 and Schedule 7 to the Data Protection Act 1998 and to more general data protection books.

3.1.2 Second Data Protection Principle – purpose limitation

Personal data shall be obtained only for one or more specified and lawful purposes, and shall not be further processed in any manner incompatible with that purpose or those purposes.[2]

Personal data are not to be processed in a manner which is inconsistent with the purpose for which they were obtained.

2 Data Protection Act 1998, Schedule 1, Part I, paragraph 2.

Such a purpose could have been made known to the data subject by the e-business either expressly or by obvious implication at the time the data were obtained. Some commentators take the view that the Second Data Protection Principle effectively imposes an obligation on an e-business to enter into contractual relations with any transferee of the data to ensure that the transferee does not use the data in a manner that is incompatible with the original purpose(s).

3.1.3 Third Data Protection Principle – adequacy, relevance and excessiveness

> Personal data shall be adequate, relevant and not excessive in relation to the purpose or purposes for which they are processed.[3]

The Third Data Protection Principle essentially provides that only the bare minimum of personal data required by an e-business for its purposes for processing should be stored by that business. This Principle is commonly breached by e-commerce businesses requesting excessive personal data on the user registration page of their websites – see section 2.4.

3.1.4 Fourth Data Protection Principle – accuracy and currency

> Personal data processed shall be accurate and, where necessary, kept up to date.[4]

The Data Protection Act 1998 gives little guidance in relation to accuracy. However, it does give some guidance in relation to *inaccuracy*[5] – an organisation will not be treated as having breached the Fourth Data Protection Principle, notwithstanding the inaccuracy of any relevant personal data, where those data accurately record the information given to the e-business by the data subject or a third party (ie where the inaccuracy is not of the e-business's own making). However, the e-business must take reasonable steps to ensure the accuracy of data. Thus, if sensitive information is to be held, it may be incumbent on the e-business to take independent steps to verify those data. Furthermore, if the data subject notifies the controller that, in his view, the data are inaccurate, then a note should be made of this fact.

In practice, an individual is likely to complain of a breach of this Principle only where there has been some detriment to the individual as a result of the information being incorrect. Where

3   Data Protection Act 1998, Schedule 1, Part I, paragraph 3.
4   Data Protection Act 1998, Schedule 1, Part I, paragraph 4.
5   Data Protection Act 1998, Schedule 1, Part II, paragraph 7.

databases of this kind exist, then it will be sensible to ensure that there is a comments field where any information about inaccuracies/changes can be noted.

3.1.5 Fifth Data Protection Principle – data retention

> Personal data processed for any purpose or purposes shall not be kept for longer than is necessary for that purpose or those purposes.[6]

In order to comply with this provision, an organisation must consider for what duration it needs to hold data commercially. In doing so, it should take account of any legal requirements (such as the possibility of litigation) that would require it to hold data for a certain period.

Information technology systems can be set up set up in a way that ensures best data protection practice. Once relevant retention periods are set by an e-business, it will be possible to set up an auto-archive/delete system whereby data are automatically dealt with once the relevant retention period has been exceeded.

See section 3.8 for further information on the need for data retention policies.

3.1.6 Sixth Data Protection Principle – the rights of data subjects

> Personal data shall be processed in accordance with the rights of data subjects under the Act.[7]

An e-business would breach this Principle by failing to comply with one or more of data subjects' rights, ie failing to meet the terms of a subject access request, failing to comply with a request to cease direct marketing, continuing to process personal data which causes damage or distress despite having received a request to stop, failing to rectify inaccurate data at the request of the data subject or failing to comply with the provisions relating to automated decision taking.[8]

3.1.7 Seventh Data Protection Principle – security

> Appropriate technical and organisational measures shall be taken against unauthorised or unlawful processing of personal data and against accidental loss or destruction of, or damage to, personal data.[9]

6   Data Protection Act 1998, Schedule 1, Part I, paragraph 5.
7   Data Protection Act 1998, Schedule 1, Part I, paragraph 6.
8   Data Protection Act 1998, Schedule 1, Part II, paragraph 8.
9   Data Protection Act 1998, Schedule 1, Part I, paragraph 7.

In effect, the Seventh Data Protection Principle provides a statutory basis for good and appropriate security and information handling practice. In essence, there is a statutory obligation on e-businesses to ensure that personal data are processed in a secure environment.

The statutory guidance on the interpretation of this Principle[10] states that the e-business must consider the state of technological development and the cost of the implementation of any security measures. Bearing in mind these factors, the security measures that are adopted by the business must ensure a level of security that is appropriate to both the nature of data to be protected and the likely harm that would result from a breach of this Principle. In other words, the more sensitive the data, and the more adverse the consequences of a security breach for the data subject, the more stringent security requirements that should be put in place.

The Information Commissioner has indicated that security measures that are more stringent should be applied to data comprising health and financial records than to records that are drawn from publicly available sources. The Commissioner has also shown support for the use of cryptography and other privacy enhancing technologies. In the UMIST study of United Kingdom website data protection compliance,[11] e-businesses were criticised for failing to apply appropriate security arrangements for the transmission of personal data collected on a website to the relevant database where they are stored pending further processing.[12]

Appropriate measures should be put in place to ensure that non-authorised personnel are not able to gain access to personal data. The most common types of such measures are the use of passwords, swipe cards and smart cards. Security procedures also include making regular back-up copies, which should ideally be stored offsite.

The interpretation provisions to the Seventh Data Protection Principle also affect the relationship between an e-business or other organisation (data controller) and a data processor. There is an obligation on the organisation to ensure that any processors it appoints carry out processing on its behalf in a secure manner. See Chapter 5 for further detail on the formalities that are required for the controller-processor relationship.

The following general guidance has been issued by the Information Commissioner concerning security obligations:

---

10 Data Protection Act 1998, Schedule 1, Part II, paragraphs 9–12.
11 See section 3.14.
12 The Study found that 39% of respondents used some form of secure electronic link for the data transmission. For around 60% of those websites with some security measures, such security was present for all the data transferred, rather than merely for certain specific forms of data such as credit card details. The majority of United Kingdom websites used one of the following three types of data storage vehicle: Microsoft Access (24.5%), SQL Server (20.6%) and Oracle (9.7%).

Security management:

- Does the data controller have a security policy setting out management commitment to information security within the organisation?

- Is responsibility for the organisation's security policy clearly placed on a particular person or department?

- Are sufficient resources and facilities made available to enable that responsibility to be fulfilled?

Controlling access to information:

- Is access to the building or room controlled or can anybody walk in?

- Can casual passers-by read information on screens or documents?

- Are passwords known only to authorised people and are the passwords changed regularly?

- Do passwords give access to all levels of the system or only to those personal data with which that employee should be concerned?

- Is there a procedure for cleaning media (such as tapes and disks) before they are reused or are new data merely written over old? In the latter case, is there a possibility of the old data reaching somebody who is not authorised to receive it? (for example, as a result of the disposal of redundant equipment).

- Is printed material disposed of securely, for example, by shredding?

- Is there a procedure for authenticating the identity of a person to whom personal data may be disclosed over the telephone prior to the disclosure of the personal data?

- Is there a procedure covering the temporary removal of personal data from the data controller's premises, for example, for staff to work on at home? What security measures are individual members of staff required to take in such circumstances?

- Are responsibilities for security clearly defined between a data processor and its customers?

Ensuring business continuity:

- Are the precautions against burglary, fire or natural disaster adequate?

- Is the system capable of checking that the data are valid and initiating the production of back-up copies? If so, is full use made of these facilities?

- Are back-up copies of all the data stored separately from the live files?

- Is there protection against corruption by viruses or other forms of intrusion?

Staff selection and training:

- Is proper weight given to the discretion and integrity of staff when they are being considered for employment or promotion or for a move to an area where they will have access to personal data?

- Are the staff aware of their responsibilities? Have they been given adequate training and is their knowledge kept up to date?

- Do disciplinary rules and procedures take account of the requirements of the Act? Are these rules enforced?

- Does an employee found to be unreliable have his or her access to personal data withdrawn immediately?

- Are staff made aware that data should only be accessed for business purposes and not for their own private purposes?

Detecting and dealing with breaches of security:

- Do systems keep audit trails so that access to personal data is logged and can be attributed to a particular person?

- Are breaches of security properly investigated and remedied; particularly when damage or distress could be caused to an individual?

3.1.8 Eighth Data Protection Principle – export ban

> Personal data shall not be transferred to a country or territory outside the European Economic Area unless that country or territory ensures an adequate level of protection for the rights and freedoms of data subjects in relation to the processing of personal data.[13]

This Principle provides that personal data must not be transferred to a country or territory outside the European Economic Area[14] unless that country or territory has in place a legal system that ensures an acceptable level of data protection.

It is, at first instance, for the relevant exporting e-business to decide if the recipient (country or territory) of the personal data will offer adequate data protection. The European Commission can offer guidance as to which countries will be deemed adequate. However, to date, only Switzerland and Hungary have been declared wholly adequate for export purposes. Canada, which was added to the list of acceptable countries in January 2002, is adequate for certain transfers only. Most significantly, the United States has not been, and is not likely to be, declared adequate.

There are a number of exemptions to this Principle – in particular, the Principle does not apply if the individual has given consent to the transfer.

As a result of political initiatives between the European Commission and the United States Department of Commerce, the 'Safe Harbor' principles have been agreed – these allow United States organisations to declare themselves compliant with European Union data protection rules and thus to allow the transfer of personal data from EU companies.

It should be remembered that the making available of personal data on a website will be treated as a transfer of those data to every country of the world and thus prima facie unlawful.

See Chapter 6 for a full analysis of the personal data export ban and the methods for its circumnavigation.

3.2 ■ LEGITIMISING PERSONAL DATA PROCESSING

Unless there is a relevant exemption from the application of the First Data Protection Principle, personal data processing – including obtaining data on a website user registration page and

---

13 Data Protection Act 1998, Schedule 1, Part I, paragraph 8.
14 Ie the member states of the European Union plus Norway, Iceland and Liechtenstein.

transferring data to a third party – is unlawful unless one of the following six legitimising conditions (contained in Schedule 2 to the Data Protection Act 1998) exists:

- the data subject has given his consent to the processing;

- the processing is necessary –

    (a)   for the performance of a contract to which the data subject is a party; or

    (b)   for the taking of steps at the request of the data subject with a view to entering into a contract;

- the processing is necessary to comply with any legal obligation to which the data controller is subject, other than an obligation imposed by contract;

- the processing is necessary in order to protect the vital interests of the data subject;

- the processing is necessary –

    (a)   for the administration of justice;

    (b)   for the exercise of any functions conferred by or under any enactment;

    (c)   for the exercise of any functions of the Crown, a minister of the Crown or a government department;

    (d)   for the exercise of any other functions of a public nature exercised in the public interest;

- the processing is necessary for the purposes of legitimate interests pursued by the e-business or by the third party or parties to whom the data are disclosed, except where the processing is unwarranted in any particular case because of prejudice to the rights and freedoms or legitimate interests of the data subject.

As far as the last condition is concerned, the Information Commissioner takes a wide view of 'legitimate interests' and recommends that two tests be applied to establish whether this condition may be appropriate in any particular case – both tests must be satisfied. The first is the establishment of the legitimacy of the interests pursued by the e-business or the third party to whom the data are to be disclosed. The second is whether the processing is unwarranted in the particular case by reason of prejudice to the rights and freedoms or legitimate interests of the data subject. The latter balancing test is weighted in favour of the data subject by the fact that, due to the protective nature of the legislation, the interests of a data subject will usually override those of the e-business.

Consent is the most controversial of the legitimising conditions and is discussed in more detail in section 2.3.

Sensitive personal data

Under the Directive, there is a general ban in the European Union on the processing of sensitive personal data, ie information as to one or more of the matters listed in the box below. That ban may be circumnavigated where the e-business is able to avail itself of one of a set of certain legitimising conditions (see below). It should be noted that websites may collect sensitive personal data on users in one of two distinct ways: the first is by requesting such data on a data collection page (for example, the user is asked to register on the site and requested to provide information concerning his or her ethnicity or religion); the second is where the fact of the visit to a site or registration thereon itself amounts to an indication of a sensitive data issue (for example, a user registers on a site which provides regular e-mail updates on migraines or visits a site which provides information on rehabilitation following a sex-change operation).

Sensitive personal data[15]

(a)   the racial or ethnic origin of the data subject;

(b)   his or her political opinions;

(c)   his or her religious beliefs or other beliefs of a similar nature;

(d)   whether he or she is a member of a trade union;

(e)   his or her physical or mental health or condition;

(f)   his or her sexual life;

(g)   the commission or alleged commission by him or her of any offence; or

(h)   any proceedings for any offence committed or alleged to have been committed by him or her, the disposal of such proceedings or the sentence of any court in such proceedings.

Schedule 3 to the Data Protection Act 1998 contains a set of exceptions to the ban on the processing of sensitive personal data. Examples of such exemptions (or legitimising conditions) include the 'explicit consent' of the data subject, compliance with employment law obligations, equal opportunities monitoring and the vital interests of the data subject. Member states are permitted to create further exemptions – the United Kingdom has created a further ten such exemptions in the form of secondary legislation. Organisations should (as part of a data protection audit or otherwise) ensure that they are aware of all the types of sensitive personal data that they process. The 1998 Act requires any processing of sensitive personal data that is not needed for the proper or desired operation of the organisation to cease.

---

15   Data Protection Act 1998, section 2.

A full list of the exemptions from the sensitive personal data processing ban is shown below. Further detail on the scope of the exemptions is contained in Schedule 3 to the Data Protection Act 1998 and in the Data Protection (Processing of Sensitive Personal Data) Order 2000.[16]

Exemptions from the sensitive personal data processing ban

Explicit consent of the data subject

Compliance with employment law obligations

Vital interests of the data subject

Processing by not-for-profit organisation

Information made public by the data subject

Legal advice and establishing or defending legal rights

Public functions (administration of justice, etc)

Medical purposes

Records on racial equality

Detection of unlawful activity

Protection of the public

Public interest disclosure

Confidential counselling

Certain data relating to pensions

Religion and health data for equality of treatment monitoring

Legitimate political activities

Research activities which are in the substantial public interest

Police processing

3.3 ■ THE NOTIFICATION SYSTEM

Under the Directive,[17] it is generally a criminal offence to process personal data anywhere in the European Union unless there is an appropriate entry in the relevant national register of data controllers. The United Kingdom register is held and maintained by the Office of the Information Commissioner (see Appendix VI).

The register entry must both reflect the fact of processing and must list the types of processing undertaken by the registrant data controller.

16 SI 2000/417.
17 Council Directive 95/46/EC.

The register is a public document and can be inspected at the Information Commissioner's premises or on-line on the Commissioner's website (for the URL and related information, see Appendix VI). A search of the register will reveal the name of the registrant, registration number, date of expiry of current registration and the types of processing registered as undertaken by that data controller.

3.3.1 The need to notify

The obligation to notify arises out of section 17 of the Data Protection Act 1998 which provides that:

 '… personal data must not be processed unless an entry in respect of the data controller is included in the register maintained by the Commissioner …'

The requirement to have a register entry prior to carrying out personal data processing first arose under the Data Protection Act 1984. The premise behind the system is transparency, ie that individuals should be able to inspect a publicly available register to determine who is processing personal data and the reasons that they are doing so.

Certain types of processing are exempt from the need to notify – see below. But it is most important for e-businesses to realise that the Data Protection Principles (see Glossary) apply to all processing, even if such processing is exempt from the notification requirement. This means that the Office of the Information Commissioner can take action against e-businesses for breaching one or more Data Protection Principles as a result of processing that was not required to be notified.

3.3.2 How to notify

Notification can be undertaken either on-line or by telephone (for the relevant contact details, see Appendix VI). In each case the e-business will be asked for certain information – see below.

The e-business will then be sent a copy of the draft register entry and given an opportunity to amend it before it becomes available for public inspection. E-businesses should ensure that all their automated processing (unless exempt – see below) is covered in their register entry.

Manual data processing does not need to be notified, but e-businesses may volunteer to include their manual processing within their register entry. The advantage of notifying manual data processing for e-businesses that only process that type of data is that the e-business will thereby be subject to less onerous disclosure obligations where a data subject access request is made (see section 24 of the Data Protection Act 1998).

The notification fee is £35 and the register entry will be maintained for one year. About two months before the expiry of the registration, the Office of the Information Commissioner will contact the e-business to invite renewal – a further £35 fee is payable each year. Only one register entry is permitted per e-business and thus each company in a group of companies must maintain a separate register entry.

3.3.3 What to notify

The e-business will be asked for its name, address, contact information and company registration number (if relevant) and will then be expected to make general statements about the types of processing undertaken (see the box of standard purposes below) and whether or not personal data are sent outside the European Economic Area – see below.

Purposes for personal data processing

Standard business purposes

Staff administration

Advertising, marketing and public relations

Accounts and records

Other purposes

Accounting and auditing

Administration of justice

Administration of membership records

Advertising marketing and public relations for others

Assessment and collection of taxes and other revenue

Benefits, grants and loans administration

Canvassing political support amongst the electorate

Constituency casework

Consultancy and advisory services

Credit referencing

Crime prevention and prosecution of offenders

Debt administration and factoring

Education

Fundraising

Health administration and services

Information and databank administration

Insurance administration

Journalism and media

Legal services

Licensing and registration

Pastoral care

Pensions administration

Policing

Private investigation

Processing for *not for profit* organisations

Property management

Provision of financial services and advice

Realising the objectives of a charitable organisation or voluntary body

Research

Trading/sharing in personal information

The general statement includes information on the *purposes* of processing (for example, for credit referencing, fundraising, trading in personal information), the *data subjects* whose data are being processed (for example, staff, customers, agents), the *classes of data* processed (for example, personal details, employment details, family and social circumstances) and the *persons to whom the data may be disclosed* (for example, prospective employers, financial institutions, the media). In each case the e-business is given an opportunity to select from a list of available options.

When e-businesses are considering whether they send personal data outside the European Economic Area, they should bear in mind the need that some businesses have to book foreign hotel rooms or airline tickets for their employees. They should also be aware that where personal data are available on the e-business's website (for example, where photographs of staff appear on-line), such availability will effectively be a transfer to all countries of the world. If data are to be sent outside the European Economic Area then the notification must reflect this fact.

The Information Commissioner has also given specific guidance in relation to the use of personal data on the Internet.[18] The guidance suggests some free text additions to the standard

18   'Data protection and the Internet: guidance on registration', available on the Commissioner's website (see Appendix VI).

business purposes outlined above which may be used for notification. It also makes the point that providing access to personal data through the Internet could potentially allow disclosure to be made to any user of the Internet worldwide. Whether this happens in practice will depend on the access allowed to the particular site. If access is possible worldwide then the notification should make this clear.

E-businesses will additionally be expected to make a security statement. This consists of a series of questions to which the answer may be either 'Yes' or 'No'. It should be noted that there are no adverse consequences of answering with a 'No'. However, where e-businesses find that their answers are in the negative, they should be aware that their processing *may* breach the Seventh Data Protection Principle.[19] The questions are set out below as they appear on the Commissioner's website – each with a pre-ticked 'No' answer that can be changed to 'Yes' as required.

Security Questions

Have you taken any measures to guard against unauthorised or unlawful processing of personal data and against accidental loss, destruction or damage?

☐ Yes ☒ No

If yes – please answer the following questions.

Do the methods include:

Adopting an information security policy? (i.e. providing clear management direction on responsibilities and procedures in order to safeguard personal data)
☐ Yes
☒ No

Taking steps to control physical security? (for example, locking doors of the office or building where computer equipment is held)
☐ Yes
☒ No

Putting in place controls on access to information? (for example, introduction of password protection on files containing personal data and encryption)
☐ Yes
☒ No

Establishing a business continuity plan? (for example, holding a backup file in the event of personal data being lost through flood, fire or other catastrophe)
☐ Yes
☒ No

Training your staff on security systems and procedures?
☐ Yes
☒ No

Detecting and investigating breaches of security when they occur?
☐ Yes
☒ No

Adopting the British Standard on Information Security Management BS7799? (This standard is not a statutory requirement)
☐ Yes
☒ No

---

19   Data Protection Act, Schedule 1, Part I, paragraph 7.

It should be remembered that if the e-business's processing changes after a notification has been made, there is a duty to inform the Office of the Information Commissioner of this change as soon as possible – e-businesses should not wait until the expiry of their 'notification year' before informing the Commissioner of the change.

3.3.4 Standard templates

The Information Commissioner's website[20] features a number of standard templates that can be used to aid the notification process. Each template includes a pre-selected set of processing types, data subjects, data classes and classes of recipients. When using standard templates, care must be taken to check that the standard terms of each entry accurately correspond to the activities of the business that it is notifying – amendments can be made on-line to standard templates.

By way of example, the following templates appear under the 'General' and 'Services' sections (the most likely to be of relevance to e-commerce businesses) in the standard templates.

General	
N834	Airline
N830	Business specialising in direct marketing
N856	Catalogue mail order trader
N865	CCTV only
N853	Friendly society
N818	Genealogist
N874	Housing association
N900	Journalist
N840	List broking
N804	Mail order traders
N869	Manufacturer
N821	Motor trader
N884	Neighbourhood watch
N920	Petrol retailer
N873	Property management
N841	Publisher
N805	Retail/wholesale
N871	Software development
N833	Trades union
N858	Unclassified

20   www.dataprotection.gov.uk.

Services

N885	Actuaries
N803	CV services
N837	Citizens Advice Bureau
N809	Consultant
N872	Dating agency
N813	Employment and recruitment agencies
N844	Estate agent
N897	Fire service
N911	Internal drainage boards
N842	Internet Service Provider
N810	Private investigation
N811	Private investigation, debt administration and factoring
N836	Surveyor
N845	Travel agent
N863	Vet

3.3.5 Notification offences[21]

As far as the notification regime is concerned, it is generally a criminal offence to:

- process personal data without a register entry; and

- fail to notify the Office of the Information Commissioner of changes to the registrable particulars.

By virtue of section 61 of the Data Protection Act 1998, a director, manager, secretary or other officer of a corporate body may be prosecuted for the same offence as that which has been proved against the corporate body if he has been involved in the offence by way of some connivance or neglect.

---

21   Data Protection Act 1998, section 21.

3.3.6 Exemptions from the notification requirement

The rules on exemptions from the notification requirement derive from the Data Protection (Notification and Notification Fees) Regulations 2000.[22] Certain types of person are exempt from the notification requirement:

- individuals who process personal data for personal, family or household affairs (including recreational purposes);

- data controllers who only process personal data for the maintenance of a public register;

- data controllers who do not process personal data on computer; and

- some not-for-profit organisations.

The Office of the Information Commissioner has given guidance that the above reference to 'computer' includes desktop, mainframe, laptop and palmtop or hand-held device. It also includes other equipment that has some ability to process data automatically, such as automated information retrieval systems for microfilm and microfiche, audio and visual systems, electronic flexitime systems and telephone logging equipment.

Additionally, certain types of processing are exempt from the requirement to notify, namely processing undertaken for:

- national security;

- staff administration;

- advertising, marketing and public relations; and

- accounts and records.

It should be noted that the exemption from the requirement to notify will be lost where the processing undertaken by an organisation is additionally for one of the 'other purposes' listed in section 3.3.4 above.

E-businesses must then go on to comply with the Data Protection Principles – notification does not exempt e-businesses from compliance with other obligations in the Data Protection Act 1998.

3.4 ■ SUBJECT ACCESS RIGHTS

Of increasing organisational and financial burden to businesses is the right of individuals to receive certain information from businesses concerning data held by the businesses on those individuals. Section 7 of the Data Protection Act 1998 allows an individual to make a 'data subject access request' and thereby to

22   SI 2000/188.

essentially obtain a copy of all personal data held about him or her by any United Kingdom business.[23]

Section 7(1) provides as follows:

An individual is entitled—

(a)   to be informed by any data controller whether personal data of which that individual is the data subject are being processed by or on behalf of that data controller,

(b)   if that is the case, to be given by the data controller a description of—

  (i)   the personal data of which that individual is the data subject,

  (ii)   the purposes for which they are being or are to be processed, and

  (iii) the recipients or classes of recipients to whom they are or may be disclosed,

(c)   to have communicated to him in an intelligible form—

  (i)   the information constituting any personal data of which that individual is the data subject, and

  (ii)   any information available to the data controller as to the source of those data,

---

3.4.1   Form of the subject access request

The Data Protection Act 1998 does not specify any particular method of request for data subject access, save that it be 'in writing'. It is not clear on the face of the legislation whether this would include e-mail, but the better opinion is that it does.

An e-business need not comply with the request where the business is uncertain as to the identity of the person making it. It is not clear what degree of identification the data controller is

---

23   The corresponding right appears in Council Directive 95/46/EC in Article 12: 'Member States shall guarantee every data subject the right to obtain from the controller ... without constraint at reasonable intervals and without excessive delay or expense:
  •   confirmation as to whether or not data relating to him are being processed and information at least as to the purposes of the processing, the categories of data concerned, and the recipients or categories of recipients to whom the data are disclosed,
  •   communication to him in an intelligible form of the data undergoing processing and of any available information as to their source,
  •   knowledge of the logic involved in any automatic processing of data concerning him at least in the case of the automated decisions referred to in Article 15(1).'

entitled to require of the data subject, except that any such requirement must be 'reasonable'. It is suggested that where a data subject sends a personally signed letter to an e-business, that will, in most cases, constitute sufficient identification. However, there may be occasions when compliance with a subject access request that has been made by signed letter may be inappropriate, and may even constitute a breach of the 1998 Act. Take, for example, the case of a person making an access request to a travel company in the name of their partner, and requesting a copy of their partner's recent on-line holiday booking form so that they can ascertain the names of any vacation companions!

E-mail requests for subject access, if such are to be accepted by an e-business, should ideally be accompanied by appropriate identification-verifying information.

A data subject access request will be deemed, by operation of the relevant legislative provisions, to relate to *all* the personal data held by the business. However, a data subject may, by virtue of section 7(7) of the Data Protection Act 1998, expressly limit his application to certain specific data.

3.4.2 Fees for subject access

An e-business is entitled to charge a fee for subject access, but that fee must not usually be more than the statutory maximum sum of £10.[24] A higher fee may be payable in the case of certain education records – subject to a maximum of £50. Credit reference agencies must not charge more than £2 where the access request is restricted to credit-related data.

3.4.3 Identifying an access request

It is important that an e-business is able to identify a subject access request when one arrives. The statutory time-period for compliance with the request (40 days) will begin to run from receipt and failure to comply within the time limit is likely to give rise to an investigation by the Information Commissioner.[25] Given that all subject access requests must be in writing (which almost certainly includes e-mail), it is incumbent upon e-businesses to educate and train officers and employees of the organisation concerning the need to be able to identify a subject access request and to bring it to the attention of the relevant person within the organisation.

---

24 The Data Protection (Subject Access) (Fees and Miscellaneous Provisions) Regulations 2000, SI 2000/191.
25 The Commissioner is obliged, under section 42 of the Data Protection Act 1998, to investigate all complaints made to him or her concerning the processing of personal data by any United Kingdom organisation – many complaints received by the Commissioner relate to failures by businesses to comply with the rights of data subjects to receive a copy of their personal data within 40 days of the request.

3.4.4 Verifying the identity of the applicant

There may be a concern that the person making the subject access request is not the relevant data subject. Disclosing personal data on one data subject to another would constitute a breach of data protection law (notably the First and Seventh Data Protection Principles).

> **Example**
>
> Mrs X writes to the e-business and requests to see a copy of her husband's file. She writes the letter in the name of, and signs it in the name of, her husband.

It is suggested that an e-business should take reasonable steps to verify the identity of the data subject before responding to an access request, particularly where the data held by the business include sensitive personal data.

It may be possible for an appropriately authorised person to make a subject access request on behalf of another, for example, where a solicitor makes a request on behalf of her client. It is suggested that, in those circumstances, the controller should obtain written authorisation, signed by the data subject, from the agent before proceeding to comply with the request.

3.4.5 Obligations of e-businesses

The flipside of the right of an individual to make a subject access request of any United Kingdom business is the corresponding obligation of the business to perform its appropriate obligations under section 7 of the Data Protection Act 1998. The obligations to provide a *description* of the personal data being processed, the *purposes* for such processing and the *recipients* to whom those data are likely to be disclosed mean it is likely that standard responses can be formulated depending on the category of data subject making the request. It is therefore suggested that a standard template document be developed which provides the appropriate information to applicants who fall within a particular category, for example, 'staff' or 'customers'.

Section 7 further provides that the individual is entitled to have communicated to him, in an intelligible form, the *information constituting the personal data*,[26] information concerning the business's *source*[27] of that information and, where automated decision-making has taken place, information on the *logic*[28] of

26 Data Protection Act 1998, section 7(1)(c)(i).
27 Data Protection Act 1998, section 7(1)(c)(ii).
28 Data Protection Act 1998, section 7(1)(d). But also see the effect of the Data Protection (Subject Access) (Fees and Miscellaneous Provisions) Regulations 2000 below and at note 32.

such decision-making – it is less likely that standard documentation can be used for this obligation as the responses will usually differ for each data subject. Generally, the business should provide a 'printout' containing the information held on the individual making the request. However, a full copy of the data does not have to be made available to the data subject where:

(a)   the supply of such a copy is not possible;

(b)   the supply of such a copy would involve disproportionate effort; or

(c)   the data subject agrees otherwise.[29]

There is no definition of 'disproportionate effort' in the Data Protection Act 1998. However, for this exemption to be made out, the relevant 'effort' is likely to require more than mere inconvenience. It should be remembered that, even where a copy of the data does not have to be supplied (due to, for example, disproportionate effort), the remaining requirements to provide appropriate descriptions, the logic behind automated decisions and information as to the data source, remain.

The requirement on data controllers to disclose the source of the personal data is not accompanied, in the legislation, by a parallel obligation to keep records of the source. Of course, it is possible that the latter obligation will be inferred, either by the Office of the Information Commissioner, or the court, from the presence of the requirement to disclose. E-businesses should, therefore, be prepared for this. In any event most e-businesses will have some record of the source of personal data – the obligation in the legislation is to be in a position to be able to inform any relevant data subject of that source.

It is not clear how an e-business is to comply with its obligation to disclose the 'logic' behind automated decisions[30] – presumably, this will entail providing the data subject with a basic analysis of the operation of the relevant software. By virtue of regulations made under the legislation,[31] a request by a data subject for such 'logic' is not to be treated as a request for any of the other rights under section 7 of the Data Protection Act 1998. Similarly, a request for data subject access that does not specifically request information concerning such logic, may be treated as if it is not a request for such logic.

E-businesses must be prepared to comply with a subject access request within a period of 40 days, commencing the day that the request was received. In most cases, compliance should be by way of supplying copies of all the personal data held by the e-business.

29   Data Protection Act 1998, section 8(2).
30   See section 3.5 for further information on the other rights of data subjects concerning automated decisions.
31   The Data Protection (Subject Access) (Fees and Miscellaneous Provisions) Regulations 2000, SI 2000/191.

3.4.6 E-mails

The material that must be disclosed to an individual following a data subject access request includes all relevant e-mails. An e-business must therefore perform a search operation on its server or relevant hard drives (including back-ups, printouts and archived records) to retrieve all personal data on the data subject contained in e-mails sent or received by any individual within the organisation.

In practice, it can be difficult for organisations to locate e-mails. This has led to a large number of complaints to the Information Commissioner, in response to which a guidance note has been issued – *Subject Access to Personal Data contained in E-mails*[32] (see Appendix I). In this note, the Commissioner outlines how a request for assessment will be handled in relation to subject access and e-mails, and, in particular, notes that businesses will not be considered to have breached the Data Protection Act 1998 if the applicant has not given the business sufficient information to locate the information. The Commissioner suggests that businesses should request:

- the fact that the data may be held in the form of e-mails;

- the names of the authors and recipients;

- the subjects of the e-mails;

- the date or range of dates upon which the messages have been sent; and

- whether it is believed that the e-mails are held as live data or in archived or back-up form.

The Information Commissioner notes in the guidance that many disputes concern whether the e-mails actually exist; businesses may have an obligation to search back-up files and to ask individuals to search stand-alone PCs. In the event of a complaint, the Commissioner will seek to ascertain that a proper search has been carried out by the organisation.

Finally, the Commissioner distinguishes between e-mails held in a live system and those held on an archived/back-up system; an e-business is expected to go to more length to track down information on a live system. Where, however, e-mails are held elsewhere the Commissioner will balance the interests of the data subject against the effort that the controller would have to take to recover the data and in many instances may decide not to take action. In particular, the Commissioner will pay regard to the nature of the data and the impact on the individual of non-disclosure, the e-business's policy in relation to other data, how hard it would be to retrieve the data and whether the data are likely to differ substantially from live data which has been supplied to the individual.

32 V1.0, 14 June 2000.

3.4.7 Archived information

The extent to which archived material will need to be sifted for relevant data depends on the extent to which the effort involved in such activity would be 'disproportionate' to the likely benefit to the requesting data subject in gaining access to such data. There is no exemption, per se, in the legislation for archived material.

3.4.8 Third party data

There will be circumstances when compliance with a data subject access request would lead to the disclosure of another individual's personal information to the requesting data subject. In those circumstances, the e-business has the *option* to withhold such data.

However, the data controller will be acting unlawfully in refusing to disclose third party data where either:

* the third party has consented to the disclosure, or

* it is reasonable in the circumstances to make the disclosure.

In exercising its option to withhold data, it is not clear whether the data controller should keep back the whole document or e-mail on which, or in which, third party data appears or should disclose the document or e-mail with the third party data blocked out or removed.

If the third party is a limited company, then there is no specific exemption that would justify an organisation in withholding the information. However, if the information relates to an individual at that company then the balancing test set out above applies.

The Data Protection Act 1998 sets out further guidance on the balancing test at section 7(6). This states that, in assessing whether it is reasonable to release information without consent, one must have regard, in particular, to:

* any duty of confidentiality owed to the third party;

* the steps which the data controller has taken in order to seek consent;

* whether the third party is capable of giving consent; and

* any express refusal of consent by the third party.

Further, it is likely to be more reasonable to disclose information disclosing third party data that concerns the third party's business or professional activities than that concerning their personal activities.

If the information can be anonymised to protect the identity of the third party individual, then this should be done prior to the release of the information. However, the e-business must have regard to any other identifying information, which it believes is reasonably likely to be in or to come into the applicant's possession. It may not be sufficient to remove the third party's name if the third party's identity will be obvious to the applicant from the context.

The Information Commissioner has issued guidance, *Subject Access Rights and Third Party Information* (available on the Commissioner's website – see Appendix VI), that organisations should take into account in carrying out the balancing exercise. These are:

- try to anonymise the information;

- always seek consent, unless this is impractical (for example, because the third party cannot be located or because the very act of seeking consent would reveal information about the data subject to the third party);

- if consent is not given, decide if it is reasonable in all the circumstances to give access, taking into account the following points, in addition to the statutory considerations:

  (a) the impact the information has had or is likely to have on actions or decisions affecting the applicant;

  (b) whether someone is making the request on behalf of the data subject and, if so, whether the third party would be content to provide the information directly to the data subject;

  (c) the nature of the third party information; whether its release will damage the third party or whether it is sensitive;

  (d) whether the applicant is already likely to be aware of the information;

  (e) whether the applicant is likely to dispute the information; and

  (f) whether the information relates to the third party in a business capacity.

If there is any substantial doubt, the organisation should not disclose the information. The applicant could then ask the Information Commissioner to assess the situation.[33] If the Commissioner considers that the information should be disclosed then an enforcement notice can be issued. Where the organisation releases information in response to an enforcement notice, this will protect the organisation from complaints of breach of the Data Protection Act 1998.

---

33   See Data Protection Act 1998, section 42.

3.4.9 Alterations to data following a request for access

A data controller is permitted to make alterations or deletions to personal data after the date of the subject access request, but before complying with the request, where to do so is within the 'normal course' of his business.[34] Such an alteration or deletion must, however, have been one that would have been made regardless of the receipt of an access request.

3.4.10 Paper-based records

Since 24 October 2001, all paper-based records that form part of a 'relevant filing system' have been included within the ambit of a data subject access request. An e-business must therefore ascertain whether it has paper records containing personal data on the person making the request.

A 'relevant filing system' is, by virtue of section 1(1) of the Data Protection Act 1998:

'Any set of information relating to individuals to the extent that, although the information is not processed by means of equipment operating automatically in response to instructions given for that purpose, the set is structured, either by reference to individuals or by reference to criteria relating to individuals, in such a way that specific information relating to a particular individual is readily accessible.'

There is one exemption from the application of some aspects the legislation to paper records: where the paper-based personal data were subject to processing already underway before 24 October 1998 and have been held since before 24 October 1998 they are exempt from certain aspects of the legislation until the end of the so-called second transitional period, ie 24 October 2007. This is, of course, likely to be relatively rare and of increasing irrelevance and, in any event, does *not* exempt the business from the requirement to comply with a subject access request in relation to those paper-based data.

3.4.11 Automated decisions

Where any automated decision (see section 3.5) has been taken by an e-business concerning a data subject, that data subject is entitled, on making a specific request, to be informed of the logic behind that decision-taking.[35] However, the e-business does not have to comply with this aspect of the legislation

---

34   Data Protection Act 1998, section 8(6).
35   Data Protection Act 1998, section 7(1)(d).

where the information concerning the 'logic' constitutes a trade secret[36] – there is no definition of 'trade secret' in the legislation.

3.4.12 Multiple requests

In order to thwart those nuisance applicants who make repeated subject access requests, a data controller is relieved from the obligation to comply with a second or subsequent request from the same data controller where a 'reasonable time' has not elapsed since the last request.

There is no indication in the legislation of what a reasonable period of time might be in this context. However, it is likely that a subject access request that is made within one calendar month of a previous request of the same e-business in circumstances where there is no reason to believe that the information held will have substantially altered would not have to be complied with.

3.4.13 Credit reference agencies

Where the data controller is a credit reference agency, the controller is entitled to assume (unless the data subject specifies otherwise) that any data subject access request it receives relates solely to the financial standing of the data subject. The fee for the request in this event must not exceed £2 and the time limit for compliance is seven working days.

3.4.14 Advice for e-businesses

All e-businesses must be in a position to comply with a data subject access request. This is likely to mean an overhaul of existing data processing systems.

As far as paper-based records are concerned, businesses should audit all such data to ensure that there is nothing within those pages that the business would not wish the data subject to see. If certain records must not be accessed by any relevant individual, then appropriate action should be taken – this may take the form of removing the paper from any 'structured file' or, where appropriate, destroying it.

The obligation on a data controller to supply the personal data to the data subject in an intelligible form should usually be complied with by sending copies of all relevant files. Where codes have been employed by the controller, the data subject should be given either a decoded version or the key.

36   Data Protection Act 1998, section 8(5).

Businesses must be in a position to be able to ascertain the existence and location of all personal data held by the business – this information may be acquired as part of a data protection audit – and must be in a position to be able to identify subject access requests and to respond within the 40-day period.

3.4.15 Exceptions

There are a number of exceptions to the obligation to comply with a data subject access request. E-businesses should note that many of the exemptions from subject access only apply 'in any case' and 'to the extent that' releasing the information would be prejudicial. In these situations, the exemption cannot be relied upon as a blanket exemption from compliance. The Data Protection Tribunal (the predecessor of the Information Tribunal) considered the phrase 'in any case' in various hearings and established that the phrase should be interpreted as meaning 'in any specific case'. In other words, these exemptions must be applied on a case-by-case basis.

Confidential references[37]

An e-business is not obliged to provide a copy of a reference which it has *given* in connection with the actual or potential education, training, employment or appointment of the data subject. Organisations should note that this exemption only applies to references that they themselves write. It does not, therefore, cover references that are *received* from third parties, although the general law of confidentiality may protect an e-business that decides not to disclose such a reference.

Crime and taxation[38]

There is an exemption for personal data processed for the purpose of preventing or detecting crime, or the assessment or collection of any tax, duty or imposition of a similar nature. It applies to:

- the obligation to provide information to individuals on the processing being carried out (as required by the First Data Protection Principle); and

- the obligation to comply with subject access requests.

However, the exemption only applies to the extent that the disclosed information would be likely to prejudice the objective of the exemption (ie prevention or detection of crime or collection of tax).

---

37 Data Protection Act 1998, Schedule 7, paragraph 1.
38 Data Protection Act 1998, section 29(1).

Armed forces[39]

Information need not be released to a data subject in any case and to the extent that this would be likely to prejudice combat effectiveness of any of the armed forces of the Crown.

Judicial appointments and honours[40]

There is a complete exemption that applies to information processed in order to assess the suitability of a candidate for judicial office or to be appointed a QC or who may be the subject of a Crown honour or dignity.

Management forecasts[41]

Organisations may process personal data for management forecasting and planning. Such data need not be disclosed in any case to the extent that this would prejudice the organisation's ability to conduct its business. The common example is that of planning for potential staff redundancy. The organisation would not be obliged to make this information available in response to a subject access request if this would prejudice the organisation's ability to carry out the planning.

Corporate finance[42]

This exemption applies where a 'relevant person' processes personal data for 'corporate finance purposes'. Corporate finance purposes are underwriting, placing and related services and advisory services relating to capital structures, industrial strategy and related matters and services relating to mergers and acquisitions. Information may be withheld if:

- the data controller reasonably considers that releasing the information would be likely to affect share prices;

- the relevant person reasonably believes that releasing the information would affect decisions about dealing in commerce, subscribing for or issuing investments; or

- release of the information would contribute to a person's decision to act 'in a way that is likely to have an effect on any business activity' including in particular 'industrial strategy' or 'the legal or beneficial ownership of a business or asset'.

---

39   Data Protection Act 1998, Schedule 7, paragraph 2.
40   Data Protection Act 1998, Schedule 7, paragraph 3.
41   Data Protection Act 1998, Schedule 7, paragraph 5.
42   Data Protection Act 1998, Schedule 7, paragraph 6.

Negotiations[43]

Information need not be provided in response to a subject access request where: (1) the information consists of records of the organisation's intentions in relation to negotiations with the data subject; and (2) provision of this information would prejudice the conduct of those negotiations.

Examination marks[44]

Examination candidates may be refused access to marking information before it would otherwise be published or made available to the candidate.

Examination scripts[45]

Personal data recorded in academic, professional or other examination scripts are exempt from the subject access right.

Legal professional privilege[46]

Information need not be supplied to an individual following a subject access request if a claim to legal professional privilege could be maintained, in relation to the information, in legal proceedings.

Self-incrimination[47]

Information need not be disclosed if it would expose an e-business to proceedings for the commission of an offence. A business cannot withhold information because it reveals evidence of an offence under the Data Protection Act 1998 itself. However, information disclosed in this way cannot subsequently be used in proceedings for an offence under the Act.

National security[48]

There is an exemption from subject access where withholding the relevant information is required for the purposes of safeguarding national security. A Ministerial Certificate stating that an exemption is required is conclusive evidence of this fact. However, there is a right of appeal from such a certificate to the Information Tribunal, which will apply judicial review principles. If the Tribunal concludes that the minister did not have reasonable grounds for issuing the certificate then it may allow the appeal and quash the certificate. See also 3.4.16.

---

43 Data Protection Act 1998, Schedule 7, paragraph 7.
44 Data Protection Act 1998, Schedule 7, paragraph 8.
45 Data Protection Act 1998, Schedule 7, paragraph 9.
46 Data Protection Act 1998, Schedule 7, paragraph 10.
47 Data Protection Act 1998, Schedule 7, paragraph 11.
48 Data Protection Act 1998, section 28(1).

Regulatory activity[49]

This exemption benefits certain statutory, government or public bodies in the course of regulatory activities designed to prevent malpractice. The exemption applies where provision of the information would prejudice the proper discharge of these regulatory functions.

Journalism, literature and art[50]

The processing of personal data for journalistic, literary, or artistic purposes is referred to in the Data Protection Act 1998 as processing for the 'special purposes' and broad exemptions are available. In particular, there is an exemption from subject access where:

(a) the information is processed with a view to publication,

(b) the organisation reasonably believes that publication would be in the public interest, and

(c) the organisation reasonably believes that making the information available would be incompatible with the special purposes.

In considering whether the organisation's belief that publication would be in the public interest, regard should be had to the relevant code of practice that is applicable to the publication in question.[51] Secondary legislation[52] provides that the designated codes of practice for this purpose are the following:

(a) the Code on Fairness and Privacy issued by the Broadcasting Standards Commission in June 1998 pursuant to sections 107 and 108 of the Broadcasting Act 1996;

(b) the ITC Programme Code issued by the Independent Television Commission in Autumn 1998 pursuant to section 7 of the Broadcasting Act 1990;

(c) the Code of Practice published by the Press Complaints Commission in December 1997;

(d) the Producers' Guidelines issued by the BBC in November 1996; and

(e) the Programme Code issued by the Radio Authority in March 1998 pursuant to section 91 of the Broadcasting Act 1990.

49 Data Protection Act 1998, section 31.
50 Data Protection Act 1998, section 32.
51 Data Protection Act 1998, section 32(3).
52 The Data Protection (Designated Codes of Practice) Order 2000, SI 2000/418.

In the *Naomi Campbell* case (see section 1.2.4) the defendant unsuccessfully claimed that the processing for the special purposes should defeat the claimant's action.

Research history and statistics[53]

There is a limited exemption from subject access in respect of information processed solely for research purposes. To benefit from this condition the information must:

- be processed only for research purposes (which include statistical or historical purposes);

- not be processed to support measures or decisions with respect to particular individuals;

- not be processed in a way which is likely to cause substantial damage or substantial distress to the data subject; and

- not be used to generate results or statistics which are made available in a way which identifies the data subject.

Publicly available information[54]

Information need not be supplied in response to a subject access request if the data controller is already obliged to make the information available (other than under the Freedom of Information Act 2000). The fact that an authority may make a charge for the provision of this information, which may be higher than that under the Data Protection Act 1998, is not relevant.

3.4.16 The *Norman Baker* case

In *Norman Baker MP v Secretary of State for the Home Office*,[55] the Liberal Democrat MP, Norman Baker, made a subject access request to the Security Service, MI5. The Service gave him a standard non-committal reply, in accordance with its policy to 'neither confirm nor deny' whether relevant data exist. The Service relied upon a certificate issued by the Secretary of State for the Home Department exempting it from the requirement to inform applicants whether or not it had processed information relating to them. Norman Baker appealed, arguing that such a policy was unreasonable under the Data Protection Act 1998 – whilst it might be reasonable to refuse to release information on the ground that this would be prejudicial to national security, it was not reasonable to operate a blanket policy refusing to

---

53   Data Protection Act 1998, section 33.
54   Data Protection Act 1998, section 34.
55   [2001] UKHRR 1275, Information Tribunal.

inform all applicants whether any data relating to them were processed. The Information Tribunal agreed with the applicant and concluded that the certificate was too wide. The Tribunal concluded that it would be incumbent on the Service to consider applications on an individual basis to ascertain whether there was a need to claim the relevant 'national security' exemption.[56]

3.4.17 Freedom of Information Act 2000 data

Under the Data Protection Act 1998, individuals have rights to access information if the information falls within the definition of 'personal data'.[57] Once the Freedom of Information Act 2000 (see section 1.3.7) comes fully into force, public authorities will have obligations to make available any recorded information which they hold in response to a request (subject to substantial exceptions). There is no requirement for these records to be recorded in any particular format. Where an individual requests information about himself from a public authority, then the Freedom of Information Act 2000 refers the authority to the Data Protection Act 1998 and the individual's request must be handled in accordance with the 1998 Act.

In order to ensure that individuals have rights to unstructured information about themselves, the Freedom of Information Act 2000 will, when it comes fully into force, make certain changes to the Data Protection Act 1998 in relation to public authorities only. In particular, an additional category of 'data' is added to the definition of personal data in section 1:

 'recorded information held by a public authority and [which] does not fall within any of paragraphs (a) to (d).'[58]

Thus all information about living identifiable individuals held by public authorities falls within this scope of the Data Protection Act 1998 – irrespective of whether this information is held on computer, in a structured paper record or in an accessible record.

56 Following the ruling of the Information Tribunal, Norman Baker MP reminded the security service of its obligations to supply him with information for which it was unable to claim the national security exemption. At the date of publication of this work the security service had yet to comply.
57 Data which relate to a living individual who can be identified—
    (a)   from those data, or
    (b)   from those data and other information which is in the possession of, or likely to come into the possession of, the data controller
    and includes any expressions of opinion about the individual and any indication of the intentions of the data controller or any other person in respect of the individual.
    (Data Protection Act 1998, section 1.)
58 Data Protection Act 1998, section 1(1)(e), as amended.

However, this new category of personal data benefits from certain of the more generous provisions under the Freedom of Information Act 2000. Firstly, a new section 33A(2) of the 1998 Act provides a complete exemption from the 1998 Act for unstructured personal data held by public authorities for personnel purposes. Section 33A(2) provides that:

> 'Personal data which fall within paragraph (e) of the definition of "data" in section 1(1) and relate to appointments or removals, pay, discipline, superannuation or other personnel matters, in relation to—
>
> (a) service in any of the armed forces of the Crown,
>
> (b) service in any office or employment under the Crown or under any public authority, or
>
> (c) service in any office or employment, or under any contract of services in respect of which power to take action, or to determine or approve the action taken, in such matters is vested in Her Majesty, any minister of the Crown, the National Assembly for Wales, any Northern Ireland minister (within of the meaning of the Freedom of Information Act 2000) or any public authority,
>
> are also exempt from the remaining Data Protection Principles and the remaining provisions of Part II.'

The effect of this provision is that when a public authority acts in its capacity as an employer, it need only comply with the general provisions of the Data Protection Act 1998. Employees of public authorities do not acquire greater rights than their private sector counterparts to see unstructured personnel files, by virtue of the Freedom of Information Act 2000 amendments to the 1998 Act. Only structured personnel files need to be considered.

A new section 9A of the 1998 Act sets out a definition of 'unstructured personal data'. This means:

> '... any personal data falling within paragraph (e) of the definition of "data" in section 1 (1), other than information which is recorded as part of, or would be the intention that it should form part of, any set of information relating to individuals to the extent that the set is structured by reference to individuals or by reference to criteria relating to individuals.'[59]

---

59   Data Protection Act 1998, section 9A(1).

Paragraph (e) data covers paper records which are not accessible records and which fall outside the definition of a 'relevant filing system'. Relevant filing systems are structured by reference to individuals. Further, within this structure, 'specific information relating to a particular individual' must be readily accessible. The new definition of 'unstructured personal data' inserted at section 9A replicates the definition of a relevant filing system, but does not include the language about specific information being readily accessible. The effect of this is that where public authorities hold paper records which are structured in any way, shape, or form, by reference to individuals, then the normal subject access provisions apply.

Files relating to individuals where the information on file is held purely in chronological order must, therefore, be dealt with under the normal subject access rules. However, where the information is genuinely unstructured then the rules in section 9A apply. These rules provide that a public authority is not obliged to comply with a subject access request unless the request contains a description of the data sought. This is, arguably, more favourable to the e-business than the normal provisions. The latter allow an e-business to insist upon the provision of additional information that is reasonably required to locate the information.

Even if the data are described, a public authority need not comply with the request if the cost of doing so would be likely to exceed the appropriate limit set by regulations. Furthermore, the authority need not tell the individual whether any personal data are being processed in relation to him if the cost of doing this, by itself, would exceed the appropriate limit. When calculating these estimates, the authority must do so in accordance with the Freedom of Information Act 2000 regulations.

3.5 ■ AUTOMATED DECISIONS

There are two main rights in respect of 'automated decisions'. An automated decision in this context means a decision that is taken based solely on processing that has been undertaken by automated means and which substantially affects the relevant individual. E-businesses are generally more likely than offline business to take automated decisions.

The first is the right of an individual to request that no automated decisions are taken about him for the purpose of evaluating matters relating to him. Such matters might, for example, be creditworthiness (automated credit scoring), reliability (automated time-recording systems) or performance at work (automated performance indicators).

The second right of an individual is to be informed when an automated decision has been taken. This right applies only in the absence of any request having been received by an e-business for the cessation of automated decision-taking. Any e-business that takes an automated decision must inform the relevant individual that such a decision has been taken as soon as reasonably practicable. The individual then has 21 days in which to require the e-business to re-take the decision by alternative means (ie with some human intervention).

Where the individual sends such a notice (known as a 'data subject notice') to the e-business, a further period of 21 days arises during which the e-business must write to the individual specifying the steps it intends to take to comply with the notice.

Neither the right of an individual to request that no automated decisions are taken concerning him nor the obligation on a e-business to inform the individual that an automated decision has been taken, apply to an 'exempt decision'.

An exempt decision is one where *one* of the conditions from *each* of the following two lists is present. The first list, contained in section 12(6) of the Data Protection Act 1998, is:

(a)   the decision is taken in the course of steps taken for the purpose of considering whether to enter into a contract with the data subject; or

(b)   the decision is taken in the course of steps taken with a view to entering into such a contract; or

(c)   the decision is taken in the course of steps taken in the course of performing such a contract; or

(d)   the decision is authorised or required by or under any enactment.

The second list, in section 12(7) of the 1998 Act, contains the following two alternatives:

(a)   the effect of the decision is to grant a request of the data subject; or

(b)   steps have been taken to safeguard the legitimate interests of the data subject (for example, by allowing him to make representations).

As with the other rights, the right to have a decision re-taken by non-automated means is enforceable by court order.

It should be remembered that where an individual makes a data subject access request (see section 3.4), he is entitled to be informed of the *logic* involved in automated decision-taking where he specifically requests this information. In most cases, this will require an e-business to explain, in general terms, how the relevant software operates and what criteria are taken into account in drawing any relevant conclusions. Where such subject access requests are likely to be frequent, a standard statement may be developed to comply with this requirement.

3.6 ■ THE RIGHT TO DEMAND CESSATION OF PROCESSING

Under section 10 of the Data Protection Act 1998, any data subject can request any data controller to cease or not begin processing of personal data of which he is the data subject on the ground that:

'(a) the processing of those data ... is likely to cause substantial damage or substantial distress to him or another, and

(b) that damage or distress is or would be unwarranted.'

However, the right to request the cessation of processing is substantially limited by section 10(2) – it does not apply where the processing being undertaken is with the consent of the data subject, necessary for the performance of a contract with the data subject, necessary for compliance with a legal obligation or to protect the vital interests of the data subject.

Once an e-business receives a request for the cessation of processing, it must respond to the relevant individual in writing within 21 days. The response must either outline the e-business's intention to comply with the request or explain why the request is unjustified.

The right to cessation of processing is enforceable by court order where the e-business refuses to comply.

3.7 ■ RECTIFICATION, BLOCKING, ERASURE AND DESTRUCTION

The rather confusing terminology that comprises the right to 'rectification, blocking, erasure or destruction' largely means that an individual is entitled to have any inaccuracies put right in relation to data held by any e-business.

Section 14 of the Data Protection Act 1998 makes such a right enforceable by court order. Usually a data subject would become aware of inaccuracies in data either where he has received some communication from an e-business, or where he has made a data subject access request.

Where data held by an e-business are inaccurate because they were supplied to the e-business in that form, a court may order that a court-approved statement of the true facts be supplemented for those data.

In some cases, inaccurate data held by an e-business will have been passed on to a third party by that e-business. If that happens, the court may make an order that the e-business must inform the third party of the inaccuracy and of the need for rectification, blocking, erasure or destruction.

Such an order may be made by a court where the data subject is entitled to compensation for damage as a result of the failure of the e-business to comply with any provision of the 1998 Act, and there is a substantial risk of further such failure.

To overcome the financial difficulties that may be faced by data subjects wishing to avail themselves of this right, the court costs may be met by the Information Commissioner, but only in cases that involve processing for the special purposes[60] and which involve matters of 'substantial public importance'.[61]

3.8 ■ DATA RETENTION

The Fifth Data Protection Principle[62] (see section 3.1) places an obligation on an e-business not to keep personal data for longer than is necessary for the purposes of the processing. Essentially, this is a requirement to destroy data when they are no longer needed for the purpose for which they were acquired. The present Information Commissioner has indicated, at various industry conferences, that she will wish to see that e-businesses have in place a policy on data retention. Such a policy should ideally list the different types of data held or acquired by the business and state the period for which the data will be retained by that business. An active rolling destruction process should accompany the policy.

Unhelpfully, the legislation does not set any particular data retention periods in relation to any specific types of data. Clearly though, certain types of data will need to be kept for certain durations and some statutes that are particular to certain specific industries[63] will specify that information must be kept for certain minimum durations. Further, it is sensible to keep certain records, for example, those relating to injuries in the workplace, for at least the limitation period on the basis that an action may be brought against the organisation.

What is clear is that a lack of any data destruction policy or procedure[64] will inevitably breach the legislative requirements.

Surveillance data

The general principle contained in the Data Protection Act 1998, that all personal data should be destroyed when they are no longer needed, is modified in the case of certain surveillance data.

---

60 See section 3.4.15.
61 Data Protection Act 1998, section 53(1).
62 Data Protection Act 1998, Schedule 1, Part I, paragraph 5.
63 For example, financial services and the professions.
64 In the UMIST Study (see section 3.14) 24% of respondents had no formal data retention policy and 9% kept data indefinitely. A further 16% gave answers that were inappropriate to the question, indicating a misunderstanding of the concept.

For data that have been specified by the government, under the provisions of the Anti-terrorism, Crime and Security Act 2001 (see section 1.3), as being 'communications data'[65] a longer data retention period may apply. The Home Secretary, in the code of practice on data retention to be drawn up under section 102 of the Act, will specify the precise period. It should be noted that there is no duty to comply with the code and that the code itself has no statutory force per se. However, the Home Secretary has power, under section 104 of the Act, to give 'directions' which are for the purposes of safeguarding national security or for the prevention or detection of crime. Such directions may be given to:

(a) communications providers generally;

(b) communications providers of a description specified in the direction; or

(c) any particular communications providers or provider.

The code had not been produced at the time of going to press.

3.9 ■ DISCLOSURE OF DATA TO THIRD PARTIES

From time to time Internet Service Providers, website hosts and e-businesses are requested to make available information on their subscribers or contributors to third parties. Attempts to obtain such data should generally be resisted, not least due to the fact that considerable quantities of administrative time will be taken up in complying with such requests. The Data Protection Act 1998 may be used as an authority for such refusal – any transfer of personal data amounts to processing and is, therefore, often unlawful without the consent of the relevant data subject (see section 3.2)

However, in *Totalise plc v Motley Fool Ltd and Interactive Investor Ltd*,[66] an Internet Service Provider claimant required the

---

65 Defined, by reference to the Regulation of Investigatory Powers Act 2000, section 21(4) as *any of the following*:
    (a) any traffic data comprised in or attached to a communication (whether by the sender or otherwise) for the purposes of any postal service or telecommunications system by means of which it is being or may be transmitted;
    (b) any information which includes none of the contents of a communication (apart from any information falling within paragraph (a)) and is about the use made by any person—
        (i) of any postal service or telecommunications service; or
        (ii) in connection with the provision to or use by any person of any telecommunications service, of any part of a telecommunications system;
    (c) any information not falling within paragraph (a) or (b) that is held or obtained, in relation to persons to whom he provides the service, by a person providing a postal service or telecommunications service.
66 [2001] EWCA Civ 1897, [2002] 1 WLR 1242, CA.

disclosure of the name of a contributor, known as 'Zeddust', to websites maintained by the defendants so that it could bring defamation proceedings against that person. The defendants had refused disclosure based on a perceived duty on their part to protect the privacy of the individuals concerned – they cited the Data Protection Act 1998 as authority for this course of action. The High Court judge made an order for disclosure and stated that respect for privacy must take second place to the need for a party to potential litigation to gain access to identifying data. This decision therefore represents some authority for the view that, where proceedings are contemplated, an e-business should disclose the names of its relevant users or customers. However, a business that chooses not to do so will not be held to have acted inappropriately. On appeal, the Court of Appeal had to decide on the issue of costs; the High Court judge had ordered Interactive Investor to pay £4,817. The judges, citing *Norwich Pharmacal Co v Customs & Excise Commissioners*,[67] found Interactive Investor to have acted properly in its refusal to disclose the identity of Zeddust prior to a court order having been obtained and granted the appeal for the costs order to be overturned. Aldous LJ stated that, in cases such as this:

'the applicant should be ordered to pay the costs of the party making the disclosure including the costs of making the disclosure. There may be cases where the circumstances require a different order, but we do not believe they include cases where:

(a) the party required to make the disclosure had a genuine doubt that the person seeking the disclosure was entitled to it;

(b) the party was under an appropriate legal obligation not to reveal the information, or where the legal position was not clear, or the party had a reasonable doubt as to the obligations; or

(c) the party could be subject to proceedings if the disclosure was voluntary; or

(d) the party would or might suffer damage by voluntarily giving the disclosure; or

(e) the disclosure would or might infringe a legitimate interest of another.'

Generally then, e-businesses will be acting appropriately where they refuse to disclose the identity of a user of their website – and there may be commercial sense in taking such a course of action. In doing so, they can rely on the Data Protection Act

67   [1974] AC 133, [1973] 2 All ER 943, [1973] 3 WLR 164, HL.

1998, human rights legislation and the content of their own privacy policy. It may be that the party seeking disclosure will seek an order for disclosure but such party will generally be expected to pick up the costs of such an application.

3.10 ■ COOKIES

The use of cookies, small pieces of code that are deposited on a user's hard drive when the user visits a website, is as fundamental to e-commerce as it is unpopular amongst privacy proponents. Recent pressure from the European Parliament to ban the use of cookies[68] without the consent of users having first been obtained has done little to persuade the public of their efficacy.

The effect of United Kingdom law on cookie usage depends entirely on what each cookie in question is designed to do. The least invasive cookies are those that merely detect a previous visitor to a site so that the visitor's preferences (for example, layout of pages, colour scheme, etc) can be set. At the other end of the scale are those cookies which report back to the site all of a user's activities on the site (for example, pages looked at, products/services purchased, type of browser being used, etc).[69]

In many cases, the use of cookies will amount to the collection of personal data on a user and hence will have data protection implications. The most significant of those implications are first, that the personal data must be collected fairly, and second, that certain information must be provided to the user at the point of data collection.

Where sensitive personal data are to be collected by cookies, care must be taken to ensure that explicit consent has been taken from the user (see section 3.2). This will necessitate an appropriate opt-in clause on the site that must be ticked by the user prior to any sensitive personal data collection. For the drafting of opt-in clauses, see section 2.3.2.

3.10.1 Using cookies for direct marketing

Use of cookies may amount to direct marketing where offers are made to users as a direct result of the processing of data gathered

---

68 The European Parliament sought an amendment to the draft Directive on the Processing of Personal Data and the Protection of Privacy in the Electronic Communications Sector, during late 2001 and early 2002, to the effect that cookie usage would be banned without the consent of each relevant individual having first been obtained. This proposal was eventually dropped after considerable pressure from the e-commerce lobby. For further detail see Eduardo Ustaran's article in *Privacy & Data Protection* volume 2, issue 3, page 5.

69 For further detail on the technical operation of cookies, see Andrew Sharpe 'The Way the Cookie Crumbles', *Privacy & Data Protection* volume 2, issue 6, page 6.

by a cookie. In this event, the user will have the right to object to direct marketing under section 11 of the Data Protection Act 1998. See Chapter 4 for further detail.

3.10.2 Use of cookies by non-European Economic Area companies

Where an e-commerce business located in a non-European Economic Area country, for example, the United States, deposits cookies on the hard drive of a user located within the European Economic Area, the question arises as to the extent to which the Data Protection Act 1998 applies to such activity. This depends on the construction of the word 'equipment' in section 5 of the Act; that section provides that an e-business that is located neither in the United Kingdom nor in any European Economic Area state is nevertheless subject to the Act's provisions where it uses equipment in the United Kingdom for processing personal data.

Example

Jo runs an on-line underwear business – *e-underwear* – from a base in Chicago. When a user visits the site, a cookie is placed on the hard drive of the user's PC. That cookie transmits information on the user's activity on the site to *e-underwear*. Jo uses the information gained by the cookie to take decisions about her customers concerning marketing activities. Jo's use of the information will amount to the processing of personal data and *e-underwear* will be subject to the Data Protection Act 1998 if a cookie amounts to 'equipment'.

Some commentators state that a cookie should indeed be regarded as equipment for the purposes of section 5 of the Data Protection Act 1998. The better view is probably that this is not the case. In any event, the difficulties of enforcement against a non-European Economic Area e-commerce business render the argument largely academic.

3.11 ■ APPOINTING A PRIVACY OFFICER

Not all organisations will be large enough to merit the appointment of a full-time privacy or data protection officer. Those companies with less than 100 employees and a relatively small customer database are unlikely to be burdened by compliance issues which are substantial enough to make such an appointment necessary.

Medium-sized organisations will often choose to make a part-time appointment – the role of privacy officer will be added to the duties of an existing compliance officer or other similar employee. When choosing an appropriate person to be the privacy officer, whether an internal or external appointment, it should be borne in mind that the responsibilities of such a role will necessitate a relatively senior appointment. Key functions of the privacy officer will include:

(a)   the ability to trace and gain access to all personal data processed by all departments of the organisation; and

(b)   the contribution of relevant considerations in any proposed management decisions that involve new data processing or changes to existing processing.

The choice of location of the privacy officer within an organisation should be based on pragmatism. Where the organisation has substantial numbers of staff, and thus many of its privacy issues will be employee-related, it may be sensible to locate the officer within the Human Resources department. Customer Services may be an appropriate location where there are significant customer-related issues. Alternative locations for larger organisations include the Compliance department or within the in-house legal team.

3.12 ■ THE ROLE OF THE INFORMATION COMMISSIONER

Throughout this work, reference is made to the Information Commissioner. The Office of the Information Commissioner is essentially the body that performs the function of regulator for data protection compliance in the United Kingdom.

As the Commissioner heads the body responsible for enforcing the legislation, it is useful to know their thinking in relation to such issues.

The Commissioner's website[70] (see Appendix VI) is a useful tool for locating various documents that will be of considerable use to on-line businesses and for discovering the Commissioner's attitude to various controversial or ambiguous aspects of the law.

3.13 ■ SANCTIONS FOR BREACHING THE DATA PROTECTION ACT 1998

Businesses will be keen to know what the consequences for them might be in breaching the legislation. It is, after all, sensible to weigh up compliance costs against possible costs of being found to be in breach of any relevant legislative provision. Two further factors should, however, be placed into the equation before a decision is taken on whether to comply with various provisions of the Data Protection Act 1998. The first is the possible negative

---

70   www.informationcommissioner.gov.uk.

publicity (for example, 'Company X rides rough shod over privacy rights of customers') that might arise as a result of a breach of the legislation. The second is the peer pressure that exists between companies in compliance terms – some organisations will refuse to do business with potential trading partners unless the business is able to warrant that it complies with the Act in respect of its personal data processing.

This section sets out the powers of the Information Commissioner to investigate an alleged breach of the Data Protection Act 1998, briefly analyses the criminal offences in the legislation and discusses the sanctions that are available if it is determined that a breach of the legislation has occurred. All references in brackets to section numbers refer to the Data Protection Act 1998.

3.13.1   Enforcement Notices (section 40)

The Information Commissioner can serve an Enforcement Notice on an e-business where he or she feels that such business is contravening, or has contravened, any of the Data Protection Principles.[70] An Enforcement Notice will require an on-line business to do one of the following:

- stop processing any personal data;

- stop processing personal data of a particular description;

- stop processing in a certain manner; or

- take certain steps to remedy unlawful processing and set out a time limit within which this must be done.

The Enforcement Notice will usually specify a time period within which the e-business is expected to comply with the Notice's requirements. Such time period should not expire before the end of the period within which an appeal can be brought against the Notice[71] and, if such an appeal is brought, the Notice need not be complied with until there has been an appropriate determination of the appeal.[72]

Where an Enforcement Notice is issued in respect of a contravention by an e-business of the Fourth Data Protection Principle[73] and the Notice requires the e-business to rectify, block, erase or destroy any inaccurate data, such Notice may also require the rectification,

---

70   See section 3.1.
71   Data Protection Act 1998, section 40(8).
72   However, see the Data Protection Act 1998, section 40(8), which provides that a shorter period may be stipulated by the Commissioner for compliance with the Notice where the Commissioner considers that the Notice should be complied with as a matter of urgency – in this event the period must not be less than seven days from the day on which the Notice is served.
73   See section 3.1.4.

blocking, erasure or destruction of any other data held by the e-business and containing an expression of opinion which appears to the Commissioner to be based on the inaccurate fact.[74]

Enforcement Notices may be cancelled or varied by the Commissioner if it is felt appropriate to do so. Compliance with an Enforcement Notice should result in compliance with the Data Protection Principles.

In determining whether or not to serve an Enforcement Notice, the Information Commissioner will make an assessment, which may require further information. In such circumstances, the Commissioner may decide to serve an Information Notice on an on-line business.

3.13.2 Information Notices (section 43)

Where the Information Commissioner reasonably requires information to decide whether or not the e-business has complied with the Data Protection Act 1998, or in response to receiving a request for assessment (see section 3.13.4), an Information Notice may be served on an on-line business.

The Information Notice will require the e-business to provide the Commissioner with such information as is specified in the notice. The form of this information will also be specified. Certain notices are called 'Special Information Notices' – these are issued in those cases where the e-business claims that personal data are being processed for journalistic, literary or artistic purposes.

There is a right of appeal against Notices to the Information Tribunal. It should be noted that service of an Enforcement or Information Notice alone does not constitute a criminal sanction – rather the e-business will have a set amount of time within which to comply with the requests made in the Notice. If the e-business has not complied with the terms of the Notice within the given time limits, the Information Commissioner and/or the Director of Public Prosecutions may decide to issue criminal proceedings.

3.13.3 Powers of entry and inspection (Schedule 9)

If there are reasonable grounds for suspecting the e-business has contravened, or is contravening, any of the Data Protection Principles, or that an offence under the Data Protection Act 1998 has been or is being committed, and evidence of the contravention or of the commission of the offence is to be found on any premises specified in the information supplied on oath

---

74 Data Protection Act 1998, section 40(3). An Enforcement Notice may also require an e-business to notify third parties to whom the data have been disclosed of the rectification, blocking, erasure or destruction (section 40(5)).

by the Information Commissioner, then a warrant to search and enter the premises may be issued by a judge.

Before issuing a warrant, the judge must be satisfied that the Information Commissioner has given seven days' notice in writing to the occupier of the premises in question demanding access to the premises and that either:

(a)   access was demanded at a reasonable hour and was unreasonably refused, or

(b)   although entry to the premises was granted, the occupier unreasonably refused to comply with the request by the Information Commissioner or any of the Commissioner's officers or staff to permit them to search the premises, inspect, examine, or operate any equipment found there which is used or intended to be used for the processing of personal data and to inspect and seize any documents or other material found there which constitutes evidence of the offence or breach of the Data Protection Principles. However, the occupier must have been notified by the Commissioner of the application for the warrant and have had an opportunity of being heard by the judge on the question of whether it should be issued or not.

3.13.4   Request for assessment (section 42)

Any individual may make a request for assessment to the Information Commissioner if he believes himself to be directly affected by any processing of his personal data. The Commissioner must, on receiving the request, assess whether the processing is being carried out in compliance with the Data Protection Act 1998. The Commissioner has wide powers of discretion in determining how to make such an assessment and will consider all relevant information.

The request for assessment procedure is the main method by which information of a possible breach of the legislation will come to the attention of the Information Commissioner.

3.13.5   Criminal offences

A number of criminal offences are created by the Data Protection Act 1998. Criminal proceedings can only be instigated by the Information Commissioner, or by or with the consent of the Director of Public Prosecutions. Other than the offence of obstructing/failing to assist in execution of a warrant (which can only be tried summarily), all offences under the Act may be tried either in a magistrates' court or in the Crown Court. Offences set out in the Act are punishable by a fine. The maximum fine on summary conviction is £5,000; in the Crown Court there is no maximum limit.

For certain offences, the court has the power to order the forfeiture, destruction or erasure of material containing personal data and used in connection with the processing of personal data (documents, computer disks, etc). This action could result in entire databases being deleted.

The offences are:

Obstructing/failing to assist in execution of a warrant (Schedule 9, paragraph 12)

It is a criminal offence intentionally to obstruct a person in the execution of a warrant for entry and inspection, or to fail, without reasonable cause, to give any person executing such a warrant such assistance as is reasonably required.

Processing without notifying (section 21(1))

It is a criminal offence for e-businesses to process personal data without notifying the fact of such processing to the Information Commissioner.

Change in notification particulars (section 21(2))

It is a criminal offence for e-businesses not to inform the Information Commissioner of any change in registrable particulars or the measures taken to comply with the Seventh Data Protection Principle[75] (ie technical and organisational measures taken against unauthorised or unlawful processing of personal data and against accidental loss or destruction of, or damage to, personal data).

Unlawful obtaining/disclosure/selling of personal data (section 55(1))

It is a criminal offence for a person knowingly or recklessly, without the consent of the e-business, to obtain or disclose personal data or the information contained in personal data, or to procure the disclosure to another person of the information contained in personal data. It is also a criminal offence to sell, or offer to sell, personal data obtained in this way.

Director/company officer liability (section 61)

Where an offence is (1) committed with 'the consent or connivance of', or (2) is attributable to any neglect on the part of, a director, manager, secretary or other similar officer, or any person who was purporting to act in any such capacity, then he may be liable to prosecution for the same offence as that for which the company has been prosecuted.

75   Data Protection Act 1998, Schedule 1, Part 1, paragraph 7.

Failure to comply with a Notice (section 47(1))

It is a criminal offence to fail to comply with an Information Notice, Special Information Notice or Enforcement Notice unless the person charged is able to show that they exercised all due diligence to comply with the notice in question.

False information (section 47(2))

It is a criminal offence for someone to make a false statement, knowingly or recklessly, when supplying information in terms of Information or Special Information Notices.

Disclosing Commissioner's information (section 59(3))

It is a criminal offence knowingly or recklessly to disclose certain information (obtained or furnished to the Information Commissioner under the Data Protection Act 1998, relating to an identifiable individual/business which is not at the time of the disclosure, and has not in the past, been available to the public from other sources) that has been provided to the Office of the Information Commissioner unless the disclosure is made with lawful authority.

Enforced subject access (section 56(5))

Section 56(5) of the Data Protection Act 1998 provides that a person must not, in connection with the recruitment of another person as an employee, the continued employment of another person, or any contract for the provision of services to him by another person, require that other person or a third party to supply him with a relevant record or to produce a relevant record to him. A 'relevant record' is defined by reference to a list of records in a table in the Act and includes (amongst other things) records relating to cautions, criminal convictions, detention and prison records.

It is a defence for a person charged with a contravention of this provision to show that the imposition of the requirement was required or authorised by or under any enactment, by any rule of law or by order of a court, or that in the particular circumstances the imposition of the requirement was justified as being in the public interest. However this provision is not yet in force and will not be so until Part V of the Police Act 1997 is in force.

Other criminal offences

There are other offences in relation to assessable processing and failing to make certain particulars available when an e-business has lawfully chosen not to register and then receives a subject access request.

3.13.6   Other sanctions

Section 13 of the Data Protection Act 1998 entitles individuals to bring a civil action against an e-business claiming compensation, provided they can show they have suffered damage or distress (or both) as a result of processing which contravenes the Act.

It should also be remembered that companies could suffer negative publicity due to a breach of the Act. Details of some of those companies found to be in breach of the Act are published in the Information Commissioner's annual report, which now appears on the Internet as well as being produced in hard copy. Arguably it is the negative publicity that should most be feared by companies in the new era of increased privacy awareness by consumers.

Certain steps can be taken by companies to reduce the risk of breaching the Act, the simplest and cheapest of which is to ensure that an adequate notification is in place. A data protection compliance officer should be appointed within the company to monitor the development and implementation of corporate data protection policies and practices (such as e-mail, Internet and telephone monitoring, direct marketing). The officer should also keep a watchful eye on the Information Commissioner's website[76] to keep track of any new legislation or guidelines. An e-business should also consider obtaining legal advice on the content and operation of its website.

3.14 ■ UK WEBSITES STUDY 2002

In March 2002, UMIST and the Office of the Information Commissioner published a jointly branded 'Study of Compliance with the Data Protection Act 1998 by UK based websites'.

The aims of the study were to:

- assess the degree to which the operation of United Kingdom websites were in compliance with the Data Protection Act 1998;

- identify particular areas where there was a failure to comply with the Act in order that the Commissioner could target future efforts to secure compliance and therefore improve standards for on-line information processing;

- generate awareness in both data controllers and data subjects through:

  - publicity arising from the results of the study;

  - contact with those data controllers in the study sample;

- provide a basis for possible future enforcement action.

76   See Appendix VI.

Three thousand URL's were visited between January and March 2002 and the investigation team spoke to 900 companies – 170 websites were investigated fully. Websites that were apparently of particular interest to the investigators were those offering financial services, those requesting sensitive personal data, sites offering mail order services and requesting credit card information, employment agencies, websites of local authorities, websites offering travel services and websites aimed primarily at children.

Common areas identified for lack of compliance, and therefore aspects of United Kingdom websites that may be targeted by future enforcement action, were:

- insufficient safeguards in respect of the collection of free-form data (ie where the user can enter whatever information he or she chooses);

- lack of contractual provisions with website hosts requiring confidentiality and other security procedures;

- lack of sufficient information identifying the data controller;

- lack of clarity in on-line privacy statements (only 5% of privacy statements reached an adequate 'readability' level for the average reader);

- a failure to adequately state the reasons for collecting personal data;

- failure to provide opt-out/opt-in notices in relation to direct marketing;

- where opt-out/opt-in notices were included on the site, failure to comply with the user's stated preference to not receive direct marketing materials;

- lack of awareness of the nature of and the distinction between personal data and sensitive personal data; and

- inadequate security techniques and procedures.

On the use of cookies or similar devices, the study identified that over half of United Kingdom websites place a cookie on the hard drive of a user, and in nearly a quarter of cases a site will place one or more third-party cookies on the user's hard drive. In many cases, the proprietors of the business did not know that their website used cookies and the study criticised the lack of knowledge of proprietors, which it identified was caused by poor communication between the proprietors of businesses and their website designers. There was a similar lack of knowledge on the part of proprietors of businesses of the use of third-party web bugs on their sites.

4

Electronic direct marketing

Direct marketing – defined in the Data Protection Act 1998 as 'the communication (by whatever means) of any advertising or marketing material which is directed to particular individuals'[1] – is an incredibly successful (in cost-benefit analysis terms) method for businesses to promote their products and services. The direct marketing industry in the United Kingdom is worth £30 billion annually and takes many familiar forms including the use of specifically targeted commercial e-mails and 'spamming'.

The Data Protection Act 1998 represents the first legislative provision in the United Kingdom that seeks to regulate direct marketing to any significant degree. It recognises a need for individuals to be able to refuse to receive direct marketing material – in section 11 it gives an absolute right to individuals to require any United Kingdom business to stop sending him or her direct marketing information – and it provides several hurdles for direct marketers to overcome before the processing of personal data for direct marketing purposes will be lawful.

Although the Data Protection Act 1984 applied to direct marketing (in the same way as it applied to other personal data processing) generally, marketers must remember that under that legislation the processing of 'contact' information on individuals at businesses was not regulated. Due to the new, wider, definition of 'processing' (see Chapter 3) in the 1998 Act,[2] all processing of information on contacts is now caught by the legislation. This means that a database containing the name and address of the

---

1 Section 11(3).
2 Section 1(1).

'buying manager' at each of a set of corporate customers must now comply with the Data Protection Act 1998.

Those engaging in electronic direct marketing must bear in mind the effect of the Directive on the Processing of Personal Data and the Protection of Privacy in the Electronic Communications Sector[3] – from September 2003 all data protection consents taken electronically must be by way of opt-in, as opposed to opt-out (see further at 4.11.3 below).

4.1 ■ LEGITIMISING DIRECT MARKETING

It will be remembered, from the discussion of the First Data Protection Principle[4] in Chapter 3 (see section 3.1), that all processing of personal data generally requires at least one of six legitimising conditions to be applicable to the processing – in the absence of such a condition, the processing is unlawful.

In the absence of a contractual obligation to provide direct marketing information to the data subject, only two of the six legitimising conditions (see section 3.2) can apply to direct marketing:

- consent;[5] and

- legitimate interests.[6]

While there is little doubt that consent, properly obtained, will be operative to legitimise direct marketing, there is considerable controversy over the question of whether the 'legitimate interests' ground will be sufficient to do so.

4.1.1 Consent as a legitimising ground

As far as consent is concerned, Chapter 2 looked at the use of opt-out and opt-in clauses for the obtaining of consent on-line from new customers. Generally, in the United Kingdom, the use of opt-out consent has been, and will be until October 2003,[7] a sufficient method to obtain consent for most marketing purposes (but see section 4.5 on the use of sensitive personal data in direct marketing).

4.1.2 Legitimate interests

The view of the Direct Marketing Association (see Appendix VI) is that processing for direct marketing purposes can be legitimised by the condition in the Data Protection Act 1998, Schedule 2,

---

3   Council Directive 2002/58/EC.
4   Data Protection Act 1998, Schedule 1, Part I, paragraph 1.
5   Data Protection Act 1998, Schedule 2, paragraph 1.
6   Data Protection Act 1998, Schedule 2, paragraph 6(1).
7   See sections 1.3.13 and 2.3.3.

paragraph 6(1)[8] (legitimate interests) and thus that direct marketing may generally be undertaken without the consent of recipients. In promoting this opinion, the Direct Marketing Association refers to a government consultation paper, which stated that:

'In essence, the balance is between, on the one hand the legitimate interests of the data controller in doing the processing; and on the other, the data subject's interests or his fundamental rights and freedoms which might be put at risk by the processing. This is a very important provision since it is likely to be relevant to a very large proportion of processing.'

In its report on direct marketing (available on the Direct Marketing Association's website – see Appendix VI), the Association goes on to state that:

'It is therefore probable that, except where sensitive data are involved, most direct marketing processing will fall within this 'balance of interests' condition – which, after all, was incorporated in the directive as Article 7(f) following intense lobbying by the direct marketing associations of the Member States – so long as data controllers do not make direct marketing approaches to data subjects who have exercised their right to prevent the processing of their personal data for direct marketing purposes, or notified their wish not to receive unrequested direct marketing approaches by registering with Telephone, Fax, E-mail or Mailing Preference Services.'

Although direct marketing to current or existing customers is arguably legitimised by the condition in Schedule 2, paragraph 6(1) (at least as far as marketing of similar products/ services as those which form the basis of the existing relationship between the business and its customer are concerned), it is unlikely that this condition will be available for marketing to prospects. The better view[9] is probably that all direct marketing to those persons who are not existing customers will require consent.

8   The processing is necessary for the purposes of legitimate interests pursued by the data controller or by the third party or parties to whom the data are disclosed, except where the processing is unwarranted in any particular case by reason of prejudice to the rights and freedoms or legitimate interests of the data subject.
9   See, for example, the views of Jason Chess and Jamie Radford in their article in *Privacy & Data Protection*, volume 2, issue 5, page 4.

4.2 ■ THE INFORMATION REQUIREMENTS

Section 2.2 described the information that must be supplied to a data subject at the point of obtaining personal data. These 'information requirements' must be met whether or not the personal data are obtained from the data subject. It is quite likely, in the context of direct marketing, that data on prospects will be obtained from sources other than the data subjects themselves. Examples of 'prospect' data sources include list rental agencies, data 'shares' and purchases of customer databases. It must be remembered that the obligation to satisfy the 'information requirements' in the legislation is separate from the provisions on the obtaining of consent – however, it is of course possible to draft an opt-out clause in such a way that is satisfies both requirements.

Specific considerations for direct marketers in relation to the three types of information that must be supplied to data subjects include the following:

Identity of the data controller

The company performing the direct marketing must be identified as such. Care should be taken to identify *both* data controllers where the direct marketing approach results from a joint marketing scheme – for example, where two organisations have pooled their marketing databases for the purposes of advertising a joint product or service.

In many cases the identity of the data controller will be obvious from the nature and content of the marketing materials.

The purposes for which data are to be processed

E-businesses should ensure that all relevant purposes are stated. This may be done in an opt-out clause that takes consent for the desired processing or elsewhere (for example, a privacy policy[10]).

Any other information which enables the processing to be fair

There is no definition in the legislation of 'fairness' in this context. Where a bland statement is used to describe the purposes of personal data processing, an obligation may arise under this head to inform data subjects of any non-obvious uses of the data. Particular care should be taken where data are to be used for cross-marketing (ie allowing marketing approaches from related companies), host mailing (ie placing inserts into mailings) or list rental (for example, supplying a database of e-mail addresses to a third party), as none of these direct marketing activities are likely to be within the data subjects' original expectations. Even

---

10   See section 2.7.

marketing of the e-business's own goods and services (where these are not similar to the goods or services initially provided to the data subject) may require some information to have been supplied to data subjects of this intention.

Non-obvious uses for personal data will often include disclosures to third parties. Such disclosures may occur without the direct action of the data controller. Host mailings, for example, will often result in a third-party data disclosure.

Example

In its monthly e-mail newsletter, a supplier of household products includes marketing information from a third company. The information includes a link to the third company's website. By clicking on the link it may be possible for the third company to identify the origin of the data subject and for it to therefore gain access to data that it otherwise would not have possessed – ie the fact that its new customer is also a recipient of the household supplies newsletter.

Similarly, if a host mailing is carried out according to a definite selection criteria known to the person on whose behalf the mailing is undertaken, then that person will know that all respondents to the host mailing fulfilled those selection criteria.

It is sometimes suggested that use of personal data for direct marketing will result in an obligation to inform the recipients of the communication that they have a right to object to the marketing in the future (ie under section 11 of the Data Protection Act 1998[11]), particularly where the marketing constitutes the first communication with the relevant individual. The better view is probably that this is not strictly necessary, although to do so would constitute best practice. Where such communication is to take place, an appropriate place for an e-business to supply such information will be the on-line privacy policy.

In spite of the above, the Information Commissioner recognises that an overriding relationship may exist between the data controller and data subject after they have done business together for a number of years. In guidance,[12] the Commissioner refers to the relationship between a bank and a customer and the fact that the data controller (the bank in this case) may wish to make additional uses of the personal data as business practices develop. The Commissioner takes the view that some additional uses, even though not referred to in the original notification to the customer, would not be inconsistent with it. The key issue seems to be that these will be within the customer's expectations. This point was discussed in the *British Gas*[13] case – see section 4.4.3.

---

11   See section 4.6.
12   Available on the Commissioner's website – see Appendix VI.
13   *British Gas Trading Ltd v Data Protection Commissioner* 25 March 1998, unreported.

4.3 ■ THE 'FAIR OBTAINING' REQUIREMENTS

The point at which data are obtained (see Chapter 2) is crucial in determining what may be done with such data during the course of its life. The First Data Protection Principle requires that personal data must be processed fairly. Particular provisions in Schedule 1 to the Data Protection Act 1998 deal with the concept of fairness as it relates to the obtaining of personal data for the first time:

Obtaining data from friends and relatives

When obtaining personal data from an individual known to the data subject, the Information Commissioner considers that the data controller must be fair to the data subject as well as the source of the data. Where the source may reasonably be expected to be aware of and to respect the wishes of the individual, then the processing is likely to be fairer.

Obtaining data from public registers

Data obtained from a register established under statute (for example, the electoral register) are automatically regarded as fairly obtained. A data controller gathering data in this way need not comply with the fair obtaining code.

4.4 ■ CASE LAW

This section examines decisions in cases involving direct marketing. Although all but the last case discussed here was decided under the Data Protection Act 1984 (which has since been repealed by the Data Protection Act 1998), the law on which those cases were based does not differ in any material way from the relevant provisions of the 1998 Act. These cases thus represent an accurate and current indication of the attitude of both the Information Commissioner and the Information Tribunal.

4.4.1 Innovations

In the *Innovations* case,[14] the Information Tribunal scrutinised Innovations' practice of only informing customers of the fact that their personal details would be used for list rental purposes at the point at which they received an acknowledgement of receipt of an order from them. Although individuals could object to the list rental by writing to Innovations, the Tribunal took the view that it was not fair to explain this to individuals at

---

14   *Innovations (Mail Order) Ltd v Data Protection Commissioner* Case DA/92 31/49/1.

such a late stage. Notification had to be given to the data subject before he supplied the data controller with the personal data which were to be used for that purpose. The Tribunal considered that it would be possible to do this by including a statement in advertisements, or by limiting such a list to customers placing orders subsequent to receipt of the acknowledgement.

Whilst many of the issues regarding notification have been clarified now by the fair obtaining code, the case is useful in demonstrating the importance of giving sufficient information to data subjects at an appropriate time. The Tribunal also makes clear that when considering what would be fair to the data subject, the data controller must consider for how long the individual would recall that their information had been passed to the data controller and that, therefore, his personal data would be traded. It was concluded, in the *Innovations* case, that this was unlikely to extend beyond six months.

4.4.2 Linguaphone

In *Linguaphone Institute Ltd v Data Protection Registrar*[15] the Information Tribunal supported the decision in *Innovations*.[16] It was Linguaphone's practice to make its customer names and addresses available on the third-party list rental market. Linguaphone also rented out the names of persons who had made inquiries about its products. In Linguaphone's advertising materials that existed prior to 1994, there was no mention of the practice of list rental – the Tribunal had no trouble in declaring this practice to be unlawful, thus dismissing the company's appeal from the Information Commissioner's enforcement notice.

Although, in its advertising since 1994, Linguaphone included the appropriate information by way of an opt-out clause, the Tribunal had the following to say about the positioning and size of the text:

'The Tribunal requested the appellant to provide examples of their advertisements and having examined those, we are concerned that the opt-out box appears in minute print at the bottom of the order form. In the Tribunal's view the position, size of print and wording of the opt-out box does not amount to a sufficient explanation to an enquirer that the company intends or may wish to hold, use or disclose that personal data provided at the time of enquiry for the purposes of trading in personal information as required by the enforcement notice.'

15 14 July 1995, unreported.
16 *Innovations (Mail Order) Ltd v Data Protection Commissioner* Case DA/92 31/49/1.

The above extract from the Information Tribunal's decision provides an indication of what it will expect to see in future cases involving the size and text of opt-out clauses.

4.4.3 British Gas

The *British Gas* case[17] concerned the appeal by British Gas Trading Limited ('BGTL') against an enforcement notice issued by the Information Commissioner.

In 1997, BGTL issued a leaflet to all its gas bill customers with their quarterly gas bill. The leaflet stated that BGTL would like to write to its customers about its present range of products and services and any future such products and services, and to pass customer details to companies within its group. It suggested that if customers did not want to be sent such material, they should complete and return a coupon to register that they did not wish to receive this information. It was accepted by all parties that the sending of marketing information with the gas bill constituted the processing of personal data. These personal data had been collected from the gas bill database.

The Information Tribunal decision made the following points:

- There is a significant distinction between utilities and other general commercial organisations, since customers have no choice but to provide their personal details to receive a utility. This follows the Information Commissioner's own view. Processing for gas-related marketing purposes would be fair within the meaning of the legislation. However, processing for purposes wider than those which would have been obvious to the customer at the time of supply of his information without his consent, would not be fair. Expectations as to the scope of goods and services to be marketed by a particular supplier would change over time and this should be taken into account when examining fairness.

- It would be fair for BGTL to process customer data, obtained as a result of supplying gas, for:

    (a) continuing its supply of gas;

    (b) marketing and host mailing information on gas-related matters;

    (c) marketing and joint promotion with third parties of electricity-related products where these are associated with the marketing or promotion of gas,

    where the processing would not lead to any disclosure of personal data by BGTL to a third party.

---

17 *British Gas Trading Ltd v Data Protection Commissioner* 25 March 1998, unreported.

- As far as new customers were concerned, BGTL should be able to inform them of the type of marketing intended and provide them an opportunity to object either orally, or in an electronic or other relevant communication or in a document returned by the customer to BGTL. Specific reference was made to an opt-in box ticked, or an-opt out box left blank.

- For existing customers, where the relationship began in monopoly conditions when BGTL inherited the customer database from the nationalised industry, the Information Tribunal did not consider it sufficient to merely send the customer a leaflet providing him with an opportunity to object to data being processed for purposes beyond gas-related purposes. The Tribunal considered it would be sufficient for customers to be informed of the type of marketing or promotions that would be carried out given an opportunity to consent immediately, or not to object. Alternatively, the Tribunal stated that before the processing takes place the customer could return a document to BGTL, or by other means of communication indicate his/her consent to, or by not filling out an opt-out box or other means indicate no objection to, the proposed processing.

The case confirmed to direct marketers that the use of opt-out boxes is acceptable. It also makes clear that processing will be legitimised where a customer merely returns a document that indicates consent, or indicates no objection. This may be given for example by the submission of a website user registration page where the user has not ticked an opt-out box.

4.4.4 The *Robertson* case

In *R (on the application of Robertson) v City of Wakefield Metropolitan Council*,[18] the refusal by an electoral registration officer to allow an elector to have his name removed from an electoral register before that register was sold to a commercial concern for marketing purposes, was held to be both a breach of his right to respect for his private and family life and an invalid interference with his right to vote.

In the Queen's Bench Division of the High Court, Mr Justice Maurice Kay granted an application, by Brian Robertson, for judicial review of the refusal of the electoral registration officer for the first defendant, Wakefield Metropolitan District Council, to accede to his request that his name and address should not be supplied to commercial organisations. The grounds for the application were twofold: (1) the refusal was unlawful in that United Kingdom domestic law did not comply with the European Directive on the 'Protection of Individuals with regard

18   [2001] EWHC Admin 915, [2002] 2 WLR 889.

to the Processing of Personal Data and on the Free Movement of Such Data'[19] (the 'Data Protection Directive'), and (2) that it was both a breach of his right to privacy under article 8 of the European Convention on Human Rights and his right to free elections under article 3 of the First Protocol thereto.

The judge said that, by virtue of the Representation of the People Act 1983 and the Representation of the People Regulations 1986,[20] electoral registration officers were charged with the duty of preparing and publishing a register of parliamentary and local government electors for their area annually and were required, under regulation 54 to supply a copy to any person upon payment of the prescribed fee.

Although it was a criminal offence not to return the application form duly completed, the claimant had written to the electoral registration officer in Wakefield stating that he did not intend to complete the form for inclusion on the register because he opposed the practice of selling copies of the register to commercial companies. In response, the registration officer stated that the compilation of the register was separate to the uses to be made of it, and that he intended to include the claimant's name and address.

The claimant applied for judicial review on the ground that he was unlawfully being required to tolerate the dissemination of the register to commercial interests who utilised it for marketing purposes and that his enfranchisement could not lawfully be made conditional upon acceptance of that practice.

Article 14 of the Data Protection Directive provided that an individual could object to the processing of personal data relating to him which the data controller anticipated being processed for the purposes of direct marketing. That was implemented in United Kingdom law by section 11 of the Data Protection Act 1998, which was specifically concerned with the right to prevent data processing for such purposes.

Since no provision had been made in the Representation of the People (England and Wales) Regulations 2001[21] for registers to be edited pursuant to requests for exclusion, domestic law failed to comply with article 14 of the Data Protection Directive and electoral registration officers were wrongly administering the registers without regard to that Directive and section 11 of the Data Protection Act 1998.

In principle, an elector could enforce his right to object and it was incumbent on the courts to construe the 1986 Regulations and the 2001 Regulations in a manner which complied with the Data Protection Directive and was consistent with the 1998 Act.

19   Council Directive 95/46/EC.
20   SI 1986/1081.
21   SI 2001/3111.

The claimant's concern was the sale of his personal details by the authority to commercial organisations in the knowledge that they would be used for direct marketing purposes. In that the sale of the register affected electors as marketing targets and the interference with their private lives, exacerbated by technological advances, was both foreseeable and foreseen, article 8 of the European Convention on Human Rights was relevant.

As, in his Lordship's judgment, the practice of selling the register to commercial concerns without affording individual electors a right of objection was a disproportionate way in which to give effect to the legitimate objective of retaining a commercially available register, it followed that the claimant's right to privacy under article 8 was breached.

Furthermore, if and to the extent that the 1986 Regulations and 2001 Regulations made the right to vote conditional upon acquiescence in that practice, with no individual right of objection, they operated in a manner which contravened article 3 of the First Protocol to the European Convention on Human Rights on the same reasoning of justification and proportionality that had applied to the article 8 challenge.

4.5 ▩ USING SENSITIVE PERSONAL DATA IN DIRECT MARKETING

The processing of sensitive personal data (see Glossary) is subject to greater restriction than that of non-sensitive personal data. It will be remembered (see section 3.2) that there are 19 pre-conditions for the use of sensitive personal data for any purpose. Unfortunately, from the point of view of direct marketing, the 'legitimate interests' ground (see section 4.1) is not one of these. Thus 'explicit consent' is the only legitimising ground for the processing of sensitive personal data for direct marketing purposes.

> **Example**
>
> On-line Information Plc runs an Internet business directory service. Ben Andrews, who recently suffered permanent injuries from a skiing accident, uses the service to locate a wheelchair retailer close to his home. On-line Information would be unable, without his explicit consent, to use the fact of Ben's search for a wheelchair retailer for any purpose other than to provide him with the information he seeks.

Whilst this position does not outlaw the use of sensitive personal data for direct marketing activities by European Union companies per se, it does mean that such activity is subject to considerable restriction. To render such usage lawful, a method should be devised for the taking of relevant explicit consent from the individuals concerned. Probably the best method to do so, for on-line commercial activities, is to devise an opt-in arrangement on the website's user registration page. Thus, in the example above, if On-line Information wanted to target Ben with information on wheelchair servicing companies or to send his details to such companies for their own marketing purposes, it would first be required to place an appropriate opt-in box on its website.

For the drafting of opt-in clauses see section 2.3 and **Precedent 2**.

4.6 ■ THE RIGHT TO PREVENT DIRECT MARKETING

Section 11 of the Data Protection Act 1998 gives a right to individuals to require the cessation of direct marketing. Section 11 provides as follows:

> (1)   An individual is entitled at any time by notice in writing to a data controller to require the data controller at the end of such period as is reasonable in the circumstances to cease, or not to begin, processing for the purposes of direct marketing personal data in respect of which he is the data subject.
>
> (2)   If the court is satisfied, on the application of any person who has given a notice under subsection (1), that the data controller has failed to comply with the notice, the court may order him to take such steps for complying with the notice as the court thinks fit.
>
> (3)   In this section 'direct marketing' means the communication (by whatever means) of any advertising or marketing material which is directed to particular individuals.

The right, as with all other rights in the Data Protection Act 1998, must be exercised in writing. However, it need not be in any particular form – in other words, it need not mention the 1998 Act, nor the fact that a right is being exercised under it. The request could simply state 'Please do not send me any more e-mails'. There is no requirement for an e-business to acknowledge receipt of a request under section 11, nor to respond to the data subject as a result of receiving it. It is suggested, however, that this right be taken seriously by the e-business – failure to cease direct marketing to someone who has specifically asked for its cessation is likely to result in a complaint to the Information Commissioner and hence to enforcement action. It is important, therefore, for e-commerce businesses to take notice of requests they receive under section 11 and to act on them appropriately.

> For a detailed analysis of the question of whether it is possible for a commercial organisation to obtain and rely on a user's contractual promise not to exercise their section 11 right, see Jo Sanders[22] 'Personal Data As Currency', *Privacy & Data Protection* volume 2, issue 4, page 7.

22   Olswang.

4.7 ■ DIRECT MARKETING USING TELECOMMUNICATIONS SYSTEMS

Marketing by way of telephone and fax does not necessarily constitute the use of personal data. Consider, for example, an automated fax system that sends marketing literature to randomly generated telephone numbers or cold-calling a set of telephone numbers obtained from a telephone marketing list. Where personal data are not used in the marketing process, the Data Protection Act 1998 will not apply. However, the Telecommunications (Data Protection and Privacy) Regulations 1999[23] (the 'Telecommunications Regulations') regulate the use of telephone equipment for direct marketing whether or not such activity is governed by the 1998 Act. Further, the 1999 Regulations apply to anyone who uses a publicly available telecommunications network for direct marketing, not just to data controllers – thus a data processor, within the meaning of the 1998 Act, must comply with the Telecommunications Regulations. It should be noted that the 1999 Regulations are due to be replaced, from October 2003, by Directive 2002/58/EC (see 1.3.13).

The Telecommunications Regulations contain the following provisions restricting the activities of direct marketers.

A ban on the use of automated calling systems[24]

Automated systems which operate direct marketing functions without human intervention are unlawful unless the 'subscriber' (any person who is a party to a contract with a telecommunications service provider for the supply of publicly available telecommunications services) has notified the caller that he consents to such communications being made. It is, of course, most unlikely that any subscriber would notify such consent and so the use of automated calling systems is essentially outlawed.

Use of fax for unsolicited direct marketing[25]

Use of non-automated faxing (automated faxing is covered by the ban on the use of automated calling systems above) is not unlawful but anyone undertaking such an activity in the United Kingdom is obliged to consult a register of persons who have opted-out of receiving such communications and 'clean' their list as a result. The register is known as the Fax Preference Service – see further section 4.8 – and is searchable by any person upon payment of a fee.

---

23 SI 1999/2093.
24 SI 1999/2093, regulation 22.
25 SI 1999/2093, regulation 23.

It should be noted that the Telecommunications Regulations apply to all subscribers, not just those that fall within the definition of 'data subjects' in the Data Protection Act 1998. Thus companies and partnerships are included within the remit of the Telecommunications Regulations.

4.8 ■ THE PREFERENCE SERVICES

The United Kingdom Direct Marketing Association runs three preference services:

- the Telephone Preference Service;

- the Fax Preference Service;

- the Mailing Preference Service.

A fourth service, the E-mail Preference Service, is run by the United States Direct Marketing Association.

Preference services allow persons to register their details by way of notice that they do not wish to receive any direct marketing materials using the relevant media.

It is incumbent, under the Telecommunications Regulations[26] (see section 1.3.6), on organisations wishing to undertake a direct marketing campaign by telephone ('cold calling') to obtain a copy of the Telephone Preference Service list of registered numbers and to 'clean' their list prior to undertaking the campaign. Similar provisions exist in respect of marketing by fax.

Whilst consulting the remaining preference service lists is not a legal requirement in relation to marketing campaigns by post and by e-mail, it is best practice to do so.

4.9 ■ USE OF COOKIES IN DIRECT MARKETING

Cookies (see Glossary and Definitions) may be used to gather information not only on a user's activities around any given website, but also to record a user's links to other sites, thus contributing to a user's on-line profile. The controversial intention of the European Parliament to ban the use of cookies without the user's informed prior consent was modified in the Directive on the Processing of Personal Data and the Protection of Privacy in the Electronic Communications Sector[27] – a user should now be given clear information about the use of cookies and should be given the option to refuse to accept them.

Information gathered by the use of cookies can lead to the tailoring of specific advertising for specific individuals.

26   SI 1999/2093.
27   See section 1.3.13.

4.10 ■ BANNER ADVERTISEMENTS

Within the definition of direct marketing falls advertising on-line which has been specifically targeted to a particular individual, for example, banner advertisements on websites that appear only to certain specifically chosen surfers.

Example

James visits a website that provides an information directory service on United Kingdom businesses. On the home page there appears various banner advertisements for various products and services, including cars and financial services. James searches for information on plumbers in his home town. A week later James visits the site again and this time an advertisement on the homepage promotes insurance against home drainage and water supply risks. Here the e-business has gathered information on James' needs and has targeted him specifically with a relevant advertisement. Such activity will be regulated by the Data Protection Act 1998 and will give rise to various rights of the user.

4.11 ■ UNSOLICITED E-MAILS ('SPAM')

Unsolicited e-mails, sometimes known as 'spam' (but see below), sent from anywhere within the European Union are subject to the provisions of the Telecommunications Directive[28] only until the United Kingdom implements the Directive on the Processing of Personal Data and the Protection of Privacy in the Electronic Communications Sector[29] (which it is obliged to do before September 2003). Strictly, the legal position turns on whether an e-mail address does in fact amount to 'personal data' under the relevant legislation. Most e-mail addresses will be personal data on a strict interpretation of the definition, as an individual can be identified from the e-mail address. Take the following address, for example:

John.Smith@BigLawFirm.com

From this address I can ascertain which law firm employs John Smith, and I will be in with a good chance of finding him if I attend the premises of that law firm during working hours. The following e-mail address, however, would not amount to personal data on a strict construction of the definition:

Lucious.Lips@hotmail.com

---

28   Council Directive 2002/58/EC.
29   See section 1.3.13.

The distinction is, however, not significant, for two reasons. The first is that any database of existing or prospective customers will inevitably contain e-mails in both of the above two categories – the database as a whole should therefore comply with the legislation. The second is that the United Kingdom Information Commissioner has taken the view that the definition of personal data will be interpreted to cover *all* e-mail addresses.

4.11.1 Spamming defined

Spam has been described as:

'... the bulk-mailing, sometimes repeatedly, of unsolicited e-mail messages, usually of a commercial nature, to individuals with whom the mailer has had no previous contact and whose e-mail addresses the mailer collected from the public spaces of the Internet: news scripts, mailing lists, directories, websites, etc.'[30]

4.11.2 The law on spamming

The law in Europe on the sending of unsolicited commercial communications is governed by five European Directives:

- Council Directive 95/46/EC on the protection of individuals with regard to the processing of personal data and on the free movement of such data;

- Council Directive 97/66/EC concerning the processing of personal data and the protection of privacy in the telecommunications sector;

- Council Directive 97/7/EC on the protection of consumers and in respect of distance contracts;

- Council Directive 2000/31/EC on certain aspects of information society services, in particular electronic commerce, in the Internal Market; and

- Council Directive 2002/58/EC on the Processing of Personal Data and the Protection of Privacy in the Electronic Communications Sector.

As far as Council Directive 95/46/EC is concerned, the position on unsolicited communications to e-mail addresses is the same as for direct marketing by e-mail generally. The one potential difference is that there may be no 'processing' within the meaning of the legislation by the operation of software that randomly

---

30   Commission Nationale l'Informatique et des Libertés *Le publication postage électronique et la protection donnes personelles*, Report presented by Madame Cécile Alvergnat and adopted 14 October 1999.

generates e-mail addresses – once those e-mail addresses have come into existence, however, then personal data would be being processed. The application of this legislation will therefore mean that any spammer should comply with the information requirements as well as having a legitimising condition for the processing of personal data (see sections 2.2 and 3.2).

4.11.3 Effect of the Directive on the Processing of Personal Data and the Protection of Privacy in the Electronic Communications Sector[31]

The Directive on the Processing of Personal Data and the Protection of Privacy in the Electronic Communications Sector (see section 1.3.13) attempts to regulate the use of unsolicited e-mails for marketing purposes. The Directive requires opt-in consent to be obtained for the sending of future direct marketing e-mails.[32] The new Directive will be effective from September 2003. However, existing customers of an e-business may be targeted with marketing e-mails, in the absence of opt-in consent, where such e-mails promote products or services which are not dissimilar to those the user has already received from the e-business provided that all previous marketing communications from the e-business gave the customer an opportunity to opt-out of future direct marketing processing.

This approach obviously affects the practice of list-selling (where a business makes a profit from selling e-mail addresses to other business that use those addresses for direct marketing). However, even businesses that neither buy lists of e-mail addresses nor sell their customers' addresses to third parties, may face a difficult challenge if the Directive is adopted as amended by the Council. For example, targeting existing customers with substantially different products from those previously bought would be regarded as a privacy breach.

4.11.4 'Spamming' distinguished from 'unsolicited e-mails'

The activity known as 'spamming' should be distinguished from the sending of unsolicited e-mails. The latter involves targeting a select group of persons with marketing material. Spamming, on the other hand, is the dispatch of non-targeted marketing materials by automated systems.

Care should be taken when using the term spamming as it is often used to mean both of the above activities. Indeed, the European Consumers Association makes no distinction between the terms.

31 Council Directive 2002/58/EC.
32 See further section 2.3.3.

4.11.5 Effect of the E-Commerce Directive

Although The European Directive on certain legal aspects of information society services, in particular electronic commerce, in the Internal Market[33] (the 'E-Commerce Directive') does not seek to regulate the sending of commercial e-mails – the issue of consent is covered in Directive 97/7/EC (which gave rise to the Consumer Protection (Distance Selling) Regulations 2000[34]) and Directive 97/66/EC (implemented in the United Kingdom by the Telecommunications (Data Protection and Privacy) Regulations 1999[35]) – it does require such e-mails to carry material which identifies the person on whose behalf the communication is made. In other words the activity known as stealth viral marketing (see Glossary and Definitions) is essentially outlawed.

The E-Commerce Directive recognises that the sending of *unsolicited* commercial communications by e-mail may be 'undesirable' for consumers and information society services providers and may 'disrupt the smooth functioning of interactive networks'. Where a member state has not banned unsolicited commercial e-mails (the United Kingdom has not done so), the e-mails will be unlawful under article 7 of the E-Commerce Directive where they fail to identify such e-mails clearly and unambiguously as commercial communication. Further, businesses undertaking such activity must consult regularly with national opt-out registers.

4.12 ■ CHECKLIST FOR WEBSITES

When constructing or reviewing websites that will be used for collecting personal data to be used for direct marketing, the following should be checked:

- If personal data are to be collected on an on-line application form or user registration page then an opt-out clause (from September 2003, this must be an opt-in clause[36]) of sufficient size and clarity will be required.

- If sensitive personal data are to be collected, an opt-in clause on the user registration page will be needed.

- Where cookies are to be used in the direct marketing process, reference should be made to this activity in the on-line privacy policy.[37]

33   Council Directive 2000/31/EC.
34   SI 2000/2334.
35   SI 1999/2093.
36   See section 2.3.3.
37   See section 2.7.

5

Using others to process data

Organisations frequently use third-party businesses to perform one or more functions or aspects of their day-to-day activities – examples include website hosting, payroll administration and host mailing. Where such 'outsourcing' arrangements involve the processing of personal data, certain legal obligations arise.

In data protection terminology, the outsourcing organisation is the 'data controller' and the third-party processing business (the supplier) is known as the 'data processor'. It should be remembered that only data controllers are obliged to comply with data protection legislation; data processors do not, therefore, have to be data protection compliant in respect of the processing that they undertake on behalf of third parties.[1] Nevertheless, the supplier should be contractually obliged by the data controller to comply with certain security and other obligations in respect of those data it processes on behalf of the data controller.

5.1 ■ OUTSOURCING PERSONAL DATA PROCESSING

An e-commerce business may outsource many parts of its personal data processing function. The most common example of personal data processing outsourcing, in the e-commerce

---

1   It should be remembered, however, that those organisations that process personal data on behalf of data controllers will also inevitably process their own personal data, for example, staff, customer and supplier information. In respect of that processing, the organisation will be a 'data controller' and hence subject to applicable data protection legislation.

world, is the use of website 'hosts'. Here a business chooses to use a third-party company to host its website on its behalf – the website host will store the websites of its customer businesses on its server. There are many reasons for doing this, including lack of sufficient expertise or lack of IT infrastructure in the outsourcing business.

> **Example**
>
> A United Kingdom food retailer wishes to set up an on-line grocery delivery service. It asks E-Xpertise, an e-commerce solutions provider, to design and host its website. On the website, individuals will be able to register themselves with the retailer, as well as purchase food and arrange deliveries. Here, the retailer will be the data controller of the users' personal data. E-Xpertise will be the data processor.

As a result of data processing outsourcing, various obligations will arise which are discussed in this chapter. The outsourcing arrangement may or may not involve the transferring of personal data from the data controller to the third party processor. For example, in the case of website hosting, the initial recipient of the data provided by users to the site will be the processor – here the data will move from the processor to the controllerof the e-business, but not vice versa. In the case of outsourcing marketing delivery functions to a mailing house, the transfer will be from the e-business to the processor. Where there is such a transfer by the e-business, this will of course amount to personal data processing – it will usually benefit from the condition in paragraph 6(1)[2] of Schedule 2 to the Data Protection Act 1998 (see section 3.2) to legitimise the processing. However, in order to comply with the information requirements in the First Data Protection Principle[3] (see section 2.2), it will be necessary for the e-business to have made available to its customers and other relevant data subjects information concerning the outsourcing arrangements. This could be done, for example, in a privacy policy.[4]

5.2 ■ THE NATURE OF A DATA PROCESSOR

Data processors take a variety of forms but all have one common element: the fact that personal data are processed by them *on*

---

2   The processing is necessary for the purposes of legitimate interests pursued by the e-business or by the third party or parties to whom the data are disclosed, except where the processing is unwarranted in any particular case because of prejudice to the rights and freedoms or legitimate interests of the data subject. (Data Protection Act 1998, Schedule 2, paragraph 6(1)).
3   Data Protection Act 1998, Schedule 1, Part I, paragraph 1.
4   See sections 2.7 and 2.2.

behalf of another.[5] The definition of 'data processor' in section 1(1) of the Data Protection Act 1998 is:

'any person (other than an employee of the data controller) who processes personal data on behalf of the data controller.'

It should be noted that, although, commonly, data processors will be sent personal data by a data controller for processing, a business is not prevented from being a data processor where it does not receive personal data from the outsourcing business. In the example of the website host, the data processing host company will be the first processor of new data obtained via the website's user registration page. It may then perform various operations on the data, such as sorting, matching, profiling, etc, before forwarding it to the relevant data controller e-business.

5.3 ■ CHOICE OF PROCESSOR

When choosing a data processor to carry out personal data processing operations on its behalf, an e-business will take into account a variety of matters that are of usual commercial significance, such as reputation of the service provider, price and ability to do the job efficiently and satisfactorily. Additionally, a further consideration must be taken into account by virtue of the Data Protection Act 1998: the ability of the data processor to provide 'sufficient guarantees in respect of the technical and organisational security measures governing the processing to be carried out'.[6]

There is no guidance as to how this check should be made or what constitutes 'sufficient' in this context. It is suggested that the outsourcing business should make inquiries of potential data processors and take account of the responses to such inquiries in making its choice of processor. Copies of relevant correspondence should be retained in the event that the Information Commissioner investigates the processor's appointment of processor at some future stage.

5   The concept of processing 'on behalf of' the data controller derives from Council Directive 95/46/EC, article 17(2) of which provides: 'The Member States shall provide that the controller must, where processing is carried out *on his behalf,* choose a processor providing sufficient guarantees in respect of the technical security measures and organisational measures governing the processing to be carried out, and must ensure compliance with those measures.'
6   See also note 5 above.

5.4 ■ PROCESSOR VERSUS CONTROLLER

It can sometimes be difficult to identify whether a particular body is a 'controller' or 'processor' of personal data.[7] The distinction will be crucial because a data processor is not obliged to comply with data protection legislation in respect of the data that it processes on behalf of another (although it will be subject to the Data Protection Act 1998 in respect of personal data that it processes on its own behalf, such as its own staff information[8]). For this reason, some businesses will prefer to be classed as data processors – the potential downside in being a processor is that the business will be unable to use the relevant personal data for its own purposes, for example, in the marketing of its own services.

The crucial distinguishing feature between a processor and a controller is the degree of autonomy that the entity exercises over the relevant personal data processing operations. Whilst the operations may be complex and extensive, the real question is whether they are performed on behalf of a third party outsourcing controller. This is true whether or not the outsourcing controller is capable of performing the operations itself – it may of course be that the reason for the outsourcing is the very expertise that characterises the nature of, and the need for, the relationship between the two businesses.

It is possible for any given personal data processing to be performed by a number of data controllers jointly, and it should not be assumed that the transfer of personal data from one business to another for a certain specified purpose will always give rise to the controller-processor relationship. For example, two businesses may undertake to pool their client database with a view to a joint marketing operation – in this scenario each business will be a data controller in respect of the amalgamated database.

On the question of whether an Internet Service Provider should be regarded as a data processor or a data controller, see Eduardo Ustaran 'ISP's – Data Controllers or Data Processors', *Privacy & Data Protection* volume 2, issue 2, page 11.

7 There can, of course, be many joint data controllers of the same personal data.
8 See note 1 above.

5.5 ■ THE NEED FOR A WRITTEN CONTRACT

The Data Protection Act 1998 provides that the e-business will not be treated as complying with its obligations in the Act[9] unless the transaction takes place under a contract that is either in writing or 'evidenced in writing'.[10] Further, the contract must contain certain obligations on the data processor. It should be noted that it is the responsibility of the outsourcing business to ensure compliance with this provision of the legislation – reliance by the data controller on the data processor's standard contractual terms of trade will be insufficient to satisfy this obligation where the terms do not include these mandatory data protection clauses. Bearing this in mind, and the inevitable renegotiation that will be required where a data controller is properly advised, it may be sensible for processors to amend their standard contractual terms to include the relevant provisions.

The obligations that must be imposed on the data processor in the written contract are the following:

(a)   to act only on the instructions of the data controller; and

(b)   to comply with obligations equivalent to those imposed on a data controller by the Seventh Data Protection Principle.[11]

It will be remembered that the data controller's obligations under the Seventh Principle are essentially to process personal data in a secure environment, ie to ensure that appropriate steps are taken against the accidental loss, destruction or damage, or any unlawful processing of the data (see section 3.1.7). It is interesting to note that the obligations on data controllers arising under the Seventh Principle are additionally to enter into a written contract with the processor – presumably, by virtue of (b) above, a data processor wishing to engage a further data processor (thereby sub-contracting its obligations under the head processor agreement) would be obligated to do so by virtue of a written contract containing the same provisions as imposed on itself under its agreement with the data controller. See **Precedent 4** for a full agreement dealing with the provision of generic data processing services in an e-business context.

As far as existing, as opposed to new, data processor arrangements are concerned, all e-businesses must review their contractual arrangements. Those that do not meet the above requirements will require attention. For example, in cases where there are no specific provisions regarding the use of information (including personal data) and the limitations affecting such use, an agreement supplementing the confidentiality of the services provided by the supplier may be required (see **Precedent 3**).

9   Specifically, the Seventh Data Protection Principle (see section 3.1.7).
10   Data Protection Act 1998, Schedule 1, Part II, paragraph 12.
11   Data Protection Act 1998, Schedule 1, Part I, paragraph 7.

It may be a good opportunity to renegotiate the contract generally. Alternatively, a simple letter agreement can be used to vary the contract and to insert the new terms required by the Data Protection Act 1998. See **Precedent 5** for an example of such a simple letter agreement.

5.6 ■ OTHER OBLIGATIONS OF THE CONTROLLER

In addition to choosing a controller that is able to comply with relevant security standards and the need to impose certain contractual obligations on the processor, the outsourcing e-business must regularly monitor the data processor's activities to ensure that it is meeting its security obligations.[12]

In order that the e-business is able to do this, it should take appropriate contractual rights of inspection in its contract with the data processor.

5.7 ■ FOREIGN DATA PROCESSORS

Where a data processor is located outside the European Economic Area,[13] an additional concern will be the export ban contained in the Eighth Data Protection Principle.[14] The outsourcing, by United Kingdom e-commerce businesses, of website hosting to companies located in the United States is a common example of this.

The European Commission produced, in December 2001, a set of model contractual clauses for the transfer of personal data to data processors located outside the European Economic Area. These standard clauses are set out at Appendix IV.

5.8 ■ DATA RETENTION

Data processors should be aware that they may have data retention obligations under the Anti-terrorism, Crime and Security Act 2001[15] by virtue of the activity that they are performing for the relevant data controller. They will need to consult the code of practice under that Act in respect of data they process, in appropriate circumstances.

---

12 See Data Protection Act 1998, Schedule 1, Part II, paragraph 11(b), which provides that a data controller must 'take reasonable steps to ensure compliance with [the relevant] measures'.
13 Ie the member states of the European Union plus Norway, Iceland and Liechtenstein.
14 Data Protection Act 1998, Schedule 1, Part I, paragraph 8.
15 See section 1.3.11.

6

Location of server and data exports

6.1 ■ INTRODUCTION

Before 1 March 2000, there was no general restriction, in the United Kingdom, on sending personal data overseas. Hence, it was common for global organisations to back up their employee records database overnight to locations in New York, Tokyo or Hong Kong. It was also common, for reasons of efficiency or value for money, for an e-commerce business to locate its server in the United States. Further examples of global data transfers include the sending of customer records to third countries such as India or Sri Lanka for processing and the sharing of customer databases between sister companies in different jurisdictions.

Since the advent of the Data Protection Act 1998's new regime, all overseas transfers must be re-examined for legality. The controversial export ban[1] (see section 6.4) is essentially an invisible barrier that has been erected around the entire European Economic Area[2] through which personal data may not pass. This ban is of particular concern to e-commerce businesses. As Eduardo Ustaran states, the ban 'has prompted international concern about the future of partnership agreements and strategic alliances between global Internet-based businesses'.[3]

---

1   Data Protection Act 1998, Schedule 1, Part I, paragraph 8.
2   Ie the member states of the European Union plus Norway, Iceland and Liechtenstein.
3   *Privacy & Data Protection* volume 1, issue 5.

However, the following three factors should be borne in mind:

- the export ban does not prevent personal data being transferred freely between companies located in member states – Company A in the United Kingdom could transfer its customer database to Company B in Italy with nothing to fear from the data export ban;

- inherent in the ban itself is the possibility of transfer to countries outside the European Economic Area that have data privacy laws that are acceptable to the European Union; and

- the ban does not prevent the transfer of personal data overseas where one of a set of listed exemptions applies.

This chapter examines the application of the export ban, the ramifications of the ban for e-businesses and the potential ways to circumnavigate the ban.

6.2 ■ THE SIGNIFICANCE OF SERVER LOCATION

United Kingdom e-businesses often express an interest in locating their server in a third country, such as the United States. As far as the business is concerned, there may be valid and obvious reasons to do so. However, such a business should be informed that it will almost certainly be treated as exporting personal data if it collects any such data on its website (via, for example, a user registration page).

6.2.1 Advice for United Kingdom companies wishing to locate their server abroad

A United Kingdom-established company wishing to locate its e-business server in a third country is presented with something of a difficulty. If it is to collect personal data on its website (most companies wish to do so for obvious commercial reasons) then it will effectively be exporting such data to the country of the website host. As well as a written contract being required between the host and the e-business (see Chapter 5), the Eighth Data Protection Principle export ban[4] must be considered where the country of the host is outside the European Economic Area. The United Kingdom company has four main choices:

(a) relocate its server within the European Union;

(b) take the consent of every person that registers their personal details on the site to have their data processed in the relevant third country;

---

4   Data Protection Act 1998, Schedule 1, Part I, paragraph 8.

(c)   use one of the other methods to circumnavigate the export ban, such as model contracts or Safe Harbor, or

(d)   move its place of establishment to a country outside the European Economic Area.

Businesses rarely like option (b) due to a perception that customers will be irritated by constant attempts to obtain their consent on-line. Option (d) is rather drastic (although, on occasion, realistic). Option (a), locating the server within the European Union, is generally the preferred choice. Of course, if the chosen third country is the United States, then 'Safe Harbor' (option(c)) becomes a possibility – see section 6.8.

6.3 ■ THE NATURE OF THE EXPORT BAN

Both the Data Protection Directive[5] (in this chapter, referred to as 'the Directive') and the Data Protection Act 1998 provide similar restrictions on the sending of personal data outside the European Economic Area, ie to 'third countries'. The Eighth Data Protection Principle provides that:

'Personal data shall not be transferred to a country or territory outside the European Economic Area unless that country or territory ensures an adequate level of protection for the rights and freedoms of data subjects in relation to the processing of personal data.'[6]

The Directive provides, in Article 25:

'The Member States shall provide that the transfer to a third country of personal data which are undergoing processing or are intended for processing after transfer may take place only if, without prejudice to compliance with the national provisions adopted pursuant to the other provisions of this Directive, the third country in question ensures an adequate level of protection.'

6.3.1 Does the legislation apply to foreign companies?

It may be that the restrictions in the Directive and the Data Protection Act 1998, and hence the export ban, do not apply to the particular e-business or activity in question. Consider the following types of business that are not 'caught' by the law:

---

5   Council Directive 95/46/EC.
6   Data Protection Act 1998, Schedule 1, Part I, paragraph 8.

- a Chicago-based e-commerce company which sells goods by mail order to customers in Europe; and

- a Patagonian company that advertises and sells South American holidays on the Internet.

However, the *mere* fact that a company is located or established 'abroad' is not enough, by itself, to ensure the non-application of the 1998 Act. The test for whether the legislation applies, stated in section 5(1), is as follows:

'... this Act applies to a data controller in respect of any data only if—

(a) the data controller is established in the United Kingdom and the data are processed in the context of that establishment, *or*

(b) the data controller is established neither in the United Kingdom nor in any other EEA State but uses equipment in the United Kingdom for processing the data otherwise than for the purposes of transit through the United Kingdom.'

It is therefore not only the presence of a company in the United Kingdom that gives rise to the application of the Data Protection Act 1998. The Act will also apply where a foreign company 'uses equipment' in the United Kingdom for processing personal data. The precise ambit of this section is not clear, but companies that own computer equipment in the United Kingdom on which they process personal data will be clearly caught, as will foreign companies that use 'data processors' (see Chapter 5) in the United Kingdom. It is likely that the argument that foreign companies that transact e-business with consumers in the United Kingdom thereby use those consumers' computers (hence leading to the applicability of the legislation) is unlikely to hold water – in any case such an argument is largely academic as enforcement against such a foreign company would often be virtually impossible.

6.3.2 Transfer not transit

The restrictions contained in the Data Protection Act 1998 apply only to 'transfers' of personal data. Therefore, a distinction should be drawn between 'transfer' and mere 'transit'. Personal data are not *transferred* to a country merely by virtue of being sent there 'en route' to another country. Therefore, the fact that an electronic transfer of data to a European Economic Area country is routed through a third country does not bring the transfer within the provisions of the Eighth Data Protection Principle[7] where the countries of both the transferor and transferee are within the

---

7   Data Protection Act 1998, Schedule 1, Part I, paragraph 8.

European Economic Area. For example, Company A may send an e-mail containing employee information from its office in London to Company B's office in Oslo – the fact that the e-mail is actually routed via Seattle is not relevant.

However, any substantive processing of the personal data in a third country will make such a country a country of transfer and the Eighth Data Protection Principle will be applicable.

6.4 ■ TRANSFERS TO WHICH THE BAN IS IRRELEVANT

This section describes the position in relation to those transfers to which the Eighth Principle export ban does not apply.

6.4.1 Non-third countries

The ban on the transfer of personal data applies only to countries outside the European Economic Area. Hence, transfers to countries listed below (the 15 member states of the European Union plus the extra three European Economic Area members) will not breach the Eighth Data Protection Principle.

Members of the European Economic Area		
Austria	Belgium	Denmark
Finland	France	Germany
Greece	Iceland*	Ireland
Italy	Liechtenstein*	Luxembourg
Netherlands	Norway*	Portugal
Spain	Sweden	United Kingdom
* Non-European Union members		

6.4.2 'Safe' countries

The European Commission, by virtue of powers contained in the Directive,[8] has drawn up a list of countries to which the export of personal data is 'safe'. In doing so, the Commission assesses the nature of the legal regime of the third country in question and, particularly, the quality of their data protection legislation. To date, only three countries have received Commission approval:

8 Council Directive 95/46/EC. Article 25(6) provides: 'The Commission may find, in accordance with the procedure referred to in Article 31(2), that a third country ensures an adequate level of protection ... by reason of its domestic law or of the international commitments it has entered into ...'

- Canada;

- Hungary; and

- Switzerland.

In the case of Canada, the approval is qualified. The reason is the fact that there are several data protection laws in Canada – the Commission's decision relates only to those data regulated by the Canadian Personal Information Protection and Electronic Documents Act 2000. The position is further complicated by the fact that the Act is not yet fully in force (it entered partially into force on 1 January 2001), nor does it cover all organisations. The Act applies to personal information about clients and employees that federally regulated organisations (such as airlines, railways, shipping, inter-provincial trucking, banks, television, radio, telephone and telegraph) collect, use and disclose in the course of commercial activity. The law also applies to all organisations that disclose personal information for consideration outside a province or outside Canada. From 1 January 2002, the Act has also applied to health information held by these organisations. As of 1 January 2004, the Act will cover every organisation that collects, uses or discloses personal information in the course of a commercial activity, whether or not the organisation is federally regulated. Thus the transfer of personal data from within the European Union to Canada will not be as simple as may at first sight appear. For the full text of the Commission's decision on Canada, see:

europa.eu.int/comm/internal_market/en/dataprot/news/02_46.htm

Many other countries around the world are in the process of passing or amending data protection legislation with the intention of meeting the European Commission's requirements, thus ensuring free and unencumbered trade between the European Union and the relevant country. During the course of 2001, Australia's Data Protection Act came into force. After making an analysis of the legislation, the Commission determined that it was insufficient to benefit from the adequacy test exemption inherent in the Eighth Data Protection Principle.[9] The Commission is negotiating with Australia concerning amendments to its legislation. The Commission is also in discussion with Argentina and New Zealand concerning possible adequacy findings.

6.5 ◼ GETTING AROUND THE BAN

Clearly, if the ban on transferring data overseas was absolute, international trade would be substantially curtailed. The Data Protection Act 1998 envisages that certain types of transfer will be permitted by providing certain exemptions from the export ban.

9   Data Protection Act 1998, Schedule 1, Part I, paragraph 8.

6.5.1 Exempt transfers

Schedule 4 to the Data Protection Act 1998 exempts transfers of personal data from the export ban where:

1. The data subject has given his consent to the transfer.

2. The transfer is necessary:

    (a) for the performance of a contract between the data subject and the data controller; or

    (b) for the taking of steps at the request of the data subject with a view to his entering into a contract with the data controller.

3. The transfer is necessary:

    (a) for the conclusion of a contract between the data controller and a person other than the data subject which:

        (i)   is entered into at the request of the data subject; or

        (ii) is in the interests of the data subject; or

    (b) for the performance of such a contract.

4. The transfer is necessary for reasons of substantial public interest (the Secretary of State for Trade and Industry may by order specify the circumstances in which a transfer may be so necessary).

5. The transfer is for legal proceedings or to obtain legal advice or for establishing, exercising or defending legal rights.

6. The transfer is necessary in order to protect the vital interests of the data subject.

7. The transfer is of part of the personal data on a public register and any conditions subject to which the register is open to inspection are complied with by any person to whom the data are or may be disclosed after the transfer.

8. The transfer is made on terms which are of a kind approved by the Information Commissioner as ensuring adequate safeguards for the rights and freedoms of data subjects.

9. The transfer has been authorised by the Information Commissioner as being made in such a manner as to ensure adequate safeguards for the rights and freedoms of data subjects.

6.5.2 Interpreting the list of exemptions

Although there is no definition of consent in the legislation, it is likely that consent can be implied from the circumstances of the transfer and the nature of the arrangements leading up to that transfer. Of course, where the relevant data contain sensitive personal data (see Chapter 2), implied consent to the export of such data will be insufficient – here, 'explicit consent' will require an opt-in type arrangement.

An example of implied consent might be where an e-business places names, photographs and basic contact details of its key employees on its website – the global availability of this personal data would constitute an export, for Eighth Data Protection Principle purposes, to every country of the world. However, it is likely that, where they knew of the presence of their information on the site, the staff would be taken to be impliedly consenting to the arrangement.

See section 2.3 for a further discussion of consent.

As far as the remaining conditions in Schedule 4 are concerned, several have already been discussed in the context of legitimising data processing generally (see further section 3.2). The two further exemptions which should be discussed further here are those numbered 8 and 9 above.

The transfer is made on terms which are of a kind approved by the Information Commissioner as ensuring adequate safeguards for the rights and freedoms of data subjects

This exemption allows a transfer of personal data from a United Kingdom-based e-business to organisations outside the European Economic Area where the transfer is of a type which has been approved by the United Kingdom Information Commissioner – at the time of going to press the Commissioner had approved two such types of transfers: (1) 'safe harbor' and (2) model contractual clauses (see 6.6 and 6.7 below).

The transfer has been authorised by the Information Commissioner as being made in such a manner as to ensure adequate safeguards for the rights and freedoms of data subjects

This aspect of the legislation gives power to the United Kingdom Information Commissioner to specifically authorise a transfer, following a request for such authorisation from a United Kingdom organisation. At the time of going to print, no such specific requests have been authorised by the Commissioner and she has made it clear that she will not be exercising her power under this provision.

In practice, therefore, in the absence of contractual necessity, United Kingdom e-businesses will need to legitimise their personal data exports to non-European Economic Area countries by one of the following methods:

- Consent – see above.

- Safe Harbor – see section 6.7.

- Model Contractual Clauses – see section 6.6.

There is one further possibility for legitimising data exports that may benefit a global organisation wishing to transfer personal data between its various offices: the use of internal codes of conduct (see section 6.9).

6.6 ■ CONTRACTUAL SOLUTIONS

The Directive[10] effectively provides for the use of standard contractual clauses approved by the member states as a method of providing safeguards necessary for circumnavigating the export ban. Further, the European Commission is empowered to make a finding that certain standard contractual clauses offer sufficient safeguards – in that event, member states must comply with such a finding.[11]

6.6.1 The European Union approved contract terms

The European Commission's set of standard contractual clauses have been effective since 3 September 2001. According to the clauses (reproduced in Appendix III), a European Union-based e-business sharing personal data with an overseas partner must warrant and undertake:

- that the processing of personal data up to the moment of the transfer is, and will continue to be, carried out in accordance with the local data protection law;

- that, if the transfer involves *sensitive* personal data, the relevant individuals will be informed (for example, via an on-line privacy policy) that their data may be transmitted to a third country without an adequate level of data protection;

- that it will make available, upon request, to any individual to whom the data relate, a copy of the standard clauses used in the transfer contract;

- that it will respond to any inquiries of any such individual in relation to the overseas transfer and processing; and

- that it will respond to any inquiries of its national data protection authority in connection with the processing carried out by the importer of the data transferred.

10 Article 26(2) of Council Directive 95/46/EC provides that 'a Member State may authorise a transfer of a set of transfers of personal data to a third country which does not ensure an adequate level of protection ... where the controller adduces adequate safeguards with respect to the protection of the privacy and fundamental rights and freedoms of individuals and as regards the exercise of the corresponding rights; such safeguards may in particular result from appropriate contractual clauses'.

11 Article 26(4) states that 'where the Commission decides, in accordance with the [required] procedure ..., that certain standard contractual clauses offer sufficient safeguards ..., Member States shall take the necessary measures to comply with the Commission's decision'.

The standard clauses approved by the European Commission require the overseas recipient of the data to warrant and undertake that it:

- has no reason to believe that its national legislation will affect its performance of the contract;

- will process the data in accordance with the so-called nine Mandatory Data Protection Principles, which represent a minimum requirement for data protection and mirror the key requirements of the Data Protection Directive in terms of purpose limitation, data quality and proportionality, transparency, security, individuals' rights, restrictions on onward transfers, sensitive data, direct marketing and automated individual decisions;

- will deal promptly and properly with all reasonable inquiries made by its European partner or the individuals to whom the data relate;

- will co-operate with any relevant national data protection authority investigating the transfer or the processing carried out by the importer;

- will submit, upon request of the data exporter, its data processing facilities for audit; and

- will make available, upon request, to any individual to whom the data relate, a copy of the standard clauses used in the transfer contract.

Further, the data exporter and importer must agree that they will be jointly and severally liable for damage caused to any data subject as a result of a breach of any of the above obligations. This requirement does not prevent the use of an indemnity clause to benefit the non-breaching party, and indeed such a clause is included in the Commission's standard draft.

The contract in which the above clauses are contained must be governed by the law of the country of the exporting controller. **Precedent 7** mirrors the standard clauses approved by the European Commission and can be used as part of a suitable agreement drawn up in accordance with English law.

The standard contractual terms (which are the only set of terms to have been approved by the Commission to date) have been criticised as being too restrictive and commercially unworkable. Various organisations (such as the International Chamber of Commerce) have approached the Commission with a view to obtaining permission to use alternative clauses – at the time of going to press no such Commission approval had been forthcoming.[12]

---

12   The main sticking point is the issue of joint and several liability for the exporter and the importer – this appears in the model clauses but not in the suggested alternatives.

6.6.2 Data controllers versus data processors

The standard contractual clauses described at Appendix III do not apply to exports of personal data to persons who act only as data processors (for the distinction between data controllers and data processors, see section 5.4). Exports to processors require a lower standard of protection due to the control that is exercised over the processor by the exporting business. For model contractual clauses (approved by the European Commission in December 2001) and for transfers to processors located outside the European Economic Area, see Appendix IV.

See **Precedent 6** for a full agreement dealing with the provision of data processing services by a supplier based overseas that includes the relevant clauses approved by the Commission.

6.6.3 Relevant countries

The contractual terms that have been approved by the European Commission are for use for transfers to countries that do not inherently have a sufficient level of protection, in other words, those countries that do not, in the opinion of the Commission, have good enough data protection law.

It follows that contractual solutions will apply to those countries that are neither in the European Economic Area nor on the Commission's white list.[13] However, it should be borne in mind that transfers to countries that have a poor legal system or a bad human rights regime would not benefit from the use of contractual solutions – not least because the contract is unlikely to be enforceable in the country of the transferee.

Examples of countries to which it is common for United Kingdom controllers to export personal data, and hence where contractual solutions might be contemplated, include the United States, Mexico and India.

6.7 ■ SAFE HARBOR

'Safe Harbor' is the name given to the agreement that enables the transfer of personal data from any European Union country to the United States without breaching the export ban contained in the Eighth Data Protection Principle.[14] Washington and Brussels agreed the Safe Harbor Privacy Principles after an extensive negotiating period of several years – representing a triumph for trans-Atlantic trade negotiations. The Principles became effective on 30 November 2000.

13 See section 6.4.2.
14 Data Protection Act 1998, Schedule 1, Part I, paragraph 8.

In order for the provisions of Safe Harbor to apply to the transfer of personal data from the European Union to the United States companies, the activities of the United States companies must be subject to the jurisdiction of, and overseen by, a United States government body willing to enforce the Data Protection Principles. At present, the only United States bodies overseeing these activities are the Federal Trade Commission and the Department of Transportation. Therefore, financial institutions and telecommunications companies are excluded from the operation of Safe Harbor, which leads to justified criticism of the system.

Safe Harbor is a self-certification system that allows a United States company to state publicly that it complies with a set of privacy rules regarding the processing of personal information that it has acquired from the European Union. At the time of writing, some 20 months after the commencement of the Safe Harbor regime, 208 companies had certified compliance with the Safe Harbor Privacy Principles. In its Staff Working Paper, published on 13 February 2002, the European Union Commission stated that:

'The number of companies to have self-certified and that can therefore be assured of the benefits of the Safe Harbor is lower than expected, but this does not seem to have affected the effectiveness of the arrangement. Companies that choose not to join have to provide adequate safeguards in other ways, for example through contracts. It is expected that Safe Harbor membership will continue to grow steadily, now that the Safe Harbor has got off to a relatively trouble-free start.'

6.7.1 Benefits of Safe Harbor

Those organisations that self-certify their compliance with the Safe Harbor Privacy Principles are able lawfully to receive personal data from the European Union. Essentially, the benefits to United States companies are fourfold:

- all 15 member states of the European Union are bound by the European Commission's finding of the 'adequacy' of the Safe Harbor regime, thus personal data transfers may take place to the relevant United States company from a substantial part of the European continent;

- companies participating in the Safe Harbor regime will be deemed 'privacy-compliant' for the purposes of data flows to those companies;

- member state requirements for prior approval of data transfers will either be waived or approval will be automatically granted; and

- claims brought by European citizens against United States companies will be heard in the United States, subject to limited exceptions.

For United Kingdom organisations, the main advantages of the regime are that exports to Safe Harbor companies can take place without breaching the data export ban and that there is no need continually to review contractual terms prior to new types of transfers taking place.

6.7.2 The Safe Harbor companies

During the course of the first year of operation of the Safe Harbor rules, over 100 companies, including BMW, Hewlett Packard, Marriott International, Microsoft, Eastman Kodak and Compaq, chose to take advantage of the flexibility that comes with Safe Harbor certification.

To obtain an up-to-date list of the Safe Harbor companies, visit the Safe Harbor website[15] (see Appendix VI).

6.7.3 How to obtain Safe Harbor status

United States companies wishing to obtain Safe Harbor status should first analyse the Safe Harbor requirements to ensure that they are able to comply.

To qualify for Safe Harbor status, United States organisations can either:

1. join a self-regulatory privacy programme that adheres to the Safe Harbor's requirements; or

2. develop their own self-regulatory privacy policy that conforms to the Safe Harbor requirements.

Examples of the former include the rules of various trade associations that have been amended to oblige members to comply with privacy rules that would automatically give them Safe Harbor status. In the case of both the self-regulatory privacy programmes and the individual privacy policies, would-be Safe Harbor organisations must comply with the principles listed at section 6.7.4.

Once a United States company has taken the decision to proceed, it must make its privacy policy accessible and declare in that policy that it complies with the Safe Harbor rules. To ensure continued Safe Harbor status, the United States organisation must renew its self-certification annually to the Department of Commerce in writing.

---

15   www.export.gov/safeharbor.

The Department of Commerce publishes a list of all organisations which have sent such self-certification letters (see Appendix VI for the address of the website from which the list of Safe Harbor companies may be accessed).

6.7.4 What does Safe Harbor require?

An organisation must comply with the eight Safe Harbor principles. The principles require the following:[16]

'**Notice:** An organization must inform individuals about the purposes for which it collects and uses information about them, how to contact the organization with any inquiries or complaints, the types of third parties to which it discloses the information, and the choices and means the organization offers individuals for limiting its use and disclosure. This notice must be provided in clear and conspicuous language when individuals are first asked to provide personal information to the organization or as soon thereafter as is practicable, but in any event before the organization uses such information for a purpose other than that for which it was originally collected or processed by the transferring organization or discloses it for the first time to a third party.

Choice: An organization must offer individuals the opportunity to choose (opt out) whether their personal information is (a) to be disclosed to a third party or (b) to be used for a purpose that is incompatible with the purpose(s) for which it was originally collected or subsequently authorized by the individual. Individuals must be provided with clear and conspicuous, readily available, and affordable mechanisms to exercise choice.

Safe Harbor Sensitive Information Principle: For sensitive information (ie personal information specifying medical or health conditions, racial or ethnic origin, political opinions, religious or philosophical beliefs, trade union membership or information specifying the sex life of the individual), they must be given affirmative or explicit (opt in) choice if the information is to be disclosed to a third party or used for a purpose other than those for which it was originally collected or subsequently authorized by the individual through the exercise of opt in choice. In any case, an organization should treat as sensitive any information received from a third party where the third party treats and identifies it as sensitive.

16   The text in the Table derives from the Safe Harbor principles, located at www.export.gov/safeharbor. Whilst accurate at the time of going to press, these principles are updated from time to time and practitioners are advised to refer to the original source.

Onward Transfer: To disclose information to a third party, organizations must apply the Notice and Choice Principles. Where an organization wishes to transfer information to a third party that is acting as an agent, as described in the endnote, it may do so if it first either ascertains that the third party subscribes to the Principles or is subject to the Directive or another adequacy finding or enters into a written agreement with such third party requiring that the third party provide at least the same level of privacy protection as is required by the relevant Principles. If the organization complies with these requirements, it shall not be held responsible (unless the organization agrees otherwise) when a third party to which it transfers such information processes it in a way contrary to any restrictions or representations, unless the organization knew or should have known the third party would process it in such a contrary way and the organization has not taken reasonable steps to prevent or stop such processing.

Security: Organizations creating, maintaining, using or disseminating personal information must take reasonable precautions to protect it from loss, misuse and unauthorized access, disclosure, alteration and destruction.

Data Integrity: Consistent with the Principles, personal information must be relevant for the purposes for which it is to be used. An organization may not process personal information in a way that is incompatible with the purposes for which it has been collected or subsequently authorized by the individual. To the extent necessary for those purposes, an organization should take reasonable steps to ensure that data is reliable for its intended use, accurate, complete, and current.

Access: Individuals must have access to personal information about them that an organization holds and be able to correct, amend, or delete that information where it is inaccurate, except where the burden or expense of providing access would be disproportionate to the risks to the individual's privacy in the case in question, or where the rights of persons other than the individual would be violated. See FAQ 8.

Enforcement: Effective privacy protection must include mechanisms for assuring compliance with the Principles, recourse for individuals to whom the data relate affected by non-compliance with the Principles, and consequences for the organization when the Principles are not followed. At a minimum, such mechanisms must include (a) readily available and affordable independent recourse mechanisms by which each individual's complaints and disputes are investigated and resolved by reference to the Principles and damages awarded where the applicable law or private sector initiatives so provide; (b) follow up procedures for verifying that the attestations and

> assertions businesses make about their privacy practices are true
> and that privacy practices have been implemented as presented; and
> (c) obligations to remedy problems arising out of failure to comply
> with the Principles by organizations announcing their adherence to
> them and consequences for such organizations. Sanctions must be
> sufficiently rigorous to ensure compliance by organizations.'

It should be noted that a United States company is required to comply with the above principles only in respect of data that it has received from a European Union organisation. The United States company must, therefore, when designing its policies for Safe Harbor compliance, make a determination as to whether *all* of the data held by the United States company will be subject to the above eight principles, or whether the company will maintain two separate databases.

6.7.5 Enforcement of the Safe Harbor principles

In general, enforcement of the Safe Harbor principles will take place in the United States in accordance with United States law and will be carried out primarily by the private sector. Private sector self-regulation and enforcement will be backed up by government enforcement.

Private sector enforcement

As part of their Safe Harbor obligations, organisations are required to have in place procedures for verifying compliance and a dispute resolution system (see section 6.7.6) that will investigate and resolve individual complaints and disputes. They are also required to remedy problems arising out of a failure to comply with the principles. Sanctions that dispute resolution bodies can apply must be severe enough to ensure compliance by the organisation; they must include the possibility of publicity for findings of non-compliance and deletion of data in certain circumstances. They may also include suspension from membership in a privacy programme (and thus effectively suspension from the Safe Harbor) and injunctive orders.

The verification requirement can be fulfilled either through a self-assessment or through an outside review. The organisation should state the in-house arrangement for resolving complaints, including the mechanism of initiating the complaint. Furthermore, the organisation must state that it has independent ways of handling complaints (see section 6.7.6).

Government enforcement

Depending on the industry sector, the Federal Trade Commission or the Department of Transportation may enforce non-compliance of the stated privacy policy. Comparable United

States government agencies and/or the states may provide overarching government enforcement of the Safe Harbor principles. Since the Safe Harbor regime relies on self-regulation in complying with the Safe Harbor enforced data protection principles, an organisation's failure to comply with such self-regulation must be actionable under federal or state law prohibiting unfair and deceptive acts, or it is not eligible to join the Safe Harbor. At present, United States organisations that are subject to the jurisdiction of the Federal Trade Commission or the Department of Transportation with respect to air carriers and ticket agents may participate in the Safe Harbor. The Federal Trade Commission and the Department of Transportation with respect to air carriers and ticket agents have both stated in letters to the European Commission that they will take enforcement action against organisations that state that they are in compliance with the Safe Harbor framework but then fail to live up to their statements.

Under Section 5 of the Federal Trade Commission Act 1914, 'unfair methods of competition in or affecting commerce, and unfair or deceptive acts or practices in or affecting commerce, are hereby declared unlawful'. If an organisation were to publish a privacy policy and subsequently breach that policy, that action would be a deceptive act, and the Federal Trade Commission could punish that breach with penalties up to $12,000 per day, and prevent future breaches. Furthermore, there are similar state statutes that could be enforced. The effect of these statutes is to give an organisation's privacy policy and Safe Harbor commitments the force of law in respect of deceptive acts.

6.7.6 Dispute resolution

As part of their obligations under Safe Harbor, United States organisations are required to have in place a dispute resolution system that is readily available, affordable and independent. They can choose to either:

(a) engage a private sector organisation to fulfil their obligation; or

(b) commit to co-operate with European Union data protection authorities.

The six private sector organisations that offer a dispute resolution service at the time of going to press are:

- BBBOn-line;

- TRUST-e;

- the Direct Marketing Safe Harbor Program;

- Entertainment Software Rating Board Privacy On-line European Union Safe Harbor Program;

- the Judicial Arbitration and Mediation Service; and

- the American Arbitration Association.

Approximately half of the United States Safe Harbor companies have chosen to take up the services of one of these organisations.

If a company chooses to co-operate with the Data Protection Authorities (DPAs), then the advice of the DPAs will be delivered through an informal panel of DPAs established at the European Union level. Those United States companies that have chosen to be regulated by the Data Protection Panel are expected to pay a fee to meet the operating costs of the Panel.

Importantly, in order to obtain Safe Harbor status for the transfer of human resources data under Safe Harbor, the company must agree to co-operate with the European DPAs. The reason for this requirement is that primary responsibility for the employees' data remains with the company in the European Union. Therefore, if the European employee is unable to resolve a complaint about the handling of his or her data, the complaint will eventually reach the DPA of the member state where the employee works. In order to resolve overlapping rights of labour laws and data protection law, the DPA must be able to address and remedy any action taken in the United States.

6.7.7 Failure to comply with the Safe Harbor requirements

If a Safe Harbor company fails to comply with the ruling of the private dispute resolution body, then that body must notify the Department of Commerce and the ruling governmental body (Federal Trade Commission or Department of Trade) of that non-compliance.

If an organisation persistently fails to comply with the Safe Harbor requirements, it is no longer entitled to benefit from the Safe Harbor agreement. Persistent failure to comply will arise where an organisation refuses to comply with a final determination by any self-regulatory or government body or where such a body determines that an organisation frequently fails to comply with the requirements to the point where its claim to comply is no longer credible. In these cases, the organisation must promptly notify the Department of Commerce of such facts. Failure to do so may be actionable under the False Statements Act.[17]

The Department of Commerce will indicate, on the public list it maintains of organisations self-certifying adherence to the Safe

18   18 USC § 1001.

Harbor requirements, any notification it receives of persistent failure to comply, and will make clear which organisations are assured and which organisations have and do not have Safe Harbor benefits.

An organisation applying to participate in a self-regulatory body for the purposes of re-qualifying for the Safe Harbor must provide that body with full information about its prior participation in the Safe Harbor.

6.8 ■ UNITED STATES TRANSFERS – CONTRACT OR SAFE HARBOR?

It can be seen from the above that, in the absence of consent, there are two main methods of legitimising transfers of personal data between the European Union and the United States. The choice of which method to use will usually come down to the willingness of the relevant United States company to self-certify Safe Harbor compliance. However, the following factors should also be borne in mind when considering the issue:

- Under the model contractual clauses, both the exporter and importer will be jointly and severally liable for damages awarded as a result of any breach of those provisions which are covered by the third party beneficiary clause. This does not apply to Safe Harbor.

- Unlike the Safe Harbor regime, once the model contractual clauses have been entered into, nothing further need be done to legitimise the export of personal data between the relevant parties. Under Safe Harbor, the United States company must renew its certification annually.

- The model contractual clauses can be inserted into standard contracts that are used for transfers to companies in several different jurisdictions. Safe Harbor applies to transfers to the United States only.[18]

- Transfers can be made, without further formality, from European Union companies to United States Safe Harbor companies without fear of breaching the export ban contained in the Eighth Data Protection Principle[19] – it is a simple matter to visit the relevant website[20] (see Appendix VI) to check that the transferee is registered as a Safe Harbor company.

---

18 Recent attempts to persuade the Commission that exports of data to third party countries can be legitimised by using contracts which incorporate the Safe Harbor obligations (as opposed to the model contractual clauses) have failed.
19 Data Protection Act 1998, Schedule 1, Part 1, paragraph 8.
20 A list of companies which have registered with the Safe Harbour regime is available at www.export.gov/safeharbor.

- A United States Safe Harbor-certified company is 'cleared' to import personal data from a variety of sources in the European Union. There is no need to enter into a written contract (containing the model clauses) with each and every European Union exporter.

- Compliance with the Safe Harbor is generally enforced by the United States Federal Trade Commission. Exports under the model contractual clauses are subject to the jurisdiction and enforcement regime of the member states' national data protection authorities.

- Negotiation of contractual provisions can often be protracted and expensive. No such negotiation is necessary under Safe Harbor.

- Model contracts contain third-party beneficiary clauses. Safe Harbor is not enforceable by data subjects.

It should be noted that, even under the Safe Harbor regime, it would be wise to have in place an appropriate contract for the transfer of personal data to the United States Safe Harbor company – see **Precedent 8**.

6.9 ■ CODES OF CONDUCT

Although it is unable to make a finding of adequacy in relation to them,[21] Codes of Conduct have met with some cautious and informal Commission approval as a method of legitimising the export of personal data to foreign offices of a single organisation. In order for such a code to be effective, the following factors should be present:

- the code must ensure an adequate level of protection for the rights and freedoms of data subjects;[22] and

- all relevant global data processing must be in accordance with the code.

The principle disadvantage of Codes of Conduct, as far as the member states' national data protection authorities are concerned, is the lack of sufficient enforcement mechanism that is inherent in the use of codes. Nevertheless, given the impracticality of taking consent from each relevant data subject

---

21 The Commission is able to make adequacy findings under articles 25(6) and 26(4) of Council Directive 95/46/EC. In the opinion of the Commission, neither of these paragraphs is sufficiently wide to include codes of conduct.

22 Essentially, the global data processing within the organisation must meet very high data privacy standards – in most cases this will mean that the code should impose standards approximately equivalent to those required by Council Directive 95/46/EC.

(employees and customers) and the current lack of sufficient flexibility in the alternative methods of circumnavigating the export ban, global organisations have little choice but to make judicious use of Codes of Conduct.

6.10 ■ CHECKLIST FOR WEBSITES

- Where the website has personal data available generally on its pages, it will be treated as making a data export to all countries of the world. Safe Harbor, model contacts and the 'safe list' of countries therefore become irrelevant – the consent of each relevant data subject must be obtained for such export.

- If the relevant United Kingdom company's website is operated by a United States company, and that United States company seeks to benefit from Safe Harbor status, the website's privacy policy must state that it is Safe Harbor compliant.

- A United Kingdom company's website which is hosted on a server located in a third country not on the European Union's 'safe' list must have a data protection notice and opt-out clause which effectively takes the consent of all registrants to have their details processed in that foreign country, unless there is an appropriate data processor contract in place between the company and its website host.

- Where the operator of the website plans to transfer sensitive personal data to a third party outside the European Economic Area, the website must contain a notice which informs users of that intended transfer. Further, explicit consent may be required for the data export.

7

E-surveillance at work

Surveillance in the workplace can take many forms – from automated scanning of e-mails for 'key' words, to remote monitoring of websites visited by staff, to covert surveillance by electronic CCTV systems. The law relating to this type of surveillance differs from the law of interception of communications generally in one important respect: the restrictions in the Regulation of Investigatory Powers Act 2000 (see section 1.3) do not usually apply to workplace monitoring due to the wide exemptions contained in Regulations (see 7.1.1).

The monitoring of workers' communications is generally permissible provided that:

- notification of the monitoring has been provided to staff in a clear and accessible manner; and

- The activities which constitute the monitoring comply with the principles of transparency and proportionality.

This chapter will examine the law on e-surveillance in the workplace and the methods of ensuring that the above requirements are met.

7.1 ■ E-MAILS

The monitoring of employee e-mails is a justified activity for a variety of reasons, including to the need to:

- check e-mails received by the business when an employee recipient is absent from work;

- ensure that the employee's work is being carried out with appropriate regard to the employer's instructions;

- investigate whether an employee is passing on the employer's trade secrets to a third party competitor; and

- investigate other unauthorised use of the e-mail system.

Considerable controversy exists over the application of the law in this field. One reason for this is that there are a numerous legal provisions that potentially apply to the monitoring, by employers, of employee e-mails. The main such provisions are the following:

- Data Protection Act 1998;

- Human Rights Act 1998;

- Regulation of Investigatory Powers Act 2000; and

- Telecommunications (Interception of Communications) (Lawful Business Practice) Regulations 2000.[1]

7.1.1 Why the Regulation of Investigatory Powers Act 2000 does not apply

The Regulation of Investigatory Powers Act 2000 generally renders unlawful the interception, by non-government bodies, of communications without the consent of both the sender and the recipient (see section 1.3.8). In the case of e-mails sent and received by employees, the obtaining of consent by the employer of both the sender and receiver of such e-mails would be problematic. However, the Telecommunications (Lawful Business Practice) (Interception of Communications) Regulations 2000 (the 'Lawful Business Practice Regulations') provide for an exemption to the operation of the 2000 Act to benefit employers. The Lawful Business Practice Regulations were created by the Secretary of State for Trade and Industry by virtue of his powers under the 2000 Act, and came into force on 24 October 2000.

The Lawful Business Practice Regulations authorise businesses to *monitor or record* employees' communications for the following specific purposes:

- to establish the existence of facts relevant to the business;

- to ascertain compliance with regulatory or self-regulatory practices or procedures;

- to ascertain or demonstrate standards which are or ought to be achieved by the employees;

- to prevent or detect crime;

- to investigate or detect the unauthorised use of the businesses' systems; and

- to ensure the effective operation of those systems.

1   SI 2000/2699.

In addition, the Regulations authorise businesses to monitor (but *not to record*) employees' communications to determine whether such communications are relevant to the business. However, before monitoring or recording employees' communications for these purposes, businesses must make all reasonable efforts to inform those employees that their communications may be intercepted.

The above permissions given to employers effectively mean that, at least as far as the Regulation of Investigatory Powers Act 2000 is concerned, the interception of e-mails can be undertaken on very wide grounds. It should be remembered, however, that the Lawful Business Practice Regulations are permissive as opposed to mandatory – the conduct constituting the interception must therefore comply with other applicable legislation.

7.1.2 Other restrictions

The monitoring and interception of employees' e-mails will necessarily involve the processing of personal data. As such, employers will require a Data Protection Act 1998, Schedule 2 condition to legitimise the activity (see section 3.2). Consent is problematic due to (1) the ambiguity in the legislation on how to obtain consent, and (2) the attitude of the Information Commissioner (as demonstrated in the Employment Code published in March 2002), ie that consent will be difficult to obtain in the employer-employee relationship due to the 'inequality of bargaining power' that exists in that relationship.

Nevertheless, it is possible to argue that the monitoring of employee e-mails is in the 'legitimate interests' of the business, thus utilising paragraph 6(1) of Schedule 2 to the Data Protection Act 1998 as the legitimising condition. As will be remembered (see section 3.2), however, the legitimate interests ground requires a balancing test – the interests of the employer in monitoring e-mails must be weighed against the privacy expectations and rights of employees. This is the aspect of the legislation that gives rise to a need for proportionality in type and method of surveillance used.

The fair processing requirements of the First Data Protection Principle[2] will additionally oblige the employer clearly to inform the employees that their e-mails will be monitored.

7.1.3 The Commissioner's Code of Practice

The present Information Commissioner has drawn up a code of practice which sets out her views on the monitoring of employee e-mails.

2   Data Protection Act 1998, Schedule 1, Part I, paragraph 1.

By way of so-called 'benchmarks', the Commissioner suggests that employers should take account of the items specified in the table below, always bearing in mind that the monitoring that is undertaken should utilise the least intrusive methods that are available to the employer.

1.	Identify who within the organisation can authorise the monitoring of workers and notify them of their responsibilities under the Act.
2.	Before monitoring, establish the specific business risk or risks which monitoring might address. Assess the impact of monitoring on the privacy, relationship of trust and other legitimate rights of workers and others. Make a realistic assessment of the likely effectiveness of monitoring in reducing or eliminating these risks and tailor the monitoring, if any, to achieving this. Do not introduce monitoring where the impact is not justified by the reduction in risk. Document your assessment.
3.	In making this assessment consult trade unions or other workers' representatives, if any, or workers themselves.
4.	If monitoring is to be used to enforce the organisation's rules and standards make sure that the rules and standards are clearly set out in a policy which also refers to any associated monitoring. Make workers aware of the policy.
5.	Tell workers that monitoring is taking place and why, and periodically remind them of this, unless covert monitoring is justified.
6.	If sensitive data are processed in the course of monitoring, ensure that a sensitive data condition is satisfied.
7.	Keep to a minimum those who have access to personal information obtained through monitoring. Subject them to confidentiality and security requirements and ensure that they are properly trained where the nature of the information requires this.
8.	Avoid using personal information collected through monitoring for purposes other than those for which the monitoring was introduced unless it is clearly in the worker's interest to do so or it reveals criminal activity or gross misconduct.
9.	If the information gathered from monitoring might have an adverse impact on workers, present them with the information and allow them to make representations.
10.	Ensure that the right of access of workers to information about them kept for or obtained through monitoring is not compromised. Monitoring equipment must be capable of meeting this and other data protection requirements.

7.2 ■ WEBSITE MONITORING

Similar considerations to monitoring e-mails apply to the keeping track of which websites are being visited by staff. Such activity will have human rights implications – always remembering that, although article 8 of the European Convention on Human Rights – the privacy right (see section 1.3.5) – will be enforceable only against public authorities per se, the courts must interpret national legislation to comply with the rights in the Convention. It should be remembered that a breach of an employee's human rights may be taken into account by an Employment Tribunal when deciding on the fairness or otherwise of an employer's actions in relation to a claim for unfair dismissal or discrimination. Where records are kept of which members of staff are visiting which sites (as opposed to a general record of sites visited generally) there will also be data protection implications.

Generally then, website monitoring will be lawful provided that staff are informed of the monitoring and for what purpose it is undertaken – this would most usefully done in a Communications Policy (see section 7.4). Appropriate measures should be adopted to ensure that the confidentiality of information gathered through monitoring is preserved.

The Commissioner's Code of Practice makes it clear that the focus of an employer's monitoring activities should be on the amount of time an employee spends viewing websites rather than on the identity of the sites visited.

7.3 ■ CCTV

The use of CCTV (closed-circuit television camera) systems to monitor and record the activities of staff at work will have considerable privacy implications. The main statutory provisions that regulate the use of CCTV in the workplace are the Data Protection Act 1998 and the Human Rights Act 1998.

An employer using a CCTV camera system will usually be processing personal data due to the fact that individual employees will be capable of being identified from the images recorded. There may also be the processing of sensitive personal data, due to the presence of images that tend to indicate that a person is guilty of a criminal offence – indeed the possibility of capturing such images may be the reason that the employer has chosen to deploy a CCTV system.

Generally, data controllers must process personal data fairly and the processing will be subject to rights of access. However, in the case of CCTV processing, the exemption in section 29 of the Data Protection Act 1998 provides an exception to these two requirements. Section 29(1) provides that personal data processed for the purposes of:

(a)   the prevention or detection of crime; or

(b)   the prosecution of offenders,

are exempt from the First Data Protection Principle (except to the extent that it requires the need for a Data Protection Act 1998, Schedule 2 and/or a Schedule 3 legitimising condition) and data subject access requests.

The Information Commissioner has produced a code of practice on the use of CCTV camera systems.[3] The code deals with the implications of the Data Protection Principles as well as such practical matters as the citing of cameras, the need for appropriate signage and the purposes for which the data are processed. The code can be downloaded from the Commissioner's website – see Appendix VI.

The Commissioner's recently published code on employee monitoring goes on to state that covert monitoring (the installation of non-visible CCTV cameras) should be done only in circumstances where the activity being monitored is of sufficient seriousness to merit the involvement of the police.

7.4 ■ COMMUNICATIONS POLICIES

As can be seen from the forgoing, a communications monitoring policy will be a desirable item to demonstrate compliance with the legislation. It will also be a useful vehicle with which to inform employees of the monitoring activity – an essential prerequisite to the lawfulness of such activity. The Employment Tribunal has been faced, in recent months, with arguments by employee claimants (in unfair dismissal actions) that the reliance by the employer on evidence obtained through e-mail monitoring is unacceptable due to the unlawfulness of the monitoring process. At the time of going to press there was no conclusive legal pronouncement from an appeal court on this point in the United Kingdom jurisdiction. However, a recent decision in the French Supreme Court[4] confirms that in drafting a communications usage policy, the employer should consider:

•   the purpose for requiring the monitoring of e-mails (the invasiveness of the monitoring must be proportionate to the 'harm' that may result from the lack of it);

•   the method of monitoring, for example, automated scanning for selected words or random selection for reading (the less invasive the monitoring the more likelihood of the activity being lawful); and

•   whether one or more terminals exist upon which e-mails are not monitored (arguably the human rights legislation requires such a terminal for staff to send personal e-mails).

3   The CCTV Code of Practice, July 2000.
4   *Frederic Onof v Nikon France SA* reported in brief in *Privacy & Data Protection*, volume 2, issue 5.

Employers should note that merely having a communications policy in place will not be enough for compliance with the legislation. Employers must also ensure that employees are made aware of, and have access to, the policy as well as any revisions to it that are made from time to time.

7.5 ■ SUMMARY

Taking into account the regulatory framework described above, practical recommendations to ensure compliance with the relevant laws are as follows:

• Draw up an internal *Communications Policy* setting out the authorised and restricted uses of all of the means of communications available to employees (such as the telephone, e-mail and Internet access) and make sure that all employees are at least *aware of its content*. Consider the possibility of inserting a clause requiring informed consent to the Policy in all contracts of employment.

• Do not monitor communications unless there is a *specific and legitimate business reason* to do it and that reason is set out in the Policy.

• Carry out *selective monitoring* rather than continuous surveillance. Only undertake continuous surveillance if the selective monitoring indicates that an employee is engaged in a prohibited activity.

• Do not use personal information collected through monitoring for purposes that are not specified in the Policy.

• Ensure that any members of staff who are responsible for any monitoring activities are fully aware of the principles and limitations that apply to those activities. To achieve this, those members of staff should be properly trained as part of the internal data protection compliance programme.

• Put in place appropriate technical and organisational measures to protect the confidentiality of any personal data collected through monitoring.

• Consider the installation of software that automatically restricts access to particular Internet websites.

Appendices

Appendix I

Various guidance from the Office of the Information Commissioner

INTERNET: PROTECTION OF PRIVACY-DATA CONTROLLERS

In using the Internet for their business dealings, data controllers must take into account the privacy rights of individuals and their own responsibilities under privacy and data protection legislation. The following points should be considered by data controllers in planning their Internet strategies.

Personal data placed on the Internet is available worldwide. In many countries the use of personal data is not protected by legislation. Because of this it is always advisable and will often be essential to obtain consent from individuals before publishing their personal data on your website.

When collecting information via the Internet **always inform the user of who you are**, what personal data you are collecting, processing and storing and for what purpose. Do this before a user gives you *any* information, when they visit your site and wherever they are asked to provide information, for example, via an on-line application form. It is good practice to ask for consent for the collection of all data and it is usually essential to get consent if you want to process **sensitive** personal data.

It is good practice for a data controller who sets up a website to provide a statement of its privacy policy. A 'privacy statement' helps individuals to decide whether or not to visit a site and, when they do visit, whether or not to provide any personal information to the data controller.

Always let individuals know when you intend to use 'cookies' or other covert software to collect information about them.

Never collect or retain personal data unless it is strictly necessary for your purposes. For example you should not require a persons name and full address to provide an on-line quotation. If extra information is required for marketing purposes this should be made clear and the provision of the information should be optional.

Design your systems in such a way as to avoid or minimise the use of personal data.

Upon a user's request you should **correct, change or delete inaccurate details.** If information is altered notify the third parties to whom the original information was communicated. **Regularly delete data which is out of date or no longer required.**

Stop processing data if the user objects to it because the processing is causing them damage or distress.

Only use personal data collected on-line for marketing purposes where the user has already been told that his information was to be used in this way. If a user asks you to stop using his data for marketing purposes you must do so and the individual should always be given the opportunity to opt out of the use of his or her data for marketing. It is also good practice to obtain the individual's consent before using their information for marketing. It will always be necessary to obtain their consent where the data is sensitive.

Use the most up-to-date technologies to protect the personal data collected or stored on your site. Especially sensitive or valuable information, such as financial details, should be protected by reliable encryption technologies.

January 2000

Version 4

INTERNET: PROTECTION OF PRIVACY – DATA SUBJECTS

It is easy to see and understand the benefits the Internet offers individuals, allowing immediate access to global information and markets and facilitating direct global communications. It is however worth remembering a few points.

The Internet is not secure. There is a risk that information provided over the Internet might be intercepted by people who you would not want to read it.

Information you provide to a website or send via e-mail may be made available anywhere in the world and may not be protected by data protection legislation.

Never provide information on-line unless you are confident you know what the website intends to use the information for.

Is more information being collected than is absolutely necessary? Be aware of this when accessing a website or making a transaction, especially if it not clear why this additional information is being requested. Do not be afraid to ask. Just because you are asked a question does not mean you have to answer it.

Show caution with your credit card and account numbers, for example, are your details security-protected? Remember, your information can be used and abused.

The best way to protect your privacy when using services over the Internet is to avoid giving your name or other personal details out over the Internet. If **Anonymity** is impractical you may use a pseudonym (if permitted by law) so that only yourself and your Internet Service Provider know your personal identity, for example, when signing on to use a 'chatroom'.

Information may be collected from you on the Internet without your knowledge. Your Internet Service Provider will have access to a lot of detailed information relating to you. Always choose a reliable Internet Service Provider. Inquire what data they collect, process and store, in what way, and for what purpose. Do this periodically. If you want to know what information your Internet Service Provider or any other service or website provider (based in the European Economic Area[1]) holds about you can make a **subject access** request.

Websites you visit may also implant software known as '**cookies**' on your machine. Some of these cookies serve a useful purpose, for example, they can be used to facilitate on-line 'shopping baskets', but some are used to track your movements on the Internet. **Check your cookie files and consider deleting those you do not want.**

E-mail addresses are personal data. If you find yourself on a directory or user list you can request to be omitted from it.

You can also ask not to be sent 'junk e-mail or spam' and where the sender is based in the European Economic Area they should comply with your request.

Consider using reliable **encryption** techniques for confidential e-mail.

Try and keep up to date with the latest privacy and security risks on the Internet. Try the Internet search engine facilities using the words 'privacy' and 'security'.

January 2000

Version 4

SUBJECT ACCESS TO PERSONAL DATA CONTAINED IN E-MAILS

Background

The Data Protection Act 1998 provides that the Data Protection Commissioner may be asked to carry out an assessment of whether any particular processing operation is likely or unlikely to breach section 42 of the Act. This provision replaces that under the Data Protection Act 1984 whereby the Data Protection Registrar could be asked to consider complaints. An increasing number of complaints and requests for assessments have involved allegations that data subjects have been denied their right of subject access to

---

1   Ie the member states of the European Union plus Norway, Iceland and Liechtenstein.

personal data held in the form of e-mails. Typically, such complaints come from people who themselves make regular use of e-mail and may have some knowledge of the systems and of the 1998 Act. In some cases the e-mails in question are held on 'live' systems in sent or received mail folders. In some cases the e-mails have been deleted from the 'live' systems but may be retained as back-up or archive records. Alternatively, they may have been 'deleted' by the sender or recipient although they may be retrievable with greater or lesser difficulty by the data controller.

This section sets out the approach taken by the Information Commissioner to requests for assessment involving access to personal data held as e-mails. It also explains the basis for 'good practice' advice which the Commissioner may offer to controllers.

An organisation which operates an e-mail system falls within the definition of a data controller if the e-mails processed or stored within its system:

- identify living individuals, and

- are held in automated form in live, archive or back-up systems, or have been 'deleted' from the live system but are still capable of recovery, or

- are stored, as printouts, in relevant filing systems (that is non-automated or 'manual' systems, organised according to criteria relating to individuals and allowing ready access to specific pieces of information).

In some cases data controllers may be able to take advantage of the transitional provisions contained in the Data Protection Act 1998. In brief, transitional relief may be claimed if the processing of personal data was already underway immediately before 24 October 1998. If a data controller operated the same e-mail system before that date, then it is likely that transitional relief may be claimed. The effect of the transitional provisions (if applicable) was that up until 23 October 2001, the personal data contained in e-mails will be exempt from subject access if:

- they exist only as printouts;

- they are held only for back-up purposes; or

- they are not processed by reference to data subjects.

(The term 'processing by reference to the data subject' derives from the Data Protection Act 1984. In effect, data are removed from the scope of the 1998 Act for the duration of the transitional period, even though they identify living individuals, if it is not possible or not intended to extract the information about those individuals from the data automatically. Thus e-mails which are indexed by the names of senders, recipients or subjects are caught, whereas an e-mail the text of which contains information about individuals although there is no intention to access that information in relation to the individual falls outside the scope of the Data Protection Act 1998.)

In making an assessment of an alleged failure by a data controller to give access to personal data held in e-mails, the Information Commissioner will consider a number of questions, including:

- Has the data subject provided sufficient information to the data controller to enable him to locate the data in question?

- Do the e-mails exist?

- Do they contain personal data covered by the Act?

- Do they contain personal data relating to third parties and, if so, should this information be withheld or disclosed?

- What information (other than a copy of the personal data) should be provided in response to a subject access request?

- If access has not been granted, should enforcement action be taken?

Each of these questions is considered in turn.

Information necessary to locate the data

Data subjects frequently make open-ended requests for access ('Give me a copy of all the data you have on me'). However, section 7(3) of the Data Protection Act 1998 specifies that 'a data controller is not obliged to comply with a request ... unless he is supplied with such information as he may reasonably require in order to ... locate the information which that person seeks'. In most cases an open-ended request will not satisfy this provision.

Information which may assist the data controller might include:

- the fact that the data may be held in the form of e-mails;

- the names of the authors and recipients of the messages;

- the subjects of the e-mails;

- the dates or range of dates upon which the messages have been sent;

- whether it is believed that e-mails are held as 'live' data or in archived or back-up form; and

- any other information which may assist the data controller in locating the data.

In making an assessment, the Information Commissioner must take a view as to whether the data subject has failed to provide information that the data controller reasonably needs to narrow down the search. If so, then it is likely to be concluded that there has been no breach of the Data Protection Act 1998. By contrast, where a data controller appears to be making demands for information which the data subject cannot reasonably be expected to give and where it appears that a copy of at least some of the personal data requested could be provided, then it is likely to be judged that there has been a breach.

Disputes about the existence of e-mails

Data subjects often allege that they have not been given all the information to which they are entitled. In the first instance those requesting an assessment must provide the Information Commissioner with information necessary to identify the processing in question. Where evidence submitted by the data subject that the e-mails in question exist or existed in the past is inconclusive, the Commissioner must form a judgment based not only on the information supplied but also upon other similar cases, particularly ones involving the same data controller.

If the Information Commissioner is satisfied that the e-mails are likely to exist, then the alleged failure to respond to the access request will generally be put to the data controller for comment.

E-mails may be held locally, for instance on a stand-alone PC, and not be immediately accessible by data protection officers/systems administrators. In putting the concerns of data subjects to data controllers, therefore, the Information Commissioner will seek to ascertain that a proper search has been carried out for the e-mails in question.

Do the e-mails contain personal data covered by the Data Protection Act 1998?

There are a number of different aspects to this question. In particular, it will be important to determine whether the transitional provisions are relevant and whether the e-mails are held in the form of 'live' data or otherwise, for example, as back-up or archive data.

General considerations

E-mails are caught if they contain information about identifiable living individuals unless they have been printed off, deleted and stored in manual filing systems falling outside the scope of the Data Protection Act 1998 (for example, references to an individual in the e-mailed minutes of a meeting which have been printed off and stored on the 'Meetings File').

In all other cases (subject to the transitional provisions below), with the implementation of the 1998 Act, the e-mails will be caught because of the ending of provisions contained in the Data Protection Act 1984, in particular:

- the text preparation exception which took outside the scope of the Data Protection Act 1984 the processing of personal data for the sole purpose of the preparation of the text of a document;

- the exemption relating to back-up data; and

- the part of the definition of 'processing' which specified that in order to process personal data, processing must take place 'by reference to the data subject'.

Even though data may have been 'deleted' from the live system, the e-mails will be caught if they can be recovered by, say, the systems administrator before their final destruction.

Transitional provisions

Where processing was already underway immediately before 24 October 1998, there may, however, be some limited exemptions if:

- the e-mails have been 'deleted' or are only held in paper form;

- the data are not processed by reference to the data subject; or

- the data are only held for back-up purposes.

As is noted above, a 'deleted' e-mail may still constitute personal data if it can be retrieved, albeit with some difficulty, by the data controller. However, if the transitional provisions apply, such e-mails are unlikely to constitute personal data since they will no longer be in a form in which they have been or it is intended that they should be processed.

Some e-mails contain personal data but fall outside the scope of the Data Protection Act 1998 since those data are not processed by reference to the data subject. An example may be a reference to an individual in the minutes of a meeting which are kept as a record of the meeting. Others will clearly fall within the scope of the 1998 Act, for example, where the name of the data subject appears in the title of the e-mail or he is the sender or recipient. Other cases will be less clear cut. However, the Data Protection Tribunal decision in the *Equifax*[2] enforcement case is of assistance. This suggests that if an e-mail is stored because it contains information about an individual and may be accessed to discover information about an individual then processing takes place by reference to the data subject regardless of how the search is carried out.

Third Party Data

By their very nature e-mails are likely to contain personal data relating to third parties. In responding to subject access requests, therefore, controllers will need to have regard to the tests set out in section 7(4)-(6) of the Data Protection Act 1998. In making assessments, the Information Commissioner will seek to assure herself that the tests have been properly applied as they would whenever a record contains information relating to a third party

In addition, the Commissioner will consider the effect of article 8 of the European Convention on Human Rights. This specifies that:

'Everyone has the right to respect for his private and family life, his home *and his correspondence.*' (Emphasis added.)

and:

'There shall be no interference by a public authority with the exercise of this right except such as in accordance with the law and is necessary in a democratic society in the interests of national security ... or for the protection of the rights and freedoms of others.'

If an e-mail was written in a private rather than an official capacity, then it is likely that only exceptional circumstances will justify disclosure of third party information without the consent of the individual concerned. Cases which involve possible breaches of article 8 provisions will be considered on their individual merits.

Other section 7 rights

Section 7 of the Data Protection Act 1998 contains a number of rights in addition to the right to be given a copy of personal data. In particular, individuals have the right:

• to be informed whether they are the subject of personal data being processed by the controller;

2   *Equifax Europe Ltd v Data Protection Registrar* June 1991, unreported.

and, if so, to be given a description of:

- the personal data in question;

- the purposes of the processing;

- the recipients or classes of recipients; and

- the sources of the personal data (if known to the controller).

While it may be difficult for a controller to reconstitute data which have been deleted from the live system in order to provide a copy to the data subject, he may still be able to provide some of this information. In particular, it may be helpful to explain that the purposes of the processing are to erase the data and that only in exceptional circumstances would those data be reconstituted and used for other purposes (for example, as evidence in serious criminal cases or as evidence in industrial tribunals).

As a matter of good practice controllers should develop clear policies as to the circumstances under which they would reconstitute 'deleted' data before they are faced with subject access requests.

The Information Commissioner's enforcement policy

Unless the personal data contained in e-mails are covered by the transitional provisions in the Data Protection Act 1998, in principle data subjects have a right of access and the Information Commissioner has the power to take enforcement action in the event of non-compliance. Notices are not served automatically, however, and in deciding whether it is proper in particular cases to serve a notice, the Commissioner will take a number of factors into account.

The Commissioner will consider first whether the data controller has been given sufficient evidence to locate the data. If transitional relief is available to the data controller, exempting back-up data and processing which does not take place by reference to the data subject, this question may be relatively simple. If the Commissioner considers that the controller can locate the data but has not provided a copy to the data subject then she will be more inclined to recommend enforcement.

If transitional relief is not available and the Data Protection Act 1998 extends to data not held on 'live systems', then the data subject may have had to provide more information to enable the data controller to locate the data. Data held other than on 'live systems' may include back-up data and data which have been 'deleted' but not yet finally erased.

In practice, however, the Information Commissioner might exercise her discretion and not seek to enforce a data subject's rights if she is satisfied that to give access would involve disproportionate effort on the part of the controller. In forming a judgment as to whether the effort involved would be disproportionate, she will consider:

- What is the nature of the data and the likely effect on the individual if the data are or are not retrieved? The more serious, the more likely it will be that the Information Commissioner will take action.

- What is the controller's policy in relation to archive or other 'non-live' data? If it is to retrieve data only in exceptional circumstances (for example, serious criminal allegations) then it may be disproportionate to have to retrieve data in response to a request from a data subject who only wants a copy out of interest. In attempting to determine what a data controller's policy is, the Commissioner may request sight of policy documents and/or an account of the practices followed by the controller in the past.

- How hard would it be for the controller to retrieve the data? Is it possible to retrieve small amounts of data or is it necessary to reconstitute large computer archives? How much will it cost?

- In the case of back-up data is there any evidence to suppose that this version differs materially from that held on the live system?

To summarise, the Information Commissioner's approach is that where e-mails are held on live systems and can be located, she will seek to enforce subject access if this has been denied. Where data are held elsewhere, the Commissioner will weigh the interests of the data subject against the effort that the controller would have to take to recover the data and in many instances may be likely to decide not to take action.

The decision not to take action does not imply that a complaint will not be assessed nor does it deny the individual the right to seek access through the courts.

14 June 2000

Version 1.0

Appendix II

Article 29 Data Protection Working Party Recommendation on certain minimum requirements for collecting data on-line in the European Union

5020/01/EN/FINAL

WP 43

RECOMMENDATION 2/2001 ON CERTAIN MINIMUM REQUIREMENTS FOR COLLECTING PERSONAL DATA ON-LINE IN THE EUROPEAN UNION

Adopted on 17 May 2001.

The Working Party has been established by Article 29 of Directive 95/46/EC. It is the independent EU Advisory Body on Data Protection and Privacy. Its tasks are laid down in Article 30 of Directive 95/46/EC and in Article 14 of Directive 97/66/EC. The Secretariat is provided by:

The European Commission, Internal Market DG, Functioning and impact of the Internal Market. Co-ordination. Data Protection. Rue de la Loi 200, B-1049 Bruxelles/Wetstraat 200, B-1049 Brussels - Belgium - Office: C100-6/136. Internet address: http://europa.eu.int/comm/internal_market/en/media/dataprot/wpdocs/index.htm

THE WORKING PARTY ON THE PROTECTION OF INDIVIDUALS WITH REGARD TO THE PROCESSING OF PERSONAL DATA

set up by Directive 95/46/EC of the European Parliament and of the Council of 24 October 1995,[1]

---

1   Official Journal no L 281 of 23/11/1995, p 31, available at: http://europa.eu.int/comm/internal_market/en/media/dataprot/index.htm

having regard to Articles 29 and 30 paragraphs 1 (a) and 3 of that Directive,

having regard to its Rules of Procedure and in particular to articles 12 and 14 thereof,

has adopted the present Recommendation:

I. Introduction

1. In its working document entitled 'Privacy on the Internet – an integrated EU approach to on-line data protection' of 21 November 2001,[2] the Working Party stressed the importance of ensuring that adequate means are put in place to guarantee that individual Internet users get all the information they need to place their trust, in full knowledge of the facts, in the sites with which they enter into contact, and if need be, to exercise certain choices in accordance with their rights under European legislation. This is particularly important given that Internet use multiplies the opportunities for collecting personal data and consequently the risks to the fundamental rights and liberties of individuals, in particular their private life. In its Opinion No 4/2000 of 16 May 2000 on the level of protection provided by the 'safe harbour principles', the Working Party invited the Commission to consider as a matter of urgency the creation of a EU seal system for Internet sites, based on common criteria of data protection assessment that could be determined at the Community level.

    This recommendation follows on from the two above-mentioned documents. It aims to contribute to the effective and homogeneous application of the national provisions adopted in compliance with the personal data protection Directives,[3] by providing <u>concrete indications</u> on how the rules set out in the Directives should be applied to the most common processing tasks carried out via the Internet. Such processing occurs, in particular, in the course of 'an initial contact' between an Internet user and a website, whether this is solely for the purpose of seeking information or to conclude a commercial transaction on a step-by-step basis.

    The indications given below mainly concern the collection of personal data on the Web and are intended to identify the concrete measures to be put in place by the players concerned for ensuring that processing is fair and lawful (application of Articles 6, 7, 10 and 11 of Directive 95/46/EC). They focus in particular on when, how and which information must be provided to the individual user but add practical details on other rights and obligations arising from the Directives.

---

2   WP 37 (5063/00): Working Document – Privacy on the Internet – An integrated EU approach to on-line data protection. Adopted on 21 November 2000. Available at: <u>http://europa.eu.int/comm/internal_market/en/media/dataprot/wpdocs/wp37en.htm</u>

3   Directive 95/46/EC of 24 October 1995 on the protection of individuals with regard to the processing of personal data and on the free movement of such data, and Directive 97/66/EC of 15 December 1997 concerning the processing of personal data and the protection of privacy in the telecommunications sector. Available at: http://europa.eu.int/comm/internal_market/en/media/dataprot/law.htm.

The main objective of this Recommendation is thus to give practical added value for the implementation of the general principles of the directive. The Working Party considers the present Recommendation as a first initiative to spell out on the European level a 'minimum' set of obligations in a way that can easily be followed by controllers (the natural or legal person responsible for the processing of personal data in the context of a web-site)[4] operating web sites which may need to be completed by adding further detail or subject matter.[5] This does of course not dispense the controllers from their present obligations to check their processing against the full range of requirements and conditions set up in the applicable national law in order to make it lawful.

This recommendation applies, if the controller is established in one of the Member States of the European Union. In that case the national law of the Member State concerned will apply to the processing of personal data in the context of the activities of that establishment. The recommendation also applies, where the controller is not established on Community territory, but for the purpose of processing personal data, makes use of equipment, automated or otherwise, situated on the territory of one of the Member States of the EU. Such processing is covered by the national law of the Member State where the technical facilities or means are situated.[6]

4   For ease of reference, Article 2 of Directive 95/46/EC defines the controller as 'the natural or legal person, public authority, agency or any other body which alone or jointly with others determines the purposes and means of the processing of personal data; where the purposes and means of processing are determined by national or Community laws or regulations, the controller or the specific criteria for his nomination may be designated by national or Community law'.

5   The concrete recommendations made in this recommendation represent minimum requirements in the sense that they are not the only ones. They should be supplemented in future by additional recommendations on the processing of more sensitive personal data, such as processing in connection with health sites, sites addressed to children or portal services. As regards certain other specific processing, such as the dissemination of personal data on a site or the storage of traffic data by Internet service providers or Internet Content and Service providers, reference is made to the Working Party's recommendations in the document mentioned in footnote 1 and to other relevant positions taken by the Working Party, for example WP 25 (5085/99): Recommendation 3/99 on the preservation of traffic data by Internet Service Providers for law enforcement purposes. Adopted on 7 September 1999. WP 18 (5005/99): Recommendation 2/99 concerning the privacy in the context of interceptions. Adopted on 3 May 1999. WP 17 (5093/98): Recommendation 1/99 on Invisible and Automatic Processing of Personal Data on the Internet performed by Software and Hardware. Adopted on 23 February 1999. All available at: see footnote 1.

6   cf. Article 4 1(a) and (c) of Directive 95/46/EC. This should be clearly distinguished from the question whether personal data may be lawfully transferred from the EU to a third country. That question is dealt with by Articles 25 and 26 of Directive 95/46/EC, and the related decisions of the European Commission concerning the adequacy of the level of protection in a third country. For instance, if an American website makes use of equipment within the EU to collect and process personal data, the legislation of the European country in question will apply to the collection, and processing operations, irrespective of whether this company is or not considered to provide an adequate level of protection, in accordance with the decision of the EU Commission regarding the Safe Harbour. This question whether a data recipient has adhered to the Safe Harbour will only be relevant for the lawfulness of the subsequent transfers of personal data from a company established in the EU to that company.

2. To achieve this objective, the recommendation is addressed in particular:

    – to the <u>controllers</u> collecting data on-line, by supplying them with a practical guide listing the <u>minimum set</u> of concrete measures to be put in place;

    – to <u>individual Internet users</u> so that they are informed about their rights and can exercise them;

    – to the <u>bodies wishing to award a label</u> certifying conformity of the processing procedures used with the European data protection Directives, by providing them with reference criteria for awarding such a label as regards the information to be given and the collection of personal data. It goes without saying that in addition to these reference criteria, other criteria concerning other obligations and rights must necessarily be taken into account also when awarding labels. The Working Party will publish a comprehensive document on this question later;

    – to the <u>European data protection authorities</u> in order to provide them with a <u>common</u> reference frame for their task of checking compliance with the national provisions adopted by Member States in accordance with the above mentioned Directives.

3. In addition, the Working Party is of the opinion that this recommendation should also serve as reference for <u>developing standards for software and hardware</u> intended for the collection and processing of personal data on the Internet.

II. Recommendations on the information to be provided when personal data are collected on the territory of European Union Member States.

2.1. What information should be provided to the data subject and when?

4. Any collection of personal data from an individual via a web site implies prior supply of certain information. In terms of content, compliance with this obligation makes it necessary:

5. <u>to state the identity and physical and electronic address of the controller</u> and, where applicable, that of the representative appointed pursuant to Article 4.2 of the Directive;

6. to state clearly the purpose(s) of the processing for which the controller is collecting data via a site. For example, when data are collected both to execute a contract (Internet subscription, ordering a product, etc) and also for direct marketing, the controller must clearly state these two purposes;

7. to state clearly the obligatory or optional nature of the information to be provided. Obligatory information is information, which is necessary to carry out the service requested. The obligatory or optional nature could be indicated, for example, by a star referring to the obligatory nature of the information, or alternatively, by adding 'optional' besides non-obligatory information. The fact that the data subject does not supply optional information cannot count against him/her in any way;

8. to mention the existence of and conditions for exercising the rights to consent or to object, as the case may be, to the

processing of personal data[7] as well as to access and to rectify and delete data. Information should be provided firstly regarding the person or service to be addressed to exercise these rights and secondly regarding the possibility of exercising them both on-line and at the physical address of the controller;

9. to list the recipients or categories of recipients of the collected information. When collecting any data, the sites should state whether the collected data will be disclosed or made available to third parties - such as business partners, subsidiaries etc. in particular – and why (for purposes other than providing the requested service and for the purposes of direct marketing[8]).

If this is the case, the Internet users must have a real possibility of objecting to this on-line by clicking a box in support of disclosure of data for purposes other than providing the requested service. Since the right to object can be exercised at any time, the possibility of exercising it on line should also be mentioned in the information provided to the data subject. Conscious of the disadvantage of over-loading the screens with information, the Working Party is of the opinion that where there is no mention of recipients, this is equivalent to the controller undertaking not to communicate or disclose the information collected to third parties whose name and address have not been provided, unless the identity of the third party is obvious and the communication of the data to it is strictly necessary to provide the service requested by the internet user and the disclosure is made only for that purpose.

10. Where it is anticipated that the data will be transmitted by the controller to countries outside the European Union, to indicate whether or not that country provides adequate protection of individuals with regard to the processing of their personal data within the meaning of Article 25 of Directive 95/46/EC. In that case, specific information must be provided on the identity and address of the recipients (physical and/or electronic address);[9]

7   A processing for a specified purpose is only legitimate if it is based on one of the grounds enumerated in Article 7 of Directive 95/46/EC *(inter alia* if the individual concerned has unambiguously given his consent, if the processing is necessary for the performance of a contract with the individual concerned, if processing is necessary for compliance with a legal obligation of the controller, if necessary for the purposes of the legitimate interests pursued by the controller or by the third party to whom the data are disclosed unless the interest of the individual concerned is prevailing).
     The right to object (see Article 14) shall be granted by Member States at least in two situations covered by Article 7 including the last one cited above. The individual has the right, save where otherwise provided by national law, to object at any time on compelling legitimate grounds relating to his particular situation to the processing of data relating to him. The right to object on request and free of charge exists in any case when the processing in question is intended for the purposes of direct marketing. In addition the data subject can also object free of charge (once informed and from the first disclosure) to personal data being disclosed to third parties or used on behalf of third parties for the purposes of direct marketing.
8   Disclosure to third parties may be authorised only if the anticipated purpose is not incompatible with that for which the data were collected and if it is based on one of the grounds enumerated in Article 7 which make the processing legitimate.
9   Information regarding adequacy decisions is available on the Commission website at the following address: http://europa.eu.int/comm/internal_market/en/media/dataprot/index.htm.

11. to give the name and address (physical and electronic address) of the service or person responsible for answering questions concerning the protection of personal data;

12. to mention clearly the existence of automatic data collection procedures, before using such a method to collect any data.[10]

   Where such procedures are used, the data subject must be given the information mentioned in this document. In addition, he/she should also be informed of the domain name of the site server transmitting the automatic collection procedures, the purpose of these procedures, their period of validity, whether or not acceptance of such procedures is necessary to visit the site and the option available to any Internet user to object to their use, as well as the consequences of de-activating such procedures. In cases where other data controllers are involved in collection of personal data, the data subject should be provided with information on the data controller's identity, purposes of processing in relation to each data controller.

   The information and the possibility of opposing to the collection must be communicated before using any automatic procedures, which trigger the user's PC to connect to another Website. eg when the user is automatically led by one website to contact another to view advertising in the form of 'banners' to avoid that this second site could collect data without any knowledge of the user.

   For example if a cookie is placed by the server of a controller, the information must be provided before it is being sent to the Internet user's hard disk in addition to the information provided by existing technology which is limited to automatically giving the name of the transmitting site and the period of validity of the cookie.[11]

13. To point out the security measures guaranteeing the authenticity of the site, the integrity and confidentiality of the information transmitted over the network taken in application of the national legislation applicable.[12]

14. The information should be provided in all the languages used on the site and in particular at those places where personal data are to be collected.

15. The controllers should check the consistency of the information contained in the various 'documents' which commit the site ('personal data and privacy protection' heading, electronic forms, text relating to the general conditions of sale and other commercial communications).

10 'Invisible' and automatic processing of Personal Data is subject to the same terms, conditions and guarantees as other processing of personal data. See Recommendation 1/99 of the Working Party on Invisible and Automatic Processing of Personal Data on the Internet Performed by Software and Hardware (23 February 1999), available on the website mentioned in footnote 1.

11 If a cookie is placed by an organisation through its own website and only this organisation can access the content of the cookie, there is no additional requirement for information identifying the organisation responsible for placing the cookie to be given, provided that the organisation hosting the website has already been adequately identified.

12 See the specific rules in Article 17 (1) and (3), second indent of Directive 95/46/EC.

2.2. How should the information be provided?

16. The Working Party considers that, the following information should be shown <u>directly on the screen</u> before the collection in order to ensure fair processing of data. This information concerns:

    – the identity of the controller;

    – the purpose(s);

    – the obligatory or optional nature of the information requested;

    – the recipients or the categories of recipients of the collected data;

    – the existence of the right of access and rectification;

    – the existence of the right to oppose any disclosure of the data to third parties for purposes other than the provision of the requested service and the way to do so (for example, by placing a box to be ticked)

    – the information which must be supplied when using automatic collection procedures;

    – the level of security during all processing stages including transmission, for example over networks.

    In such cases, the information should be provided interactively and on screen. Thus, in the case of automatic data collection methods, if necessary this information could be provided using the technique of a 'pop-up' window.

    As regards the level of security during the transmission of the data from the user's equipment to the web site, this might be a heading such as 'You are entering a secure session' or the automatic information procedures present in the navigators, such as the appearance of specific icons in the form of a key or a padlock.

17. Furthermore, the Working Party considers that complete information on the privacy policy (including the way to exercise the right of access) should be directly accessible on the home page of the site and anywhere where personal data are collected on-line. The title of the heading to click on should be sufficiently highlighted, explicit and specific to allow the Internet user to have a clear idea of the content to which he/she is being sent. For example, the heading could state 'We are collecting and processing personal data relating to you. For further information, click here' or 'Personal Data or Privacy Protection'. The content of the information to which the Internet user is directed should also be sufficiently specific.

III. Recommendations for implementing other rights and obligations

The Working Party would also like to draw the attention of the addresses of this Recommendation to some other rights of the individuals and obligations of controllers based on the directives which are of particular relevance in the context of collecting personal data on web sites. As with the indications on information, the Working Party considers that the recommendations below are of immediate practical value for both controllers and Internet users.

18. Collect only data as far as necessary in view of achieving the purpose specified;

19. ensure that data is processed only in so far as it is legitimate on the basis of one of the criteria enumerated in article 7 of the directive 95/46/EC;

20. ensure effective exercise of the right to access and to rectify, rights which it should be possible to exercise both at the physical address of the controller and on-line. Security measures should exist to guarantee that only the data subject has on-line access to the information, which concerns him/her;

21. implement the 'finality' or 'purpose' principle, which requires personal data only, be used where necessary for a specific purpose. In other words, without a legitimate reason, personal data cannot be used and the individual remains anonymous (Article 6 (1) b of Directive 95/46/EC). This principle is also sometimes called 'data minimisation principle'.

22. In the same context as described under point 21, provide for and promote anonymous consultation of a commercial site without requests for identification of the users by name, first name, e-mail address or other identifying data.

    Where a link to a person is needed without however full identification, propose and accept the use of pseudonyms of all kinds.

    Where no legal identification requirement exists, promote and accept the use of pseudonyms, even in the case of certain transactions. One example is the use of pseudonym certificates for electronic signatures (see Article 8 of Directive 1999/93/EC on a Community framework for electronic signatures).

23. Fix a storage period for the data collected. Data can only be kept for as long as this is justified by the purpose of the processing specified and pursued (Article 6 of Directive 95/46/EC and Article 6 of Directive 97/66/EC).

24. Take the steps necessary to ensure data security during processing including transmission (for example restrict and define the persons authorised to have access to the data, use strong encryption etc. Article 17 of Directive 95/46/EC).

25. Where a processor is involved, for example to host a web site, conclude a contract requiring the processor to put in place appropriate security measures in accordance also with the law of the Member State where the processor is located and only process personal data on the data controller's instructions.

26. As appropriate under national law, notify the supervisory authority (when the site controller is established in the European Union or when he has a representative in the European Union). The registration number of the notification can appear on the site, to great advantage, under the heading dedicated to data protection.

27. When transferring information to a third country where adequate protection is not guaranteed, ensure that the transfer of data only takes place if it is in line with one of the derogations provided for in Article 26 of Directive 95/46/EC. In such cases, inform the individual about the adequate guarantees provided in order to make the transfer lawful.

IV. Collection of addresses for direct marketing by e-mail and the dispatch of newsletters

28. As regards direct marketing by <u>e-mail</u>:

    – the Working Party reiterates its view that e-mail addresses picked up in public areas of the Internet such as news groups without the informed knowledge of the individual are not lawfully collected. They can thus not be used for any other purpose than the one for which they have been made public, in particular not for direct marketing.[13]

    – use of e-mail addresses for direct marketing solely where these have been collected fairly and lawfully. Fair and lawful collection implies that the data subjects have been informed of the possibility of this information being used for commercial direct marketing and that they have been placed in a position to consent to such use directly at the time the information is collected (click box on line).[14] The sending of e-mail of a promotional nature under these conditions must also be accompanied by the possibility of on-line withdrawal from the mailing list used.[15]

29. As regards the dispatch of newsletters:

    – Secure the prior agreement of the data subjects and ensure that they can effectively unsubscribe at any time, which will require informing them of this possibility each time a newsletter is sent.

13   See WP 28 (5007/00): 'Opinion 1/2000 on certain data protection aspects of electronic commerce', adopted on 3.2.2000, WP 29 (5009/00): 'Opinion 2/2000 concerning the general review of the telecommunications legal framework', adopted on 3.2.2000, and, in particular, as to the application of Articles 6 and 7 of Directive 95/46/EC, WP 36 (5042/00): 'Opinion 7/2000 on the European Commission proposal for a Directive of the European Parliament and of the Council concerning the processing of personal data and the protection of privacy in the electronic communications sector of 12 July 2000 (COM(2000)385)', adopted on 2.11.2000 and WP 37 (5063/00): 'Working document: Privacy on the Internet, an integrated approach to on-line data protection', adopted on 21.11.2000.

14   Within the European Union, five Member States (Germany, Austria, Italy, Finland and Denmark) have adopted measures aimed at banning unsolicited commercial communications. In the other Member States, either an opt-out system exists or the situation is not fully clear. It should be noted that the Commission proposal for a directive on the processing of personal data and the protection of privacy in the electronic communications sector (COM(2000)385) of 12 July 2000 favours a harmonised solution based on the 'opt-in' approach which had been unanimously supported by the Working Party in its Opinion 7/2000 (WP 36 cited above); see also the study of S. Gauthronet and E. Drouard (ARETE) for the Commission, 'Unsolicited Commercial Communications and Data Protection, January 2001, available at: http://europa.eu.int/comm/internal_market/en/media/dataprot/studies/spamsum.htm.

15   Additional requirements concerning unsolicited commercial communications in cases where opt-out is allowed on the basis of Directive 97/66/EC are laid down in the Directive on electronic commerce.

The Working Party invites the Council, the European Commission, the European Parliament and Member States to take into account this Recommendation.

The Working Party reserves the possibility to issue further comments.

Done at Brussels, 21 May 2001

For the Working Party

The Chairman

Stefano RODOTA

Appendix III

The model contractual clauses for the transfer of personal data to data controllers outside the European Economic Area[1]

Standard contractual clauses

for the purposes of Article 26(2) of Directive 95/46/EC for the transfer of personal data to third countries which do not ensure an adequate level of protection

Name of the data exporting organisation:

. . . .

Address . . . .

. . . .

Tel.: . . . .;   *fax*: . . . .;   *e-mail*: . . . .

Other information needed to identify the organisation . . . .

. . . .

("the Data **Exporter**")

and

Name of the data importing organisation:

. . . .

Address . . . .

. . . .

Tel.: . . . .;   *fax*: . . . .;   *e-mail*: . . . .

Other information needed to identify the organisation . . . .

. . . .

("the Data **Importer**")

1   Ie the member states of the European Union plus Norway, Iceland and Liechtenstein.

HAVE AGREED on the following contractual clauses ('the **Clauses**') in order to adduce adequate safeguards with respect to the protection of privacy and fundamental rights and freedoms of individuals for the transfer by the Data Exporter to the Data Importer of the personal data specified in Appendix 1.

Clause 1

Definitions

For the purposes of the Clauses:

(a) *"personal data"*, *"special categories of data"*, *"process/ processing"*, *"controller"*, *"processor"*, *"Data Subject"* and *"Supervisory Authority"* shall have the same meaning as in Directive 95/46/EC of 24 October 1995 on the protection of individuals with regard to the processing of personal data and on the free movement of such data ("the Directive");

(b) "the *Data Exporter*" shall mean the Controller who transfers the Personal Data;

(c) "the *Data Importer*" shall mean the Controller who agrees to receive from the Data Exporter personal data for further processing in accordance with the terms of these Clauses and who is not subject to a third country's system ensuring adequate protection.

Clause 2

Details of the Transfer

The details of the transfer, and in particular the categories of personal data and the purposes for which they are transferred, are specified in Appendix 1 which forms an integral part of the Clauses.

Clause 3

Third-party beneficiary clause

The Data Subjects can enforce this Clause, Clause 4 (b), (c) and (d), Clause 5 (a), (b), (c) and (e), Clause 6 (1) and (2), and Clauses 7, 9 and 11 as third-party beneficiaries. The parties do not object to the Data Subjects being represented by an association or other bodies if they so wish and if permitted by national law.

Clause 4

Obligations of the Data Exporter

The Data Exporter agrees and warrants:

(a) that the processing, including the transfer itself, of the personal data by him has been and, up to the moment of the transfer, will continue to be carried out in accordance with all the relevant provisions of the Member State in which the Data Exporter is established (and where applicable has been notified to the relevant Authorities of that State) and does not violate the relevant provisions of that State;

(b)   that if the transfer involves special categories of Data the Data Subject has been informed or will be informed before the transfer that his data could be transmitted to a third country not providing adequate protection;

(c)   to make available to the Data Subjects upon request a copy of the Clauses; and

(d)   to respond in a reasonable time and to the extent reasonably possible to enquiries from the Supervisory Authority on the processing of the relevant Personal Data by the Data Importer and to any enquiries from the Data Subject concerning the processing of his Personal Data by the Data Importer.

Clause 5

Obligations of the Data Importer

The Data Importer agrees and warrants:

(a)   that he has no reason to believe that the legislation applicable to him prevents him from fulfilling his obligations under the contract and that in the event of a change in that legislation which is likely to have a substantial adverse effect on the guarantees provided by the Clauses, he will notify the change to the Data Exporter and to the Supervisory Authority where the Data Exporter is established, in which case the Data Exporter is entitled to suspend the transfer of data and/or terminate the contract;

(b)   to process the Personal Data in accordance with the Mandatory Data Protection Principles set out in Appendix 2;

or, if explicitly agreed by the parties by ticking below and subject to compliance with the Mandatory Data Protection Principles set out in Appendix 3, to process in all other respects the data in accordance with:

 •   the relevant provisions of national law (attached to these Clauses) protecting the fundamental rights and freedoms of natural persons, and in particular their right to privacy with respect to the processing of personal data applicable to a Data Controller in the country in which the Data Exporter is established, or,

 •   the relevant provisions of any Commission decision under Article 25(6) of Directive 95/46/EC finding that a third country provides adequate protection in certain sectors of activity only, if the Data Importer is based in that third country and is not covered by those provisions, in so far those provisions are of a nature which makes them applicable in the sector of the transfer;

(c)   to deal promptly and properly with all reasonable inquiries from the Data Exporter or the Data Subject relating to his processing of the Personal Data subject to the transfer and to cooperate with the competent Supervisory Authority in the course of all its inquiries and abide by the advice of the Supervisory Authority with regard to the processing of the data transferred;

(d)   at the request of the Data Exporter to submit its data processing facilities for audit which shall be carried out by the Data

Exporter or an inspection body composed of independent members and in possession of the required professional qualifications, selected by the Data Exporter, where applicable, in agreement with the Supervisory Authority;

(e)   to make available to the Data Subject upon request a copy of the Clauses and indicate the office which handles complaints.

Clause 6

Liability

1.   The Parties agree that a Data Subject who has suffered damage as a result of any violation of the provisions referred to in Clause 3 is entitled to receive compensation from the parties for the damage suffered. The Parties agree that they may be exempted from this liability only if they prove that neither of them is responsible for the violation of those provisions.

2.   The Data Exporter and the Data Importer agree that they will be jointly and severally liable for damage to the Data Subject resulting from any violation referred to in paragraph 1. In the event of such a violation, the Data Subject may bring an action before a court against either the Data Exporter or the Data Importer or both.

3.   The parties agree that if one party is held liable for a violation referred to in paragraph 1 by the other party, the latter will, to the extent to which it is liable, indemnify the first party for any cost, charge, damages, expenses or loss it has incurred*.

    [* paragraph 3 is optional]

Clause 7

Mediation and Jurisdiction

1.   The parties agree that if there is a dispute between a Data Subject and either party which is not amicably resolved and the Data Subject invokes the third-party beneficiary provision in Clause 3, they accept the decision of the Data Subject:

    (a)   to refer the dispute to mediation by an independent person or, where applicable, by the Supervisory Authority;

    (b)   to refer the dispute to the courts in the Member State in which the Data Exporter is established.

2.   The Parties agree that by agreement between a Data Subject and the relevant party a dispute can be referred to an arbitration body, if that party is established in a country which has ratified the New York Convention on enforcement of arbitration awards.

3.   The parties agree that paragraphs 1 and 2 apply without prejudice to the Data Subject's substantive or procedural rights to seek remedies in accordance with other provisions of national or international law.

Clause 8

Cooperation with Supervisory Authorities

The parties agree to deposit a copy of this contract with the Supervisory Authority if it so requests or if such deposit is required under national law.

Clause 9

Termination of the Clauses

The parties agree that the termination of the Clauses at any time, in any circumstances and for whatever reason does not exempt them from the obligations and/or conditions under the Clauses as regards the processing of the data transferred.

Clause 10

Governing Law

The Clauses shall be governed by the law of the Member State in which the Data Exporter is established, namely

. . . .

Clause 11

Variation of the contract

The parties undertake not to vary or modify the terms of the Clauses.

On behalf of the Data Exporter:

Name (written out in full): . . . .

Position: . . . .

Address: . . . .

Other information necessary in order for the contract to be binding

(if any): . . . .

Signature . . . .

(stamp of organisation)

On behalf of the Data Importer:

Name (written out in full): . . . .

Position: . . . .

Address: . . . .

Other information necessary in order for the contract to be binding

(if any): . . . .

Signature . . . .

(stamp of organisation)

APPENDIX 1
to the Standard Contractual Clauses

This Appendix forms part of the Clauses and must be completed and signed by the parties

(*The Member States may complete or specify, according to their national procedures, any additional necessary information to be contained in this Appendix)

Data Exporter

The Data Exporter is (*please specify briefly your activities relevant to the transfer*):

. . . .

. . . .

. . . .

Data Importer

The Data Importer is (*please specify briefly your activities relevant to the transfer*):

. . . .

. . . .

. . . .

Data Subjects

The personal data transferred concern the following categories of Data Subjects (*please specify*):

. . . .

. . . .

. . . .

Purposes of the transfer

The transfer is necessary for the following purposes (*please specify*):

. . . .

. . . .

. . . .

Categories of data

The personal data transferred fall within the following categories of data (*please specify*):

. . . .

. . . .

. . . .

Sensitive Data (if appropriate)

The personal data transferred fall within the following categories of sensitive data (*please specify*):

. . . .

. . . .

. . . .

Recipients

The personal data transferred may be disclosed only to the following recipients or categories

of recipients (*please specify*):

. . . .

. . . .

. . . .

Storage limit

The personal data transferred may be stored for no more than (*please indicate*): . . . . (months/years)

DATA EXPORTER	DATA IMPORTER
Name:	. . . .
Authorised	
Signature	. . . .

APPENDIX 2
to the Standard Contractual Clauses

> Mandatory Data Protection Principles referred to in the first paragraph of Clause 5(b).

These data protection principles should be read and interpreted in the light of the provisions (principles and relevant exceptions) of Directive 95/46/EC.[2]

They shall apply subject to the mandatory requirements of the national legislation applicable to the Data Importer which do not go beyond what is necessary in a democratic society on the basis of one of the interests listed in Article 13(1) of Directive 95/46/EC, that is, if they constitute a necessary measure to safeguard national security, defence, public security, the prevention, investigation,

2   Directive 95/46/EC of the European Parliament and of the Council of 24 October 1995 on the protection of individuals with regard to the processing of personal data and on the free movement of such data, *Official Journal of the European Communities*, L 281, 23.11.1995, p 31.

detection and prosecution of criminal offences or of breaches of ethics for the regulated professions, an important economic or financial interest of the State or the protection of the Data Subject or the rights and freedoms of others.

(1) **Purpose limitation**

Data must be processed and subsequently used or further communicated only for the specific purposes in Appendix 1 to the Clauses. Data must not be kept longer than necessary for the purposes for which they are transferred.

(2) **Data quality and proportionality**

Data must be accurate and, where necessary, kept up to date. The data must be adequate, relevant and not excessive in relation to the purposes for which they are transferred and further processed.

(3) **Transparency**

Data Subjects must be provided with information as to the purposes of the processing and the identity of the data controller in the third country, and other information insofar as this is necessary to ensure fair processing, unless such information has already been given by the Data Exporter.

(4) **Security and confidentiality**

Technical and organisational security measures must be taken by the data controller that are appropriate to the risks, such as unauthorised access, presented by the processing. Any person acting under the authority of the data controller, including a processor, must not process the data except on instructions from the controller.

(5) **Rights of access, rectification, erasure and blocking of data**

As provided for in Article 12 of Directive 95/46/EC, the Data Subject must have a right of access to all data relating to him that are processed and, as appropriate, the right to the rectification, erasure or blocking of data the processing of which does not comply with the principles set out in this Appendix, in particular because the data are incomplete or inaccurate.

He should also be able to object to the processing of the data relating to him on compelling legitimate grounds relating to his particular situation.

(6) **Restrictions on onward transfers**

Further transfers of personal data from the Data Importer to another controller established in a third country not providing adequate protection or not covered by a Decision adopted by the Commission pursuant to Article 25(6) of Directive 95/46/EC (onward transfer) may take place only if either:

(a) Data Subjects have, in the case of special categories of data, given their unambiguous consent to the onward transfer or, in other cases, have been given the opportunity to object. The minimum information to be provided to Data Subjects must contain in a language understandable to them:

  – the purposes of the onward transfer,

  – the identification of the Data Exporter established in the Community,

  – the categories of further recipients of the data and the countries of destination, and

      –   an explanation that, after the onward transfer, the data may be processed by a controller established in a country where there is not an adequate level of protection of the privacy of individuals;

or

(b)   the Data Exporter and the Data Importer agree to the adherence to the Clauses of another controller which thereby becomes a party to the Clauses and assumes the same obligations as the Data Importer.

(7)   Special categories of data

Where data revealing racial or ethnic origin, political opinions, religious or philosophical beliefs or trade union memberships and data concerning health or sex life and data relating to offences, criminal convictions or security measures are processed, additional safeguards should be in place within the meaning of Directive 95/46/EC, in particular, appropriate security measures such as strong encryption for transmission or such as keeping a record of access to sensitive data.

(8)   Direct marketing

Where data are processed for the purposes of direct marketing, effective procedures should exist allowing the Data Subject at any time to 'opt-out' from having his data used for such purposes.

(9)   Automated individual decisions

Data Subjects are entitled not to be subject to a decision which is based solely on automated processing of data, unless other measures are taken to safeguard the individual's legitimate interests as provided for in Article 15(2) of Directive 95/46/EC. Where the purpose of the transfer is the taking of an automated decision as referred to in Article 15 of Directive 95/46/EC, which produces legal effects concerning the individual or significantly affects him and which is based solely on automated processing of data intended to evaluate certain personal aspects relating to him, such as his performance at work, creditworthiness, reliability, conduct, etc., the individual should have the right to know the reasoning for this Decision.

APPENDIX 3
to the Standard Contractual Clauses

> Mandatory Data Protection Principles referred to in the second paragraph of Clause 5(b).

(1)   Purpose limitation

Data must be processed and subsequently used or further communicated only for the specific purposes in Appendix 1 to the Clauses. Data must not be kept longer than necessary for the purposes for which they are transferred.

(2)   Rights of access, rectification, erasure and blocking of data

As provided for in Article 12 of Directive 95/46/EC, the Data Subject must have a right of access to all data relating to him that are processed and, as appropriate, the right to the rectification, erasure or blocking of data the processing of which does not comply with the principles set out in this Appendix, in particular because the data is incomplete or inaccurate. He should also be able to object to the processing of the data relating to him on compelling legitimate grounds relating to his particular situation.

(3) **Restrictions on onward transfers**

Further transfers of personal data from the Data Importer to another controller established in a third country not providing adequate protection or not covered by a Decision adopted by the Commission pursuant to Article 25(6) of Directive 95/46/EC (onward transfer) may take place only if either:

(a) Data Subjects have, in the case of if special categories of data, given their unambiguous consent to the onward transfer, or, in other cases, have been given the opportunity to object.

The minimum information to be provided to Data Subjects must contain in a language understandable to them:

- the purposes of the onward transfer,

- the identification of the Data Exporter established in the Community,

- the categories of further recipients of the data and the countries of destination, and,

- an explanation that, after the onward transfer, the data may be processed by a controller established in a country where there is not an adequate level of protection of the privacy of individuals;

or

(b) the Data Exporter and the Data Importer agree to the adherence to the Clauses of another controller which thereby becomes a party to the Clauses and assumes the same obligations as the Data Importer.

Appendix IV

The model contractual clauses for the transfer of personal data to data processors located outside the European Economic Area[1]

Standard Contractual Clauses (processors)

For the purposes of Article 26(2) of Directive 95/46/EC for the transfer of personal data to processors established in third countries which do not ensure an adequate level of data protection

Name of the data exporting organisation:

. . . .

Address . . . .

. . . .

Tel.: . . . .;   fax: . . . .;   e-mail: . . . .

Other information needed to identify the organisation . . . .

. . . .

(the data **exporter**)

and

Name of the data importing organisation:

. . . .

Address . . . .

. . . .

Tel.: . . . .;   fax: . . . .;   e-mail: . . . .

Other information needed to identify the organisation . . . .

. . . .

(the data **importer**)

1   Ie the member states of the European Union plus Norway, Iceland and Liechtenstein.

HAVE AGREED on the following Contractual Clauses (the Clauses) in order to adduce adequate safeguards with respect to the protection of privacy and fundamental rights and freedoms of individuals for the transfer by the data exporter to the data importer of the personal data specified in Appendix 1.

Clause 1

Definitions

For the purposes of the Clauses:

(a) 'personal data', 'special categories of data', 'process/ processing', 'controller', 'processor', 'data subject' and 'supervisory authority' shall have the same meaning as in Directive 95/46/EC of the European Parliament and of the Council of 24 October 1995 on the protection of individuals with regard to the processing of personal data and on the free movement of such data (the Directive);[2]

(b) 'the data exporter' shall mean the controller who transfers the personal data;

(c) 'the data importer' shall mean the processor who agrees to receive from the data exporter personal data intended for processing on his behalf after the transfer in accordance with his instructions and the terms of these Clauses and who is not subject to a third country's system ensuring to adequate protection;

(d) 'the applicable data protection law' shall mean the legislation protecting the fundamental rights and freedoms of natural persons and, in particular, their right to privacy with respect to the processing of personal data applicable to a data controller in the Member State in which the data exporter is established;

(e) 'technical and organisational security measures' shall mean those measures aimed at protecting personal data against accidental or unlawful destruction or accidental loss, alteration, unauthorised disclosure or access, in particular where the processing involves the transmission of data over a network, and against all other unlawful forms of processing.

Clause 2

Details of the transfer

Details of the transfer and in particular the special categories of personal data where applicable are specified in Appendix 1 which forms an integral part of the Clauses.

Clause 3

Third-party beneficiary clause

The data exporter agrees and warrants:

(a) that the processing, including the transfer itself, of the personal data has been and will continue to be carried out in accordance with the relevant provisions of the applicable data protection law

2   Parties may reproduce definitions and means contained in Directive 95/46/EC within this Clause if they consider it better for the contract to stand alone.

(and, where applicable, has been notified to the relevant authorities of the Member State where the data exporter is established) and does not violate the relevant provisions of that State;

(b)   that he has instructed and throughout the duration of the personal data processing services will instruct the data importer to process the personal data transferred only on the data exporter's behalf and in accordance with the applicable data protection law and these clauses;

(c)   that the data importer shall provide sufficient guarantees in respect of the technical and organisational security measures specified in Appendix 2 of this contract;

(d)   that after assessment of the requirements of the applicable data protection law, the security measures are appropriate to protect personal data against accidental or unlawful destruction or accidental loss, alteration, unauthorised disclosure or access, in particular where the processing involves the transmission of data over a network, and against all other unlawful forms of processing, and that these measures ensure a level of security appropriate to the risks presented by the processing and the nature of the data to be protected having regard to the state of the art and the cost of their implementation;

(e)   that he will ensure compliance with the security measures;

(f)   that, if the transfer involves special categories of data, the data subject has been informed or will be informed before, or as soon as possible after, the transfer that his data could be transmitted to a third country not providing adequate protection;

(g)   that he agrees to forward the notification received from the data importer pursuant to Clause 5(b) to the data protection supervisory authority if he decides to continue the transfer or to lift his suspension;

(h)   to make available to the data subjects upon request a copy of the Clauses set out in this Annex, with the exception of Appendix 2 which shall be replaced by a summary description of the security measures.

Clause 5

Obligations of the data importer[3]

The data exporter agrees and warrants:

(a)   to process the personal data only on behalf of the data exporter and in compliance with his instructions and the clauses; if he

---

3   Mandatory requirements of the national legislation applicable to the data importer which do not go beyond what is necessary in a democratic society on the basis of one of the interests listed in Article 13(1) of Directive 95/46/EC, that is, if they constitute a necessary measure to safeguard national security defence, public security, the prevention, investigation, detection and prosecution of criminal offences or of breaches of ethics for the regulated professions, an important economic or financial interest of the State or the protection of the data subject or the rights and freedoms of others, are not in contradiction with the standard contractual clauses. Some examples of such mandatory requirements which do not go beyond what is necessary in a democratic society are, inter alia, internationally recognised sanctions, tax-reporting requirements or anti-money-laundering reporting requirements.

cannot provide such compliance for whatever reasons, he agrees to inform promptly the data exporter of his inability to comply, in which case the data exporter is entitled to suspend the transfer of data and/or terminate the contract;

(b)   that he has no reason to believe that the legislation applicable to him prevents him from fulfilling the instructions received from the data exporter and his obligations under the contract and that in the event of a change in this legislation which is likely to have a substantial adverse effect on the warranties and obligations provided by the Clauses, he will promptly notify the change to the data exporter as soon as he is aware, in which case the data exporter is entitled to suspend the transfer of data and/or terminate the contract;

(c)   that he has implemented the technical and organisational security measures specified in Appendix 2 before processing the personal data transferred;

(d)   that he shall promptly notify the data exporter about:

(i)   any legally binding request for disclosure of the personal data by a law enforcement authority unless otherwise prohibited, such as a prohibition under criminal law to preserve the confidentiality of a law enforcement investigation;

(ii)   any accidental or unauthorised access; and

(iii)   any request received directly from the data subjects without responding to that request, unless he has been otherwise authorised to do so;

(e)   to deal promptly and properly with all inquiries from the data exporter relating to his processing of the personal data subject to the transfer and to abide by the advice of the supervisory authority with regard to the processing of the data transferred;

(f)   at the request of the data exporter to submit his data processing facilities for audit of the processing activities covered by the clauses which shall be carried out by the data exporter or an inspection body composed of independent members and in possession of the required professional qualifications bound by a duty of confidentiality, selected by the data exporter, where applicable, in agreement with the supervisory authority;

(g)   to make available to the data subject upon request a copy of the Clauses set out in this Annex, with the exception of Appendix 2 which shall be replaced by a summary description of the security measures in those cases where the data subject is unable to obtain a copy from the data exporter.

Clause 6

Liability

1   The parties agree that a data subject, who has suffered damage as a result of any violation of the provisions referred to in Clause 3 is entitled to receive compensation from the data exporter for the damage suffered.

2   If a data subject is not able to bring the action referred to in paragraph 1 arising out of a breach by the data importer of any of his obligations referred to in Clause 3 against the data exporter has disappeared factually or has ceased to exist in

law or became insolvent, the data importer agrees that the data subject may issue a claim against the data importer as if he were the data exporter.

3   The parties agree that if one party is held liable for a violation of the clauses committed by the other party, the latter will, to the extent to which it is liable, indemnify the first party for any cost, charge, damages, expenses or loss it has incurred.

Indemnification is contingent upon:

(a)   the data exporter notifying the data importer of a claim; and

(b)   the data importer being given the possibility to co-operate with the data exporter in the defence and settlement of the claim.[4]

Clause 7

Mediation and jurisdiction

1   The data importer agrees that if the data subject invokes against him third-party beneficiary rights and/or claims compensation for damages under the clauses, the data importer will accept the decision of the data subject:

(a)   to refer the dispute to mediation, by an independent person or, where applicable, by the supervisory authority;

(b)   to refer the dispute to the courts in the Member State in which the data exporter is established.

2   The data importer agrees that, by agreement with the data subject, the resolution of a specific dispute can be referred to an arbitration body if the data importer is established in a country which has ratified the New York Convention on enforcement of arbitration awards.

3   The parties agree that the choice made by the data subject will not prejudice his substantive or procedural rights to seek remedies in accordance with other provisions of national or international law.

Clause 8

Co-operation with supervisory authorities

1   The data exporter agrees to deposit a copy of this contract with the supervisory authority if it so requests or if such deposit is required under the applicable data protection law.

2   The parties agree that the supervisory authority has the right to conduct an audit of the data importer which has the same scope and is subject to the same conditions as would apply to an audit of the data exporter under the applicable data protection law.

Clause 9

Governing Law

The Clauses shall be governed by the law of the Member State in which the data exporter is established, namely . . . .

---

4   Paragraph 3 is optional.

Clause 10

Variation of the contract

The parties undertake not to vary or modify the terms of the Clauses.

Clause 11

Obligation after the termination of personal data processing services

1   The parties agree that on the termination of the provision of data processing services, the data importer shall, at the choice of the data exporter, return all the personal data transferred and the copies thereof to the data exporter or shall destroy all the personal data and certify to the data exporter that he has done so, unless legislation imposed upon the data importer prevents him from returning or destroying all or part of the personal data transferred. In that case, the data importer warrants that he will guarantee the confidentiality of the personal data transferred and will not actively process the personal data transferred anymore.

2   The data importer warrants that upon request of the data exporter and/or of the supervisory authority, he will submit his data processing facilities for an audit of the measures referred to in paragraph 1.

On behalf of the data exporter:

Name (written out in full):

Position:

Address:

Other information necessary in order for the contract to be binding (if any):

Signature

(stamp of organisation)

On behalf of the data importer:

Name (written out in full):

Position:

Address:

Other information necessary in order for the contract to be binding (if any):

Signature

(stamp of organisation)

Appendix 1
to the Standard Contractual Clauses

This Appendix forms part of the Clauses and must be completed and signed by the parties

(*) The Member States may complete or specify, according to their national procedures, any additional necessary information to be contained in this Appendix)

Data exporter

The data exporter is (please specify briefly your activities relevant to the transfer):

Data importer

The data importer is (please specify briefly activities relevant to the transfer):

Data subjects

The personal data transferred concern the following categories of data subjects (please specify):

Categories of data

The personal data transferred concern the following categories of data (please specify):

Special categories of data (if appropriate)

The personal data transferred concern the following special categories of data (please specify):

Processing operations

The personal data transferred will be subject to the following basic processing activities (please specify):

DATA EXPORTER	DATA IMPORTER
Name:	. . . .
Authorised	
Signature:	. . . .

Appendix 2
to the Standard Contractual Clauses

This Appendix forms part of the Clauses and must be completed and signed by the parties

Description of the technical and organisational security measures implemented by the data importer in accordance with Clauses 4(d) and 5(c) (or document/legislation attached):

Appendix V

Interception of Communications – Code of Practice

Interception of Communications Code of Practice

**Pursuant to Section 71 of the Regulation of
Investigatory Powers Act 2000**

CONTENTS

1. GENERAL

1.1 This code of practice relates to the powers and duties conferred or imposed under Chapter I of Part I of the Regulation of Investigatory Powers Act 2000 ("the Act"). It provides guidance on the procedures that must be followed before interception of communications can take place under those provisions. It is primarily intended for use by those public authorities listed in section 6(2) of the Act. It will also prove useful to postal and telecommunication operators and other interested bodies to acquaint themselves with the procedures to be followed by those public authorities.

1.2 The Act provides that all codes of practice relating to the Act are admissible as evidence in criminal and civil proceedings. If any provision of this code appears relevant before any court or tribunal considering any such proceedings, or to the Tribunal established under the Act, or to one of the Commissioners responsible for overseeing the powers conferred by the Act, it must be taken into account.

2. GENERAL RULES ON INTERCEPTION WITH A WARRANT

2.1 There are a limited number of persons by whom, or on behalf of whom, applications for interception warrants may be made. These persons are:

- The Director-General of the Security Service.

- The Chief of the Secret Intelligence Service.

- The Director of GCHQ.

- The Director-General of the National Criminal Intelligence Service (NCIS handle interception on behalf of police forces in England and Wales).

- The Commissioner of the Police of the Metropolis (the Metropolitan Police Special Branch handle interception on behalf of Special Branches in England and Wales).

- The Chief Constable of the Police Service of Northern Ireland.

- The Chief Constable of any police force maintained under or by virtue of section 1 of the Police (Scotland) Act 1967.

- The Commissioners of Customs and Excise.

- The Chief of Defence Intelligence.

A person who, for the purposes of any international mutual assistance agreement, is the competent authority of a country or territory outside the United Kingdom.

Any application made on behalf of one of the above must be made by a person holding office under the Crown.

2.2 All interception warrants are issued by the Secretary of State. Even where the urgency procedure is followed, the Secretary of State personally authorises the warrant, although it is signed by a senior official.

2.3 Before issuing an interception warrant, the Secretary of State must believe that what the action seeks to achieve is necessary for one of the following section 5(3) purposes:

- in the interests of national security;

- for the purpose of preventing or detecting serious crime; or

- for the purpose of safeguarding the economic well-being of the UK and that the conduct authorised by the warrant is proportionate to what is sought to be achieved by that conduct.

Necessity and Proportionality

2.4   Obtaining a warrant under the Act will only ensure that the interception authorised is a justifiable interference with an individual's rights under Article 8 of the European Convention of Human Rights (the right to privacy) if it is necessary and proportionate for the interception to take place. The Act recognises this by first requiring that the Secretary of State believes that the authorisation is necessary on one or more of the statutory grounds set out in section 5(3) of the Act. This requires him to believe that it is necessary to undertake the interception which is to be authorised for a particular purpose falling within the relevant statutory ground.

2.5   Then, if the interception is necessary, the Secretary of State must also believe that it is proportionate to what is sought to be achieved by carrying it out. This involves balancing the intrusiveness of the interference, against the need for it in operational terms. Interception of communications will not be proportionate if it is excessive in the circumstances of the case or if the information which is sought could reasonably be obtained by other means. Further, all interception should be carefully managed to meet the objective in question and must not be arbitrary or unfair.

Implementation of Warrants

2.6   After a warrant has been issued it will be forwarded to the person to whom it is addressed, in practice the intercepting agency which submitted the application. The Act (section 11) then permits the intercepting agency to carry out the interception, or to require the assistance of other persons in giving effect to the warrant. Warrants cannot be served on those outside the jurisdiction of the UK.

Provision of Reasonable Assistance

2.7   Any postal or telecommunications operator (referred to as communications service providers) in the United Kingdom may be required to provide assistance in giving effect to an interception. The Act places a requirement on postal and telecommunications operators to take all such steps for giving effect to the warrant as are notified to them (section 11(4) of the Act). But the steps which may be required are limited to those which it is reasonably practicable to take (section 11(5)). What is reasonably practicable should be agreed after consultation between the postal or telecommunications operator and the Government. If no agreement can be reached it will be for the Secretary of State to decide whether to press forward with civil proceedings. Criminal proceedings may also be instituted by or with the consent of the Director of Public Prosecutions.

2.8   Where the intercepting agency requires the assistance of a communications service provider in order to implement a warrant, they should provide the following to the communications service provider:

- A copy of the warrant instrument signed and dated by the Secretary of State (or in an urgent case, by a senior official);

- The relevant schedule for that service provider setting out the numbers, addresses or other factors identifying the communications to be intercepted;

- A covering document from the intercepting agency requiring the assistance of the communications service provider and specifying any other details regarding the means of interception and delivery as may be necessary. Contact details with respect to the intercepting agency will either be provided in this covering document or will be available in the handbook provided to all postal and telecommunications operators who maintain an intercept capability.

Provision of Intercept Capability

2.9 Whilst all persons who provide a postal or telecommunications service are obliged to provide assistance in giving effect to an interception, persons who provide a public postal or telecommunications service, or plan to do so, may also be required to provide a reasonable intercept capability. The obligations the Secretary of State considers reasonable to impose on such persons to ensure they have such a capability will be set out in an order made by the Secretary of State and approved by Parliament. The Secretary of State may then serve a notice upon a communications service provider setting out the steps they must take to ensure they can meet these obligations. A notice will not be served without consultation over the content of the notice between the Government and the service provider having previously taken place. When served with such a notice, a communications service provider, if he feels it unreasonable, will be able to refer that notice to the Technical Advisory Board (TAB) on the reasonableness of the technical requirements and capabilities that are being sought. Details of how to submit a notice to the TAB will be provided either before or at the time the notice is served.

2.10 Any communications service provider obliged to maintain a reasonable intercept capability will be provided with a handbook which will contain the basic information they require to respond to requests for reasonable assistance for the interception of communications.

Duration of Interception Warrants

2.11 All interception warrants are valid for an initial period of three months. Upon renewal, warrants issued on serious crime grounds are valid for a further period of three months. Warrants renewed on national security/ economic well-being grounds are valid for a further period of six months. Urgent authorisations are valid for five working days following the date of issue unless renewed by the Secretary of State.

2.12 Where modifications take place, the warrant expiry date remains unchanged. However, where the modification takes place under the urgency provisions, the modification instrument expires after five working days following the date of issue unless renewed following the routine procedure.

2.13 Where a change in circumstance prior to the set expiry date leads the intercepting agency to consider it no longer necessary or practicable for the warrant to be in force, it should be cancelled with immediate effect.

Stored Communications

2.14 Section 2(7) of the Act defines a communication in the course of its transmission as also encompassing any time when the communication is being stored on the communication system in such a way as to enable the intended recipient to have access to it. This means that a warrant can be used to obtain both communications that are in the process of transmission and those that are being stored on the transmission system.

2.15 Stored communications may also be accessed by means other than a warrant. If a communication has been stored on a communication system it may be obtained with lawful authority by means of an existing statutory power such as a production order (under the Police and Criminal Evidence Act 1984) or a search warrant.

3. SPECIAL RULES ON INTERCEPTION WITH A WARRANT

Collateral Intrusion

3.1 Consideration should be given to any infringement of the privacy of individuals who are not the subject of the intended interception, especially where communications relating to religious, medical, journalistic or legally privileged material may be involved. An application for an interception warrant should draw attention to any circumstances which give rise to an unusual degree of collateral infringement of privacy, and this will be taken into account by the Secretary of State when considering a warrant application. Should an interception operation reach the point where individuals other than the subject of the authorisation are identified as directly relevant to the operation, consideration should be given to applying for separate warrants covering those individuals.

Confidential Information

3.2 Particular consideration should also be given in cases where the subject of the interception might reasonably assume a high degree of privacy, or where confidential information is involved. Confidential information consists of matters subject to legal privilege, confidential personal information or confidential journalistic material (see paragraphs 3.9-3.11). For example, extra consideration should be given where interception might involve communications between a minister of religion and an individual relating to the latter's spiritual welfare, or where matters of medical or journalistic confidentiality or legal privilege may be involved.

Communications Subject to Legal Privilege

3.3   Section 98 of the Police Act 1997 describes those matters that are subject to legal privilege in England and Wales. In relation to Scotland, those matters subject to legal privilege contained in section 33 of the Criminal Law (Consolidation) (Scotland) Act 1995 should be adopted. With regard to Northern Ireland, Article 12 of the Police and Criminal Evidence (Northern Ireland) Order 1989 should be referred to.

3.4   Legal privilege does not apply to communications made with the intention of furthering a criminal purpose (whether the lawyer is acting unwittingly or culpably). Legally privileged communications will lose their protection if there are grounds to believe, for example, that the professional legal advisor is intending to hold or use the information for a criminal purpose. But privilege is not lost if a professional legal advisor is properly advising a person who is suspected of having committed a criminal offence. The concept of legal privilege applies to the provision of professional legal advice by any individual, agency or organisation qualified to do so.

3.5   The Act does not provide any special protection for legally privileged communications. Nevertheless, intercepting such communications is particularly sensitive and is therefore subject to additional safeguards under this Code. The guidance set out below may in part depend on whether matters subject to legal privilege have been obtained intentionally or incidentally to some other material which has been sought.

3.6   In general, any application for a warrant which is likely to result in the interception of legally privileged communications should include, in addition to the reasons why it is considered necessary for the interception to take place, an assessment of how likely it is that communications which are subject to legal privilege will be intercepted. In addition, it should state whether the purpose (or one of the purposes) of the interception is to obtain privileged communications. This assessment will be taken into account by the Secretary of State in deciding whether an interception is necessary under section 5(3) of the Act and whether it is proportionate. In such circumstances, the Secretary of State will be able to impose additional conditions such as regular reporting arrangements so as to be able to exercise his discretion on whether a warrant should continue to be authorised. In those cases where communications which include legally privileged communications have been intercepted and retained, the matter should be reported to the Interception of Communications Commissioner during his inspections and the material be made available to him if requested.

3.7   Where a lawyer is the subject of an interception, it is possible that a substantial proportion of the communications which will be intercepted will be between the lawyer and his client(s) and will be subject to legal privilege. Any case where a lawyer is the subject of an investigation should be notified to the Interception of Communications Commissioner during his inspections and any material which has been retained should be made available to him if requested.

3.8   In addition to safeguards governing the handling and retention of intercept material as provided for in section 15 of the Act, caseworkers who examine intercepted communications should be alert to any intercept material which may be subject to legal privilege.

Where there is doubt as to whether the communications are subject to legal privilege, advice should be sought from a legal adviser within the intercepting agency. Similar advice should also be sought where there is doubt over whether communications are not subject to legal privilege due to the "in furtherance of a criminal purpose" exception.

Communications involving Confidential Personal Information and Confidential Journalistic Material

3.9 Similar consideration to that given to legally privileged communications must also be given to the interception of communications that involve confidential personal information and confidential journalistic material. Confidential personal information is information held in confidence concerning an individual (whether living or dead) who can be identified from it, and the material in question relates to his physical or mental health or to spiritual counselling. Such information can include both oral and written communications. Such information as described above is held in confidence if it is held subject to an express or implied undertaking to hold it in confidence or it is subject to a restriction on disclosure or an obligation of confidentiality contained in existing legislation. For example, confidential personal information might include consultations between a health professional and a patient, or information from a patient's medical records.

3.10 Spiritual counselling is defined as conversations between an individual and a Minister of Religion acting in his official capacity, and where the individual being counselled is seeking or the Minister is imparting forgiveness, absolution or the resolution of conscience with the authority of the Divine Being(s) of their faith.

3.11 Confidential journalistic material includes material acquired or created for the purposes of journalism and held subject to an undertaking to hold it in confidence, as well as communications resulting in information being acquired for the purposes of journalism and held subject to such an undertaking.

4. INTERCEPTION WARRANTS (SECTION 8(1))

4.1 This section applies to the interception of communications by means of a warrant complying with section 8(1) of the Act. This type of warrant may be issued in respect of the interception of communications carried on any postal service or telecommunications system as defined in section 2(1) of the Act (including a private telecommunications system). Responsibility for the issuing of interception warrants rests with the Secretary of State.

Application for a Section 8(1) Warrant

4.2 An application for a warrant is made to the Secretary of State. Interception warrants, when issued, are addressed to the person who submitted the application. This person may then serve a copy upon any person who may be able to provide assistance in giving effect to that warrant. Each application, a copy of which must be retained by the applicant, should contain the following information:

- Background to the operation in question.

- Person or premises to which the application relates (and how the person or premises feature in the operation).

- Description of the communications to be intercepted, details of the communications service provider(s) and an assessment of the feasibility of the interception operation where this is relevant.

- Description of the conduct to be authorised as considered necessary in order to carry out the interception, where appropriate.

- An explanation of why the interception is considered to be necessary under the provisions of section 5(3).

- A consideration of why the conduct to be authorised by the warrant is proportionate to what is sought to be achieved by that conduct.

- A consideration of any unusual degree of collateral intrusion and why that intrusion is justified in the circumstances. In particular, where the communications in question might affect religious, medical or journalistic confidentiality or legal privilege, this must be specified in the application.

- Where an application is urgent, supporting justification should be provided.

- An assurance that all material intercepted will be handled in accordance with the safeguards required by section 15 of the Act.

Authorisation of a Section 8(1) Warrant

4.3   Before issuing a warrant under section 8(1), the Secretary of State must believe the warrant is necessary:

- in the interests of national security;

- for the purpose of preventing or detecting serious crime; or

- for the purpose of safeguarding the economic well-being of the United Kingdom.

4.4   In exercising his power to issue an interception warrant for the purpose of safeguarding the economic well-being of the United Kingdom (as provided for by section 5(3)(c) of the Act), the Secretary of State will consider whether the economic well-being of the United Kingdom which is to be safeguarded is, on the facts of each case, directly related to state security. The term "state security", which is used in Directive 97/66/EC (concerning the processing of personal data and the protection of privacy in the telecommunications sector), should be interpreted in the same way as the term "national security" which is used elsewhere in the Act and this Code. The Secretary of State will not issue a warrant on section 5(3)(c) grounds if this direct link between the economic well-being of the United Kingdom and state security is not established. Any application for a warrant on section 5(3)(c) grounds should therefore explain how, in the applicant's view, the economic well-being of the United Kingdom which is to be safeguarded is directly related to state security on the facts of the case.

4.5   The Secretary of State must also consider that the conduct authorised by the warrant is proportionate to what it seeks to achieve (section 5(2)(b)). In considering necessity and proportionality, the Secretary of State must take into account whether the information sought could reasonably be obtained by other means (section 5(4)).

Urgent Authorisation of a Section 8(1) Warrant

4.6 The Act makes provision (section 7(1)(b)) for cases in which an interception warrant is required urgently, yet the Secretary of State is not available to sign the warrant. In these cases the Secretary of State will still personally authorise the interception but the warrant is signed by a senior official, following discussion of the case between officials and the Secretary of State. The Act restricts issue of warrants in this way to urgent cases where the Secretary of State has himself expressly authorised the issue of the warrant (section 7(2)(a)), and requires the warrant to contain a statement to that effect (section 7(4)(a)). A warrant issued under the urgency procedure lasts for five working days following the day of issue unless renewed by the Secretary of State, in which case it expires after three months in the case of serious crime or six months in the case of national security or economic well-being in the same way as other non-urgent section 8(1) warrants. An urgent case is one in which interception authorisation is required within a twenty four hour period.

Format of a Section 8(1) Warrant

4.7 Each warrant comprises two sections, a warrant instrument signed by the Secretary of State listing the subject of the interception or set of premises, a copy of which each communications service provider will receive, and a schedule or set of schedules listing the communications to be intercepted. Only the schedule relevant to the communications that can be intercepted by the specified communications service provider will be provided to that service provider.

4.8 The warrant instrument should include:

- The name or description of the interception subject or of a set of premises in relation to which the interception is to take place.

- A warrant reference number.

- The persons who may subsequently modify the scheduled part of the warrant in an urgent case (if authorised in accordance with section 10(8) of the Act).

4.9 The scheduled part of the warrant will comprise one or more schedules. Each schedule should contain:

- The name of the communication service provider, or the other person who is to take action.

- A warrant reference number.

- A means of identifying the communications to be intercepted.

Modification of Section 8(1) warrant

4.10 Interception warrants may be modified under the provisions of section 10 of the Act. The unscheduled part of a warrant may only be modified by the Secretary of State or, in an urgent case, by a senior official with the express authorisation of the Secretary of State. In these cases, a statement of that fact must be endorsed on the modifying instrument, and the modification ceases to have effect after five working days following the day of issue unless it is renewed by the Secretary of State. The modification will then expire upon the expiry date of the warrant.

4.11   Scheduled parts of a warrant may be modified by the Secretary of State, or by a senior official acting upon his behalf. A modification to the scheduled part of the warrant may include the addition of a new schedule relating to a communication service provider on whom a copy of the warrant has not been previously served. Modifications made in this way expire at the same time as the warrant expires. There also exists a duty to modify a warrant by deleting a communication identifier if it is no longer relevant. When a modification is sought to delete a number or other communication identifier, the relevant communications service provider must be advised and interception suspended before the modification instrument is signed.

4.12   In an urgent case, and where the warrant specifically authorises it, scheduled parts of a warrant may be modified by the person to whom the warrant is addressed (the person who submitted the application) or a subordinate (where the subordinate is identified in the warrant). Modifications of this kind are valid for five working days following the day of issue unless the modification instrument is endorsed by a senior official acting on behalf of the Secretary of State. Where the modification is endorsed in this way, the modification expires upon the expiry date of the warrant.

Renewal of a Section 8(1) Warrant

4.13   The Secretary of State may renew a warrant at any point before its expiry date. Applications for renewals must be made to the Secretary of State and should contain an update of the matters outlined in paragraph 4.2 above. In particular, the applicant should give an assessment of the value of interception to the operation to date and explain why he considers that interception continues to be necessary for one or more of the purposes in section 5(3).

4.14   Where the Secretary of State is satisfied that the interception continues to meet the requirements of the Act he may renew the warrant. Where the warrant is issued on serious crime grounds, the renewed warrant is valid for a further three months. Where it is issued on national security/ economic well-being grounds, the renewed warrant is valid for six months. These dates run from the date of signature on the renewal instrument.

4.15   A copy of the warrant renewal instrument will be forwarded by the intercepting agency to all relevant communications service providers on whom a copy of the original warrant instrument and a schedule have been served, providing they are still actively assisting. A warrant renewal instrument will include the reference number of the warrant and description of the person or premises described in the warrant.

Warrant Cancellation

4.16   The Secretary of State is under a duty to cancel an interception warrant if, at any time before its expiry date, he is satisfied that the warrant is no longer necessary on grounds falling within section 5(3) of the Act. Intercepting agencies will therefore need to keep their warrants under continuous review. In practice, cancellation instruments will be signed by a senior official on his behalf.

4.17   The cancellation instrument should be addressed to the person to whom the warrant was issued (the intercepting agency) and should include the reference number of the warrant and the description of the person or premises specified in the warrant. A copy of the cancellation instrument should be sent to those communications service providers who have held a copy of the warrant instrument and accompanying schedule during the preceding twelve months.

Records

4.18   The oversight regime allows the Interception of Communications Commissioner to inspect the warrant application upon which the Secretary of State based his decision, and the applicant may be required to justify the content. Each intercepting agency should keep the following to be made available for scrutiny by the Commissioner as he may require:

*   all applications made for warrants complying with section 8(1) and applications made for the renewal of such warrants;

*   all warrants, and renewals and copies of schedule modifications (if any);

*   where any application is refused, the grounds for refusal as given by the Secretary of State;

*   the dates on which interception is started and stopped.

4.19   Records shall also be kept of the arrangements by which the requirements of section 15(2) (minimisation of copying and destruction of intercepted material) and section 15(3) (destruction of intercepted material) are to be met. For further details see section on "Safeguards".

4.20   The term "intercepted material" is used throughout to embrace copies, extracts or summaries made from the intercepted material as well as the intercept material itself.

5. INTERCEPTION WARRANTS (SECTION 8(4))

5.1   This section applies to the interception of external communications by means of a warrant complying with section 8(4) of the Act. External communications are defined by the Act to be those which are sent or received outside the British Islands. They include those which are both sent and received outside the British Islands, whether or not they pass through the British Islands in course of their transit. They do not include communications both sent and received in the British Islands, even if they pass outside the British Islands en route. Responsibility for the issuing of such interception warrants rests with the Secretary of State.

Application for a Section 8(4) Warrant

5.2 An application for a warrant is made to the Secretary of State. Interception warrants, when issued, are addressed to the person who submitted the application. This person may then serve a copy upon any person who may be able to provide assistance in giving effect to that warrant. Each application, a copy of which must be retained by the applicant, should contain the following information:

- Background to the operation in question.

- Description of the communications to be intercepted, details of the communications service provider(s) and an assessment of the feasibility of the operation where this is relevant.

- Description of the conduct to be authorised, which must be restricted to the interception of external communications, or to conduct necessary in order to intercept those external communications, where appropriate.

- The certificate that will regulate examination of intercepted material.

- An explanation of why the interception is considered to be necessary for one or more of the section 5(3) purposes.

- A consideration of why the conduct to be authorised by the warrant is proportionate to what is sought to be achieved by that conduct.

- A consideration of any unusual degree of collateral intrusion, and why that intrusion is justified in the circumstances. In particular, where the communications in question might affect religious, medical or journalistic confidentiality or legal privilege, this must be specified in the application.

- Where an application is urgent, supporting justification should be provided.

- An assurance that intercepted material will be read, looked at or listened to only so far as it is certified, and it meets the conditions of sections 16(2)-16(6) of the Act.

- An assurance that all material intercepted will be handled in accordance with the safeguards required by sections 15 and 16 of the Act.

Authorisation of a Section 8(4) warrant

5.3 Before issuing a warrant under section 8(4), the Secretary of State must believe that the warrant is necessary:

- in the interests of national security;

- for the purpose of preventing or detecting serious crime; or

- for the purpose of safeguarding the economic well-being of the United Kingdom;

5.4 In exercising his power to issue an interception warrant for the purpose of safeguarding the economic well-being of the United Kingdom (as provided for by section 5(3)(c) of the Act), the Secretary of State will consider whether the economic well-being of the United Kingdom which is to be safeguarded is, on the facts of each case, directly related to state security. The term "state security", which is used in Directive 97/66/EC (concerning the processing of personal data and the protection of privacy in the telecommunications sector), should be interpreted in the same way as the term "national security" which is used elsewhere in the Act and this Code. The Secretary of State will not issue a warrant on section 5(3)(c) grounds if this direct link between the economic well-being of the United Kingdom and state security is not established. Any application for a warrant on section 5(3)(c) grounds should therefore explain how, in the applicant's view, the economic well-being of the United Kingdom which is to be safeguarded is directly related to state security on the facts of the case.

5.5   The Secretary of State must also consider that the conduct authorised by the warrant is proportionate to what it seeks to achieve (section 5(2)(b)). In considering necessity and proportionality, the Secretary of State must take into account whether the information sought could reasonably be obtained by other means (section 5(4)).

5.6   When the Secretary of State issues a warrant of this kind, it must be accompanied by a certificate in which the Secretary of State certifies that he considers examination of the intercepted material to be necessary for one or more of the section 5(3) purposes. The Secretary of State has a duty to ensure that arrangements are in force for securing that only that material which has been certified as necessary for examination for a section 5(3) purpose, and which meets the conditions set out in section 16(2) to section 16(6) is, in fact, read, looked at or listened to. The Interception of Communications Commissioner is under a duty to review the adequacy of those arrangements.

Urgent Authorisation of a Section 8(4) Warrant

5.7 The Act makes provision (section 7(1)(b)) for cases in which an interception warrant is required urgently, yet the Secretary of State is not available to sign the warrant. In these cases the Secretary of State will still personally authorise the interception but the warrant is signed by a senior official, following discussion of the case between officials and the Secretary of State. The Act restricts issue of warrants in this way to urgent cases where the Secretary of State has himself expressly authorised the issue of the warrant (section 7(2)(a)), and requires the warrant to contain a statement to that effect (section 7(4)(a)).

5.8   A warrant issued under the urgency procedure lasts for five working days following the day of issue unless renewed by the Secretary of State, in which case it expires after three months in the case of serious crime or six months in the case of national security or economic well-being in the same way as other section 8(4) warrants.

Format of a Section 8(4) Warrant

5.9   Each warrant is addressed to the person who submitted the application. This person may then serve a copy upon such providers of communications services as he believes will be able to assist in implementing the interception. Communications service providers will not receive a copy of the certificate.

The warrant should include the following:

*   A description of the communications to be intercepted.

*   The warrant reference number.

- The persons who may subsequently modify the scheduled part of the warrant in an urgent case (if authorised in accordance with section 10(8) of the Act).

Modification of a section 8(4) warrant

5.10   Interception warrants may be modified under the provisions of section 10 of the Act. The warrant may only be modified by the Secretary of State or, in an urgent case, by a senior official with the express authorisation of the Secretary of State. In these cases a statement of that fact must be endorsed on the modifying instrument, and the modification ceases to have effect after five working days following the day of issue unless it is endorsed by the Secretary of State.

5.11   The certificate must be modified by the Secretary of State, save in an urgent case where a certificate may be modified under the hand of a senior official provided that the official holds a position in respect of which he is expressly authorised by provisions contained in the certificate to modify the certificate on the Secretary of State's behalf, or the Secretary of State has himself expressly authorised the modification and a statement of that fact is endorsed on the modifying instrument. Again the modification shall cease to have effect after five working days following the day of issue unless it is endorsed by the Secretary of State.

Renewal of a Section 8(4) Warrant

5.12   The Secretary of State may renew a warrant at any point before its expiry date. Applications for renewals are made to the Secretary of State and contain an update of the matters outlined in paragraph 5.2 above. In particular, the applicant must give an assessment of the value of interception to the operation to date and explain why he considers that interception continues to be necessary for one or more of purposes in section 5(3).

5.13   Where the Secretary of State is satisfied that the interception continues to meet the requirements of the Act he may renew the warrant. Where the warrant is issued on serious crime grounds, the renewed warrant is valid for a further three months. Where it is issued on national security/ economic well-being grounds the renewed warrant is valid for six months. These dates run from the date of signature on the renewal instrument.

5.14   In those circumstances where the assistance of communications service providers has been sought, a copy of the warrant renewal instrument will be forwarded by the intercepting agency to all those on whom a copy of the original warrant instrument has been served, providing they are still actively assisting. A warrant renewal instrument will include the reference number of the warrant and description of the communications to be intercepted.

Warrant Cancellation

5.15   The Secretary of State shall cancel an interception warrant if, at any time before its expiry date, he is satisfied that the warrant is no longer necessary on grounds falling within Section 5(3) of the Act. In practice, cancellation instruments will be signed by a senior official on his behalf.

5.16 The cancellation instrument will be addressed to the person to whom the warrant was issued (the intercepting agency). A copy of the cancellation instrument should be sent to those communications service providers, if any, who have given effect to the warrant during the preceding twelve months.

Records

5.17 The oversight regime allows the Interception of Communications Commissioner to inspect the warrant application upon which the Secretary of State based his decision, and the applicant may be required to justify the content. Each intercepting agency should keep, so to be made available for scrutiny by the Interception of Communications Commissioner, the following:

- all applications made for warrants complying with section 8(4), and applications made for the renewal of such warrants;

- all warrants and certificates, and copies of renewal and modification instruments (if any);

- where any application is refused, the grounds for refusal as given by the Secretary of State;

- the dates on which interception is started and stopped.

Records shall also be kept of the arrangements in force for securing that only material which has been certified for examination for a purpose under section 5(3) and which meets the conditions set out in section 16(2) – 16(6) of the Act in accordance with section 15 of the Act. Records shall be kept of the arrangements by which the requirements of section 15(2) (minimisation of copying and distribution of intercepted material) and section 15(3) (destruction of intercepted material) are to be met. For further details see section on "Safeguards".

6. SAFEGUARDS

6.1 All material (including related communications data) intercepted under the authority of a warrant complying with section 8(1) or section 8(4) of the Act must be handled in accordance with safeguards which the Secretary of State has approved in conformity with the duty imposed upon him by the Act. These safeguards are made available to the Interception of Communications Commissioner, and they must meet the requirements of section 15 of the Act which are set out below. In addition, the safeguards in section 16 of the Act apply to warrants complying with section 8(4). Any breach of these safeguards must be reported to the Interception of Communications Commissioner.

6.2 Section 15 of the Act requires that disclosure, copying and retention of intercept material be limited to the minimum necessary for the authorised purposes. The authorised purposes defined in section 15(4) of the Act include:

- If the material continues to be, or is likely to become, necessary for any of the purposes set out in section 5(3) – namely, in the interests of national security, for the purpose of preventing or detecting serious crime, for the purpose of safeguarding the economic well-being of the United Kingdom.

- If the material is necessary for facilitating the carrying out of the functions of the Secretary of State under Chapter I of Part I of the Act.

- If the material is necessary for facilitating the carrying out of any functions of the Interception of Communications Commissioner or the Tribunal.

- If the material is necessary to ensure that a person conducting a criminal prosecution has the information he needs to determine what is required of him by his duty to secure the fairness of the prosecution.

- If the material is necessary for the performance of any duty imposed by the Public Record Acts.

6.3 Section 16 provides for additional safeguards in relation to material gathered under section 8(4) warrants, requiring that the safeguards:

- Ensure that intercepted material is read, looked at or listened to by any person only to the extent that the material is certified.

- Regulate the use of selection factors that refer to individuals known to be for the time being in the British Islands.

The Secretary of State must ensure that the safeguards are in force before any interception under warrants complying with section 8(4) can begin. The Interception of Communications Commissioner is under a duty to review the adequacy of the safeguards.

Dissemination of Intercepted Material

6.4 The number of persons to whom any of the material is disclosed, and the extent of disclosure, must be limited to the minimum that is necessary for the authorised purposes set out in section 15(4) of the Act. This obligation applies equally to disclosure to additional persons within an agency, and to disclosure outside the agency. It is enforced by prohibiting disclosure to persons who do not hold the required security clearance, and also by the need-to-know principle: intercepted material must not be disclosed to any person unless that person's duties, which must relate to one of the authorised purposes, are such that he needs to know about the material to carry out those duties. In the same way only so much of the material may be disclosed as the recipient needs; for example if a summary of the material will suffice, no more than that should be disclosed.

6.5 The obligations apply not just to the original interceptor, but also to anyone to whom the material is subsequently disclosed. In some cases this will be achieved by requiring the latter to obtain the originator's permission before disclosing the material further. In others, explicit safeguards are applied to secondary recipients.

Copying

6.6 Intercepted material may only be copied to the extent necessary for the authorised purposes set out in section 15(4) of the Act. Copies include not only direct copies of the whole of the material, but also extracts and summaries which identify themselves as the product of an interception, and any record referring to an interception which is a record of the identities of the persons to or by whom the intercepted material was sent. The restrictions are implemented by requiring special treatment of such copies, extracts and summaries that are made by recording their making, distribution and destruction.

Storage

6.7 Intercepted material, and all copies, extracts and summaries of it, must be handled and stored securely, so as to minimise the risk of loss or theft. It must be held so as to be inaccessible to persons without the required level of security clearance. This requirement to store intercept product securely applies to all those who are responsible for the handling of this material, including communications service providers. The details of what such a requirement will mean in practice for communications service providers will be set out in the discussions they will be having with the Government before a Section 12 Notice is served (see paragraph 2.9).

Destruction

6.8 Intercepted material, and all copies, extracts and summaries which can be identified as the product of an interception, must be securely destroyed as soon as it is no longer needed for any of the authorised purposes. If such material is retained, it should be reviewed at appropriate intervals to confirm that the justification for its retention is still valid under section 15(3) of the Act.

Personnel security

6.9 Each intercepting agency maintains a distribution list of persons who may have access to intercepted material or need to see any reporting in relation to it. All such persons must be appropriately vetted. Any person no longer needing access to perform his duties should be removed from any such list. Where it is necessary for an officer of one agency to disclose material to another, it is the former's responsibility to ensure that the recipient has the necessary clearance.

7. DISCLOSURE TO ENSURE FAIRNESS IN CRIMINAL PROCEEDINGS

7.1 Section 15(3) of the Act states the general rule that intercepted material must be destroyed as soon as its retention is no longer necessary for a purpose authorised under the Act. Section 15(4) specifies the authorised purposes for which retention is necessary.

7.2 This part of the Code applies to the handling of intercepted material in the context of criminal proceedings where the material has been retained for one of the purposes authorised in section 15(4) of the Act. For those who would ordinarily have had responsibility under the Criminal Procedure and Investigations Act 1996 to provide disclosure in criminal proceedings, this includes those rare situations where destruction of intercepted material has not taken place in accordance with section 15(3) and where that material is still in existence after the commencement of a criminal prosecution, retention having been considered necessary to ensure that a person conducting a criminal prosecution has the information he needs to discharge his duty of ensuring its fairness (section 15(4)(d)).

Exclusion of Matters from Legal Proceedings

7.3   The general rule is that neither the possibility of interception nor intercepted material itself plays any part in legal proceedings. This rule is set out in section 17 of the Act, which excludes evidence, questioning, assertion or disclosure in legal proceedings likely to reveal the existence (or the absence) of a warrant issued under this Act (or the Interception of Communications Act 1985). This rule means that the intercepted material cannot be used either by the prosecution or the defence. This preserves "equality of arms" which is a requirement under Article 6 of the European Convention on Human Rights.

7.4   Section 18 contains a number of tightly-drawn exceptions to this rule. This part of the Code deals only with the exception in subsections (7) to (11).

Disclosure to a Prosecutor

7.5   Section 18(7)(a) provides that intercepted material obtained by means of a warrant and which continues to be available, may, for a strictly limited purpose, be disclosed to a person conducting a criminal prosecution.

7.6   This may only be done for the purpose of enabling the prosecutor to determine what is required of him by his duty to secure the fairness of the prosecution. The prosecutor may not use intercepted material to which he is given access under section 18(7)(a) to mount a cross-examination, or to do anything other than ensure the fairness of the proceedings.

7.7   The exception does not mean that intercepted material should be retained against a remote possibility that it might be relevant to future proceedings. The normal expectation is, still, for the intercepted material to be destroyed in accordance with the general safeguards provided by section 15. The exceptions only come into play if such material has, in fact, been retained for an authorised purpose. Because the authorised purpose given in section 5(3)(b) (*"for the purpose of preventing or detecting serious crime"*) does not extend to gathering evidence for the purpose of a prosecution, material intercepted for this purpose may not have survived to the prosecution stage, as it will have been destroyed in accordance with the section 15(3) safeguards. There is, in these circumstances, no need to consider disclosure to a prosecutor if, in fact, no intercepted material remains in existence.

7.8   Be that as it may, section 18(7)(a) recognises the duty on prosecutors, acknowledged by common law, to review all available material to make sure that the prosecution is not proceeding unfairly. 'Available material' will only ever include intercepted material at this stage if the conscious decision has been made to retain it for an authorised purpose.

7.9   If intercepted material does continue to be available at the prosecution stage, once this information has come to the attention of the holder of this material the prosecutor should be informed that a warrant has been issued under section 5 and that material of possible relevance to the case has been intercepted.

7.10   Having had access to the material, the prosecutor may conclude that the material affects the fairness of the proceedings. In these circumstances, he will decide how the prosecution, if it proceeds, should be presented.

Disclosure to a Judge

7.11   Section 18(7)(b) recognises that there may be cases where the prosecutor, having seen intercepted material under subsection (7)(a), will need to consult the trial Judge. Accordingly, it provides for the Judge to be given access to intercepted material, where there are exceptional circumstances making that disclosure essential in the interests of justice.

7.12   This access will be achieved by the prosecutor inviting the judge to make an order for disclosure to him alone, under this subsection. This is an exceptional procedure; normally, the prosecutor's functions under subsection (7)(a) will not fall to be reviewed by the judge. To comply with section 17(1), any consideration given to, or exercise of, this power must be carried out without notice to the defence. The purpose of this power is to ensure that the trial is conducted fairly.

7.13   The judge may, having considered the intercepted material disclosed to him, direct the prosecution to make an admission of fact. The admission will be abstracted from the interception; but, in accordance with the requirements of section 17(1), it must not reveal the fact of interception. This is likely to be a very unusual step. The Act only allows it where the judge considers it essential in the interests of justice.

7.14   Nothing in these provisions allows intercepted material, or the fact of interception, to be disclosed to the defence.

8. OVERSIGHT

8.1 The Act provides for an Interception of Communications Commissioner whose remit is to provide independent oversight of the use of the powers contained within the warranted interception regime under Chapter I of Part I of the Act.

8.2   This Code does not cover the exercise of the Commissioner's functions. However, it will be the duty of any person who uses the above powers to comply with any request made by the Commissioner to provide any information as he requires for the purpose of enabling him to discharge his functions.

9. COMPLAINTS

9.1   The Act establishes an independent Tribunal. This Tribunal will be made up of senior members of the judiciary and the legal profession and is independent of the Government. The Tribunal has full powers to investigate and decide any case within its jurisdiction.

9.2 This code does not cover the exercise of the Tribunal's functions. Details of the relevant complaints procedure can be obtained from the following address:

The Investigatory Powers Tribunal
PO Box 33220
London
SW1H 9ZQ

☎ 0207 273 4514

10. INTERCEPTION WITHOUT A WARRANT

10.1 Section 1(5) of the Act permits interception without a warrant in the following circumstances:

- where it is authorised by or under sections 3 or 4 of the Act (see below);

- where it is in exercise, in relation to any stored communication, of some other statutory power exercised for the purpose of obtaining information or of taking possession of any document or other property, for example, the obtaining of a production order under Schedule 1 to the Police and Criminal Evidence Act 1984 for stored data to be produced.

Interception in accordance with a warrant under section 5 of the Act is dealt with under parts 2, 3, 4 and 5 of this Code.

10.2 For lawful interception which takes place without a warrant, pursuant to sections 3 or 4 of the Act or pursuant to some other statutory power, there is no prohibition in the Act on the evidential use of any material that is obtained as a result. The matter may still, however, be regulated by the exclusionary rules of evidence to be found in the common law, section 78 of the Police and Criminal Evidence Act 1984, and/or pursuant to the Human Rights Act 1998.

Interception with the Consent of both Parties

10.3 Section 3(1) of the Act authorises the interception of a communication if both the person sending the communication and the intended recipient(s) have consented to its interception, or where the person conducting the interception has reasonable grounds for believing that all parties have consented to the interception.

Interception with the Consent of one Party

10.4 Section 3(2) of the Act authorises the interception of a communication if either the sender or intended recipient of the communication has consented to its interception, and directed surveillance by means of that interception has been authorised under Part II of the Act. Further details can be found in chapter 4 of the Covert Surveillance Code of Practice and in chapter 2 of the Covert Human Intelligence Sources Code of Practice.

Interception for the Purposes of a Communication Service Provider

10.5   Section 3(3) of the Act permits a communication service provider or a person acting upon their behalf to carry out interception for purposes connected with the operation of that service or for purposes connected with the enforcement of any enactment relating to the use of the communication service.

Lawful Business Practice

10.6   Section 4(2) of the Act enables the Secretary of State to make regulations setting out those circumstances where it is lawful to intercept communications for the purpose of carrying on a business. These regulations apply equally to public authorities.

These Lawful Business Practice Regulations can be found on the following Department of Trade and Industry website: **www.dti.gov.uk/cii/regulation.html**.

Regulation of Investigatory Powers Act page
Home Office front page

© Crown Copyright 2002

Appendix VI

Addresses and websites

To search the register of data controllers, to notify processing and for general data protection and freedom of information guidance:

The Information Commissioner

Wycliffe House

Water Lane

Wilmslow

Cheshire

SK9 5AF

Tel. 01625 545700

Fax. 01625 524510

www.informationcommissioner.gov.uk

For data protection training courses and to subscribe to *Privacy & Data Protection* journal:

Privacy & Data Protection Ltd

44 Tregarvon Road

London

SW11 5QE

Tel. 020 7924 1927

Fax. 0870 137 7871

www.privacydataprotection.co.uk

For legal advice on all data protection issues:

Berwin Leighton Paisner

Adelaide House

London Bridge

London

EC4R 9HA

Tel. 020 7760 1000

Fax. 020 7760 1111

www.blplaw.com

Charles Russell

8-10 New Fetter Lane

London

EC4A 1RS

Tel. 020 7203 5000

Fax. 020 7203 5302

www.cr-law.co.uk

To join the Direct Marketing Association and to obtain a copy of the Direct Marketing Association's code of practice on direct marketing:

Direct Marketing Association

DMA House

70 Margaret Street

London

W1W 8SS

Tel. 020 7291 3300

Fax. 020 7323 4165

www.dma.org.uk

To view a list of the companies that have joined Safe Harbor:

www.export.gov/safeharbor

(then click on 'Safe Harbor List')

For information on Safe Harbor dispute resolution mechanisms and to obtain a privacy seal:

TRUSTe

1180 Coleman Avenue

Suite 202

San Jose, CA 95110

USA

Tel. +1 408 494 4956

www.truste.org

BBBOn-line

4200 Wilson Boulevard

8th Floor

Arlington

VA 22203

USA

Tel. +1 703 247 9336 (privacy seals)

Tel. +1 888 769 3353 (dispute resolution)

www.bbbon-line.org

Precedents

Precedent 1

Website Privacy Policy

This Privacy Policy sets out the data processing practices carried out through the use of the Internet and any other electronic communications networks by [Name of the business]. If you have any requests concerning your personal information or any queries with regard to these practices please contact [Name of data protection representative] [us] at [privacy@your-domain-name.com].

Information collected

We collect personal information from visitors to this website [through the use of on-line forms] [and every time you e-mail us your details]. [We also collect information about the transactions you undertake including details of payment cards used.]

[We collect additional information automatically about your visit to our website.]

Use of personal information

We process personal information collected via this website for the purposes of:

[providing and personalising our services]

[dealing with your inquiries and requests]

[administering orders and accounts relating to our suppliers or customers]

[administering membership records]

[crime prevention and prosecution of offenders]

[fundraising]

[maintaining information as a reference tool or general resource]

[providing reservation or booking services]

[trading in personal information (selling, hiring or exchanging information)]

[carrying out market research campaigns]

[providing you with information about products and services]

Please tick the appropriate box if you do not wish to receive information about:

[our products or services [BOX]]

[products or services offered by other companies within our group [BOX]]

[products or services offered jointly with or on behalf of other organisations [BOX]]

[Alternatively, you may opt-out by sending us an e-mail at [privacy@your-domain-name.com], calling us on [Telephone number], or writing to us at the following address: [Address of the business].]

[We may also use and disclose information in aggregate (so that no individuals are identified) for marketing and strategic development purposes.]

[Use of cookies

A cookie is a small piece of information sent by a web server to a web browser, which enables the server to collect information from the browser. Find out more about the use of cookies on www.cookiecentral.com.

We use cookies to identify you when you visit this website and to keep track of your browsing patterns and build up a demographic profile.

Our use of cookies also allows registered users to be presented with a personalised version of the site, carry out transactions and have access to information about their account.

Most browsers allow you to turn off cookies. If you want to know how to do this please look at the help menu on your browser. However, switching off cookies will restrict your use of our website.]

Disclosures

We will only disclose personal information to [other companies within our group of companies,] [business partners,] [government bodies and law enforcement agencies] successors in title to our business and suppliers we engage to process data on our behalf.

[Other websites

Our website may contain links to other websites which are outside our control and are not covered by this Privacy Policy. If you access other sites using the links provided, the operators of these sites may collect information from you which will be used by them in accordance with their privacy policy, which may differ from ours.]

[Access right

You have a right to access the personal data held about you. To obtain a copy of the personal information we hold about you, please write to us at [Address].]

Internet-based transfers

Given that the Internet is a global environment, using the Internet to collect and process personal data necessarily involves the transmission of data on an international basis. Therefore, by browsing this website and communicating electronically with us, you acknowledge and agree to our processing of personal data in this way.

Explanatory notes

In order to process personal data fairly (as required by Principle 1 of the Data Protection Act 1998), a data controller must make available to the individuals to whom the data relate, details regarding:

- the identity of the data controller (this should include a reference to the group of companies to which the data controller belongs, if that is unlikely to be obvious);

- its data protection representative and contact details (if no such representative has been appointed, details of how to contact the business in order to make requests or raise queries concerning the use of personal data should be provided);

- the purposes for which the data are intended to be processed (see sample list provided under the 'Use of personal information' heading); and

* any other relevant information (including whether data are automatically collected – by means of 'cookies', for example – whether individuals will be contacted for marketing purposes, and potential recipients of the data).

The most practical and user-friendly way of providing this information is by means of a Privacy Policy available on the website operated by the data controller.

This precedent includes examples of:

- ways in which personal data are collected;

- purposes for which the data are processed;

- references to common uses of cookies; and

- typical recipients of data,

based on common practice for e-businesses, which should be tailored as appropriate.

The Privacy Policy can also be used to point out that the website may contain external links to other websites and that the use of personal information by the operators of those websites is outside the scope of the Privacy Policy.

In addition, it is good data protection practice to refer to the right of access. Including this reference is not a legal obligation under the Data Protection Act 1998, but it is something that was specifically mentioned by the 1995 Data Protection Directive[1] and is often required by self-regulatory codes of practice.

Finally, given the inherent conflict between the prohibition set out in Principle 8 of the Data Protection Act 1998 and the global nature

---

1   Council Directive 95/46/EC.

of the Internet, a Privacy Policy should include a reference to the transmission of data on an international basis, so that users acknowledge this as a normal feature in an on-line environment.

The Privacy Policy should be displayed on the website in accordance with the following guidelines:

*   Place a prominent link to the Privacy Policy on the homepage.

*   Place a prominent link to the Privacy Policy on every page that is used to collect personal data from individuals (for example, inquiry forms, subscription pages) preceded by the words: 'Your personal information will be processed in accordance with our Privacy Policy' (where the words Privacy Policy are a hypertext link to the full Privacy Policy).

*   If explicit consent is required (see Chapter 3.2 on 'sensitive personal data'), the Privacy Policy should appear by default (for example, by means of a pop-up window appearing on the screen) before any personal information is submitted by individuals and consent should be obtained by requiring individuals to click on an 'Accept' button. Pop-up windows without an 'Accept' button (ie where the user can easily bypass the Privacy Policy by shutting the window) should be avoided if sensitive personal data are collected.

Precedent 2

Opt-out and opt-in

Opt-out

I do not wish to receive:

[ ] Information about products and/or services sold by [Name of the business]

[ ] Information about other companies, products and/or services

[ ] Market research communications aimed at improving the service of [Name of the business]

I do not wish to be contacted for marketing purposes via:

[ ] post [ ] e-mail [ ] telephone

Opt-in

I wish to receive:

[ ] Information about products and/or services sold by [Name of the business]

[ ] Information about other companies, products and/or services

[ ] Market research communications aimed at improving the service of [Name of the business]

I am happy to be contacted via:

[ ] post [ ] e-mail [ ] telephone [ ] fax

Explanatory notes

A key data protection issue in the context of e-business is the right of individuals to prevent the use of their personal data for the purposes of direct marketing. This right entitles individuals to ask the data controller to stop (or not to begin) marketing-related communications by any means. In order to exercise this right, individuals must always be given the opportunity to opt-out from receiving direct marketing. This opportunity should be presented either via the Privacy Policy or on the registration form (and, ideally, in both).

Having a multiple choice opt-out form (where individuals select those marketing uses of their data they object to by ticking a box) will often allow the e-business to retain an element of direct marketing, even if an individual objects to other direct marketing activities. This principle also applies to the use of different means of communication for this purpose (see Opt-out precedent above).

The use of the telephone and fax for direct marketing is governed by a specific set of rules known as the Telecommunications (Data Protection and Privacy) Regulations 1999.[1] According to these Regulations, before sending a direct marketing fax to an individual subscriber (as opposed to a corporate subscriber), the organisation wishing to send the fax must obtain consent from the potential recipient. In other words, the opt-out regime becomes opt-in in relation to marketing faxes. Therefore, the Opt-out precedent does not deal with opting-out of marketing faxes.

The current opt-out regime in relation to e-mails will eventually be replaced by a more stringent one, where the use of e-mail for the purposes of direct marketing will only be allowed in respect of individuals who have given their prior consent (a limited opt-out will be allowed in respect of marketing e-mails concerning a businesses own products and services which are *similar* to those purchased by the recipient in the past).

As a result, a number of e-businesses are shifting their policy on direct marketing to make it entirely opt-in (see Opt-in precedent above).

1   SI 1999/2093.

Precedent 3

Confidentiality agreement between data controller and data processor

Dated

Parties

Data Controller	[Name of the data controller] company number [Registration No] whose registered address is at [Address of the data controller].
Data Processor	[Name of the data processor] company number [Registration No] whose registered address is at [Address of the data processor].

Introduction

(A) The Data Controller is [Describe nature of the business].

(B) The Data Processor carries out [Describe nature of the data processing services].

(C) The Data Controller and the Data Processor have entered into an agreement for the provision of services by the Data Processor to the Data Controller including [Describe nature of the processing of personal data on behalf of the Data Controller] dated [Insert date of data processing agreement].

(D) The Data Controller and the Data Processor have further agreed to enter into an agreement to supplement the confidentiality of the services provided by the Data Processor.

Operative provisions

1   **Definitions**

1.1 In this agreement the following expression will have the following meaning:

Confidential Information means all information relating to the trade secrets, operations, processes, plans, intentions, product information, know-how, designs, market opportunities, transactions, affairs and/or business of the other party and/or to its customers, suppliers, clients, holding companies and/or subsidiaries, and the terms of this agreement.

1.2 In this agreement:

1.2.1 clause headings are included for convenience only and will not affect the construction of the agreement; and

1.2.2 words denoting the singular will include the plural and vice versa.

2 Use of Confidential Information

2.1 Unless expressly authorised in writing by the Data Controller, the Data Processor will:

2.1.1 use the Confidential Information only in connection with the processing of personal data on behalf of the Data Controller;

2.1.2 retain the Confidential Information in confidence; and

2.1.3 take all precautions reasonably necessary to protect such Confidential Information or any information derived from it from disclosure to any third person.

3 Prohibited Uses

3.1 The Data Processor will not (whether orally, in writing or electronically) reproduce, copy, disclose or transmit any Confidential Information disclosed, in full or in part, by the Data Controller except:

3.1.1 for disclosure to its employees to the extent that they need to know the same in connection with the processing of personal data on behalf of the Data Controller;

3.1.2 for distribution to its legal or other professional advisors on a confidential basis for the purpose of obtaining legal or other professional advice; or

3.1.3 to the extent that the Data Processor is required to disclose the Confidential Information pursuant to any statutory or regulatory authority, provided the Data Controller is given prompt notice of such requirement and the scope of such disclosure is limited to the extent possible.

4 Return and Destruction of Confidential Information

The Data Processor will, promptly upon the demand of the Data Controller, return to the Data Controller or destroy all copies of the Confidential Information of the Data Controller in its possession, custody, power or control, and delete all electronic copies, hidden copies, back-ups, caches, copies in recycle bins, deleted items folders and undeletable files of the Confidential Information from systems within its possession, custody, power or control.

5   **Exceptions**

5.1   The restrictions in this agreement will not apply to any information which the Data Processor can prove:

>   5.1.1   is in the public domain and is readily available at the time of disclosure or which enters the public domain and is readily available, through no improper action or inaction by the Data Processor;

>   5.1.2   was in the possession of the Data Processor or known by it prior to receipt from the Data Controller;

>   5.1.3   was rightfully disclosed to the Data Processor by another person without restriction; or

>   5.1.4   is or was independently developed by the Data Processor without access to such Confidential Information.

6   **Duration**

The obligations of the Data Processor under this agreement will survive the termination of any processing of personal data carried out on behalf of the Data Controller.

7   **Law and Jurisdiction**

This agreement will be construed in accordance with and governed by the laws of England and each party agrees to submit to the exclusive jurisdiction of the English Courts.

Signed by the parties on the date of this agreement.

Explanatory notes

The purpose of this precedent is to supplement the confidentiality of the services provided by a supplier. This is particularly important in those cases where there is an existing agreement which involves processing of personal data by the supplier (even if this is not a core element of the relationship), but there are no specific provisions regarding the use of information (including personal data) and the limitations affecting such use.

Precedent 4

Data processing agreement with Internet Service Provider

Dated

Parties

Customer   [Name of the business] company number [Registration No] whose registered address is at [Address of the business].

Supplier   [Name of the Internet Service Provider] company number [Registration No] whose registered address is at [Address of the Internet Service Provider].

Introduction

(A)   The Customer is [Describe nature of the business].

(B)   The Supplier is [Describe nature of the Internet Service Provider].

(C)   The Customer and the Supplier have agreed to enter into an agreement for the provision of services by the Supplier to the Customer including [Describe nature of services].

Operative provisions

1   **Definitions**

1.1   In this agreement the following expressions will have the following meanings:

Confidential Information means all information relating to the trade secrets, operations, processes, plans, intentions, product information, know-how, designs, market opportunities, transactions, affairs and/or business of the other party and/or to its customers, suppliers, clients, holding companies and/or subsidiaries, and the terms of this agreement;

Data   means any personal data (as defined by the Data Protection Act 1998) processed by the Supplier as a result of, or in connection with, the provision of the Services;

Fee   means the fees to be paid by the Customer to the Supplier for the provision of the Services as set out in Schedule 2;

Intellectual Property Rights means copyright, database right, patents, registered and unregistered design rights, registered and unregistered trade marks, semiconductor topography rights and all other industrial, commercial or intellectual property rights existing in any jurisdiction and all rights to apply for the same; and

Services   means the services to be provided by the Supplier as set out in Schedule 1.

1.2 In this agreement:

    1.2.1 clause headings are included for convenience only and will not affect the construction of the agreement; and

    1.2.2 words denoting the singular will include the plural and vice versa.

2   Services

The Supplier agrees to provide the Services in accordance with the terms of this agreement and, in any event, in an efficient and professional manner using all reasonable skill, care and diligence.

3   Payment

In consideration of the provision of the Services, the Customer will pay the Fee to the Supplier in accordance with the payment structure set out in Schedule 2.

4   Intellectual property

4.1 All Intellectual Property Rights in any materials provided by the Customer for the purposes of the provision of the Services will be and remain the property of the Customer. The Customer hereby grants to the Supplier a non-exclusive licence for the duration of this agreement to use such materials solely for the purposes of providing the Services. The Supplier may not disclose or sub-license the use of such materials without the Customer's prior written consent.

4.2 All Intellectual Property Rights arising as a result of, or in connection with, the provision of the Services (with the exception of those Intellectual Property Rights arising in any of the software, programming tools, skills and techniques developed and used by the Supplier in the provision of the Services) will be and remain the property of the Customer.

5   **Data protection**

5.1   The Supplier will carry out the processing (as defined by the Data Protection Act 1998) of the Data only to provide the Services, and will not divulge the whole or any part of the Data to any person, except to the extent necessary, for the proper performance by it of this agreement. In particular, the Supplier will not:

    5.1.1   process the Data for its own purposes;

    5.1.2   disclose the Data to any individual other than for the purposes of complying with subject access requests in accordance with section 7 of the Data Protection Act 1998 on behalf of the Customer;

    5.1.3   include the Data in any product or service offered by the Supplier to third parties;

    5.1.4   carry out any research, analysis or profiling activity which involves the use of any element of the Data (including in aggregate form) or any information derived from any processing of such Data; and

    5.1.5   pass files containing the Data to any third party for further processing by that third party or its agents (except for the purposes of mere routing of the Data through a third party).

6   **Warranties**

6.1   The Customer warrants and undertakes that it has fulfilled, and will continue to fulfil, all of its obligations under the data protection laws applicable in the United Kingdom in respect of the processing of the Data.

6.2   The Supplier warrants and undertakes:

    6.2.1   that the provision of the Services will not infringe the Intellectual Property Rights of any third party;

    6.2.2   that it has, and will continue to have, full legal authority to process the Data and that it will only process the Data strictly in accordance with the data protection laws applicable in the United Kingdom and the terms of this agreement and for the purposes of performing its obligations and exercising its rights under this agreement; and

    6.2.3   that it has in place, and will maintain throughout the term of this agreement, appropriate technical and organisational measures against accidental or unauthorised destruction, loss, alteration or disclosure of the Data, and adequate security programs and procedures to ensure that unauthorised persons will not have access to any equipment used to process the Data.

7   **Indemnity**

7.1   Each party to this agreement will indemnify the other against all losses, liabilities, damages, claims, costs (including legal and other professional costs) and expenses which the other may suffer or incur arising out of or in connection with the failure of the indemnifying party to comply with any of its obligations under this agreement.

7.2 Except in relation to claims made in connection with this agreement for death or personal injury caused by any negligent act or omission or wilful misconduct, each party's liability to the other in respect of any individual claim for breach of contract, negligence, breach of statutory duty or otherwise in relation to this agreement will be limited to the sum of [£ Insert amount] and in respect of the aggregate of any such claims to [£ Insert amount] in any calendar year.

8 Confidentiality

8.1 Each party will:

    8.1.1 keep all Confidential Information strictly confidential;

    8.1.2 not disclose any Confidential Information to a third party, other than to such of its employees as will of necessity acquire it as a consequence of the performance of that party's obligations under this agreement (in which case the relevant party will ensure that such employees will keep such Confidential Information confidential and will not use any of it for any purpose or disclose it to any person, firm or company other than those for which or to whom that party may lawfully use or disclose it under this agreement); and

    8.1.3 use Confidential Information only in connection with the proper performance of this agreement.

8.2 Clause 8.1 will not apply to any Confidential Information to the extent that it:

    8.2.1 comes within the public domain other than through breach of clause 8.1;

    8.2.2 is required or requested to be divulged by any court, tribunal or governmental authority with competent jurisdiction; or

    8.2.3 is disclosed on a confidential basis for the purposes of obtaining professional advice.

8.3 This clause will continue in force after and despite the expiry of this agreement.

9 Termination

9.1 Either party may terminate this agreement at any time by giving to the other [3] months' written notice.

9.2 Either party may terminate this agreement at any time by giving written notice to the other party if the other party:

    9.2.1 commits a material breach of any of the terms of this agreement and, where such a breach is capable of remedy, fails to remedy the same within [14] days after receipt of a written notice from the other requiring it to be remedied; or

    9.2.2 is unable to pay its debts when they fall due; or

    9.2.3 takes, or there is taken in respect of the other, any step, action, application or proceeding in relation to the whole or any material part of its undertaking for a voluntary arrangement or composition or reconstruction of its debts, or winding up, dissolution, administration or receivership (administrative or otherwise).

9.3 Upon termination of this agreement for whatever cause, the Supplier will return to the Customer or destroy upon the Customer's request any copy of the Data in hard copy and/or electronic form.

10 Notices

Any notice under this agreement will be in writing and delivered by personal delivery, express courier, confirmed facsimile, confirmed e-mail or certified or registered mail, return receipt requested, and will be deemed given upon personal delivery, one (1) day after deposit with express courier, upon confirmation of receipt of facsimile or e-mail or five (5) days after deposit in the mail. Notices will be sent to a party at its registered address or such other address as that party may specify in writing pursuant to this clause.

11 Jurisdiction

This agreement will be construed in accordance with and governed by the laws of England and each party agrees to submit to the exclusive jurisdiction of the English courts.

12 General

12.1 Nothing in this agreement will be construed so as to create a partnership, joint venture or agency relationship between the parties.

12.2 This agreement embodies the whole agreement of the parties with respect to its subject matter and, once signed by both parties, supersedes all prior agreements, negotiations, representations, and proposals, written or oral, relating to its subject matter.

12.3 In the event that any of the provisions of this agreement are held to be unenforceable by a court or arbitrator, the remaining portions of the agreement will remain in full force and effect.

12.4 Neither party will assign or transfer or purport to assign or transfer all or any of its rights or obligations contained in this agreement without the prior written consent of the other or as expressly permitted pursuant to this agreement.

12.5 Any delay in or failure of performance by either party under this agreement will not be considered a breach of this agreement and will be excused to the extent caused by any occurrence beyond the reasonable control of such party including, but not limited to, acts of God, power outages and governmental restrictions.

Signed by the parties on the date of this agreement.

Schedule 1

Services

[Insert a comprehensive description of all of the data processing services to be provided by the Supplier.]

Schedule 2

Fee and payment

[Insert all fees to be paid by the Customer and a description of the payment structure.]

Explanatory notes

The Data Protection Act 1998 requires data controllers to ensure that where a third party processes data on their behalf (ie a data processor), there is a written contract between the parties whereby the data processor agrees only to act on the instructions of the data controller and to adopt appropriate technical and organisational measures to prevent (a) the unauthorised or unlawful processing of data, and (b) the accidental loss, destruction of, or damage to, data.

This precedent is a full agreement and deals with the provision of generic data processing services in an e-business context. The agreement imposes a number of data protection obligations (see clauses 5 and 6) on the suppler as required by the Act.

In particular, clause 5 is aimed at addressing the following issues:

- The supplier is allowed to disclose personal data processed on behalf of the customer for the purposes of complying with subject access requests in accordance with section 7 of the Data Protection Act 1998.

- The inclusion of personal data processed on behalf of the customer in any product or service offered by the supplier to third parties is expressly prohibited.

- Carrying out any research, analysis or profiling activity which involves the use of any element of the personal data processed on behalf of the customer (including in aggregate form) or any information derived from any processing of such data is also prohibited. This provision may be excessively restrictive in cases where Internet Service Providers wish to monitor and publicise the overall use of their services and is, therefore, likely to be negotiated by the parties.

- The supplier is not permitted to sub-contract any element of the service that may involve any substantive processing (as opposed to mere routing) of personal data by the sub-contractor.

Precedent 5

Variation to existing agreement with Internet Service Provider

[Name and address of the supplier]

[Date]

Dear [Name]

[Subject matter of the agreement]

We refer to the agreement dated [Date of the agreement] (as subsequently extended and modified) signed by [Name of the business] and [Name of the supplier] (the 'agreement').

The Data Protection Act 1998, which came into force on 1 March 2000, establishes a requirement for data controllers to ensure that where a third party processes data on their behalf, there is a written contract between the parties whereby the data processor agrees only to act on the instructions of the data controller and to adopt appropriate security measures.

Therefore, would you please countersign and date the enclosed duplicate copy of this letter to show your agreement to its terms, which will then form part of the agreement.

1. [Name of the supplier] warrants and undertakes that it has and will continue to have full legal authority to process personal data available to it in connection with the services provided under the agreement and that it will only process such personal data in accordance with the applicable data protection laws in the United Kingdom and the terms of the agreement and for the purposes of performing its obligations and exercising its rights under the agreement.

2. [Name of the supplier] warrants that it has in place, and undertakes to maintain throughout the term of the agreement, appropriate technical and organisational measures against the accidental, unauthorised or unlawful processing, destruction, loss, damage or disclosure of personal data and adequate security programmes and procedures to ensure that unauthorised persons do not have access to the personal data or to any equipment used to process personal data.

. . . .

For and on behalf of

[Name of the business]

We agree to the above:

. . . .

For and on behalf of

[Name of the supplier]

Date: . . . .

Explanatory notes

In order to comply with the requirement to ensure that a data processor agrees only to act on the instructions of the data controller and to adopt appropriate technical and organisational measures, in cases where there is already a written contract in place, the easiest way forward for the parties will be to execute a variation to the existing agreement as set out in this precedent.

Precedent 6

Data processing agreement with Internet Service Provider based outside the European Economic Area[1]

Dated

Parties

Customer	[Name of the business] company number [Registration no] whose registered address is at [Address of the business]
Supplier	[Name of the Internet Service Provider] company number [Registration No] whose registered address is at [Address of the Internet Service Provider]

Introduction

(A)   The Customer is [Describe nature of the business].

(B)   The Supplier is [Describe nature of the Internet Service Provider].

(C)   The Customer and the Supplier have agreed to enter into an agreement for the provision of services by the Supplier to the Customer including [Describe nature of services].

Operative provisions

1   **Definitions**

1.1   In this agreement the following expressions will have the following meanings:

---

1   Ie the member states of the European Union plus Norway, Iceland and Liechtenstein.

Clauses	means any provisions of this agreement specifically aimed at adducing adequate safeguards with respect to the protection of privacy and fundamental rights and freedoms of individuals for the transfer of the Data by the Customer to the Supplier;
Confidential Information	means all information relating to the trade secrets, operations, processes, plans, intentions, product information, know-how, designs, market opportunities, transactions, affairs and/or business of the other party and/or to its customers, suppliers, clients, holding companies and/or subsidiaries, and the terms of this agreement;
Data	means any personal data (as defined by the Data Protection Act 1998) processed by the Supplier as a result of, or in connection with, the provision of the Services;
Fee	means the fees to be paid by the Customer to the Supplier for the provision of the Services as set out in Schedule 2;
Intellectual Property Rights	means copyright, database right, patents, registered and unregistered design rights, registered and unregistered trade marks, semiconductor topography rights and all other industrial, commercial or intellectual property rights existing in any jurisdiction and all rights to apply for the same; and
Services	means the services to be provided by the Supplier as set out in Schedule 1.

1.2 In this agreement:

    1.2.1 clause headings are included for convenience only and will not affect the construction of the agreement; and

    1.2.2 words denoting the singular will include the plural and vice versa.

2 Services

The Supplier agrees to provide the Services in accordance with the terms of this agreement and, in any event, in an efficient and professional manner using all reasonable skill, care and diligence.

3 Payment

In consideration of the provision of the Services, the Customer will pay the Fee to the Supplier in accordance with the payment structure set out in Schedule 2.

4 **Intellectual property**

4.1 All Intellectual Property Rights in any materials provided by the Customer for the purposes of the provision of the Services will be and remain the property of the Customer. The Customer hereby grants to the Supplier a non-exclusive licence for the duration of this agreement to use such materials solely for the purposes of providing the Services. The Supplier may not disclose or sub-license the use of such materials without the Customer's prior written consent.

4.2 All Intellectual Property Rights arising as a result of, or in connection with, the provision of the Services (with the exception of those Intellectual Property Rights arising in any of the software, programming tools, skills and techniques developed and used by the Supplier in the provision of the Services) will be and remain the property of the Customer.

5 **Warranties**

5.1 The Customer warrants and undertakes:

5.1.1 that the processing including the transfer itself of the Data by it has been and will continue to be carried out in accordance with the requirements and relevant provisions of the data protection laws applicable in the United Kingdom and does not violate any such provisions;

5.1.2 that it has instructed the Supplier to process the Data transferred only on its behalf and in accordance with the data protection laws applicable in the United Kingdom and this agreement;

5.1.3 that it will ensure compliance with any technical and organisational security measures imposed on the Supplier;

5.1.4 that, if the transfer involves sensitive personal data (as defined by the Data Protection Act 1998), the relevant individuals have been informed or will be informed before the transfer that their data could be transmitted to a third country not providing adequate protection;

5.1.5 to inform the Information Commissioner of any change in the legislation applicable to the Supplier which is likely to have a substantial adverse effect on the warranties and obligations provided by the Clauses if the Customer decides to continue the transfer or lift its suspension; and

5.1.6 to make available to the individuals to whom the Data relate upon request a copy of the Clauses.

5.2 The Supplier warrants and undertakes:

5.2.1 that the provision of the Services will not infringe the Intellectual Property Rights of any third party;

5.2.2 to process the Data only on behalf of the Customer and in accordance with its instructions and this agreement and that in the event it could not provide such compliance for whatever reasons, it agrees to inform the Customer of that, in which case the Customer is entitled to suspend the transfer of Data and/or terminate this agreement;

5.2.3 that it has no reason to believe that the legislation applicable to it prevents it from fulfilling the instructions received from the Customer and its obligations under this agreement and that in the event of a change in this legislation which is likely to have a substantial adverse effect on the warranties and obligations provided by the Clauses, it will notify the change to the Customer as soon as it is aware, in which case the Customer is entitled to suspend the transfer of the Data and/or terminate this agreement;

5.2.4 that it has in place, and will maintain throughout the term of this agreement, appropriate technical and organisational measures against accidental or unauthorised destruction, loss, alteration or disclosure of the Data, and adequate security programs and procedures to ensure that unauthorised persons will not have access to any equipment used to process the Data;

5.2.5 that it will use the Data transferred solely for the provision of the Services on behalf of the Customer and that it will not disclose the Data transferred to third parties unless the Customer has given prior written authorisation and the third party has entered into the same obligations than the Supplier;

5.2.6 that it will immediately notify the Customer about any request of disclosure of the Data transferred from a public body that could eventually force it to disclose the Data, unless such notification is forbidden by law as well as any disclosure or accidental or unauthorised access made by an employee, sub-contractor or any other identified person as well as the known facts as regards the above mentioned disclosure or use;

5.2.7 that it will immediately notify the Customer about any requests received directly from the individuals to whom the Data relate acknowledging that it is not authorised to respond unless the Customer has explicitly authorised that action or a competent authority has declared that the Customer is unable to respond to requests from those individuals;

5.2.8 to deal promptly and properly with all inquiries from the Customer relating to processing of the Data subject to the transfer and to co-operate with the Information Commissioner in the course of all its enquiries and abide by the advice of the Information Commissioner with regard to the processing of the Data transferred;

5.2.9 at the request of the Customer to submit its data processing facilities for audit which will be carried out by the Customer or an inspection body composed of independent members and in possession of the required professional qualifications bound by a duty of confidentiality, selected by the Customer, where applicable, in agreement with the Information Commissioner; and

5.2.10 to make available to the individuals to whom the Data relate a copy of the Clauses upon request in those cases where those individuals are unable to obtain a copy from the Customer and indicate the Customer's office which handles complaints.

6 **Indemnity**

6.1 Each party to this agreement will indemnify the other against all losses, liabilities, damages, claims, costs (including legal and other professional costs) and expenses which the other may suffer or incur arising out of or in connection with the failure of the indemnifying party to comply with any of its obligations under this agreement.

6.2 The parties agree that an individual who has suffered damage as a result of any violation of the Clauses, committed by the Customer or the Supplier, is entitled to receive compensation from the Customer for the damage suffered.

6.3 The parties agree that the Supplier can also be considered liable for damages caused to the individuals to whom the Data relate in those cases where the Customer has disappeared or has ceased to exist in law or become insolvent and the Supplier has violated some of its obligations under this agreement.

6.4 Except in relation to claims made in connection with this agreement for death or personal injury caused by any negligent act or omission or wilful misconduct, each party's liability to the other in respect of any individual claim for breach of contract, negligence, breach of statutory duty or otherwise in relation to this agreement will be limited to the sum of [£ Insert amount] and in respect of the aggregate of any such claims to [£ Insert amount] in any calendar year.

7 **Co-operation with the Information Commissioner**

The parties agree that the Information Commissioner has the right to audit the Supplier on the same terms as, and with the same power the Information Commissioner would have in relation to the Customer under the data protection laws applicable in the United Kingdom.

8 **Confidentiality**

8.1 Each party will:

8.1.1 keep all Confidential Information strictly confidential;

8.1.2 not disclose any Confidential Information to a third party, other than to such of its employees as will of necessity acquire it as a consequence of the performance of that party's obligations under this agreement (in which case the relevant party will ensure that such employees will keep such Confidential Information confidential and will not use any of it for any purpose or disclose it to any person, firm or company other than those for which or to whom that party may lawfully use or disclose it under this agreement); and

8.1.3 use Confidential Information only in connection with the proper performance of this agreement.

8.2 Clause 8.1 will not apply to any Confidential Information to the extent that it:

8.2.1 comes within the public domain other than through breach of clause 8.1;

8.2.2 is required or requested to be divulged by any court, tribunal or governmental authority with competent jurisdiction; or

    8.2.3 is disclosed on a confidential basis for the purposes of obtaining professional advice.

8.3   This clause will continue in force after and despite the expiry of this agreement.

9 Termination

9.1   Either party may terminate this agreement at any time by giving to the other [3] months' written notice.

9.2   Either party may terminate this agreement at any time by giving written notice to the other party if the other party:

    9.2.1 commits a material breach of any of the terms of this agreement and, where such a breach is capable of remedy, fails to remedy the same within [14] days after receipt of a written notice from the other requiring it to be remedied; or

    9.2.2 is unable to pay its debts when they fall due; or

    9.2.3 takes, or there is taken in respect of the other, any step, action, application or proceeding in relation to the whole or any material part of its undertaking for a voluntary arrangement or composition or reconstruction of its debts, or winding up, dissolution, administration or receivership (administrative or otherwise).

9.3   Upon termination of this agreement for whatever cause, the Supplier will return to the Customer or destroy upon the Customer's request any copy of the Data in hard copy and/or electronic form.

10 Notices

Any notice under this agreement will be in writing and delivered by personal delivery, express courier, confirmed facsimile, confirmed e-mail or certified or registered mail, return receipt requested, and will be deemed given upon personal delivery, one (1) day after deposit with express courier, upon confirmation of receipt of facsimile or e-mail or five (5) days after deposit in the mail. Notices will be sent to a party at its registered address or such other address as that party may specify in writing pursuant to this clause.

11 Jurisdiction

This agreement will be construed in accordance with and governed by the laws of England and each party agrees to submit to the exclusive jurisdiction of the English courts.

12 General

12.1   Nothing in this agreement will be construed so as to create a partnership, joint venture or agency relationship between the parties.

12.2   This agreement embodies the whole agreement of the parties with respect to its subject matter and, once signed by both parties, supersedes all prior agreements, negotiations, representations, and proposals, written or oral, relating to its subject matter.

12.3   In the event that any of the provisions of this agreement are held to be unenforceable by a court or arbitrator, the remaining portions of the agreement will remain in full force and effect.

12.4 Neither party will assign or transfer or purport to assign or transfer all or any of its rights or obligations contained in this agreement without the prior written consent of the other or as expressly permitted pursuant to this agreement.

12.5 Any delay in or failure of performance by either party under this agreement will not be considered a breach of this agreement and will be excused to the extent caused by any occurrence beyond the reasonable control of such party including, but not limited to, acts of God, power outages and governmental restrictions.

Signed by the parties on the date of this agreement.

Schedule 1

Services

[Insert a comprehensive description of all of the data processing services to be provided by the Supplier.]

Schedule 2

Fee and payment

[Insert all fees to be paid by the Customer and a description of the payment structure.]

Explanatory notes

On 27 December 2001, the European Commission adopted a Decision[2] setting out standard contractual clauses for the transfer of personal data to data processors established in non-European Union countries that are not recognised as offering an adequate level of data protection. Although the use of the standard clauses is just one of the options available to organisations wishing to transfer data overseas, the Decision offers those organisations a straightforward means of complying with their obligation to ensure 'adequate protection' for personal data transferred to countries outside the European Union.

This precedent is a full agreement which deals with the provision of data processing services by a supplier based overseas. It includes the relevant clauses approved by the European Commission and therefore, can be used to legitimise transfers to data processors located in countries or territories without adequate data protection laws.

2   Commission Decision (ECSC) 2002/16/EC.

Precedent 7

Standard contractual clauses for transfers of personal data outside the European Economic Area[1]

Definitions

'Personal data', *'special categories of data'*, *'process/processing'*, *'controller'*, *'processor'*, *'Data Subject'* and *'Supervisory Authority'* shall have the same meaning as in Council Directive 95/46/EC of 24 October 1995 on the protection of individuals with regard to the processing of personal data and on the free movement of such data ('the Directive').

'Clauses' mean the data protection clauses inserted in this agreement for the purpose of allowing transfers of personal data in accordance with the Directive.

Obligations of the [Business]

The [Business] agrees and warrants:

(a)   that the processing, including the transfer itself, of the personal data by him has been and, up to the moment of the transfer, will continue to be carried out in accordance with all the relevant provisions of the member state in which the [Business] is established (and where applicable has been notified to the relevant Authorities of that state) and does not violate the relevant provisions of that state;

(b)   that if the transfer involves special categories of Data the Data Subject has been informed or will be informed before the transfer that his data could be transmitted to a third country not providing adequate protection;

---

1   Ie the member states of the European Union plus Norway, Iceland and Liechtenstein.

(c) to make available to the Data Subjects upon request a copy of the Clauses; and

(d) to respond in a reasonable time and to the extent reasonably possible to inquiries from the Supervisory Authority on the processing of the relevant personal data by the [Recipient] and to any enquiries from the Data Subject concerning the processing of his personal data by the [Recipient].

Obligations of the [Recipient]

The [Recipient] agrees and warrants:

(a) that he has no reason to believe that the legislation applicable to him prevents him from fulfilling his obligations under the contract and that in the event of a change in that legislation which is likely to have a substantial adverse effect on the guarantees provided by the Clauses, he will notify the change to the [Business] and to the Supervisory Authority where the [Business] is established, in which case the [Business] is entitled to suspend the transfer of data and/or terminate the contract;

(b) to process the personal data in accordance with the Mandatory Data Protection Principles set out in the Appendix;

(c) to deal promptly and properly with all reasonable inquiries from the [Business] or the Data Subject relating to his processing of the personal data subject to the transfer and to co-operate with the competent Supervisory Authority in the course of all its inquiries and abide by the advice of the Supervisory Authority with regard to the processing of the data transferred;

(d) at the request of the [Business] to submit its data processing facilities for audit which shall be carried out by the [Business] or an inspection body composed of independent members and in possession of the required professional qualifications, selected by the [Business], where applicable, in agreement with the Supervisory Authority;

(e) to make available to the Data Subject upon request a copy of the Clauses and indicate the office which handles complaints.

Liability

(a) The Parties agree that a Data Subject who has suffered damage as a result of any violation of the provisions of the Clauses is entitled to receive compensation from the parties for the damage suffered. The Parties agree that they may be exempted from this liability only if they prove that neither of them is responsible for the violation of those provisions.

(b) The [Business] and the [Recipient] agree that they will be jointly and severally liable for damage to the Data Subject resulting from any violation referred to in paragraph (a). In the event of such a violation, the Data Subject may bring an action before a court against either the [Business] or the [Recipient] or both.

Co-operation with Supervisory Authorities

The parties agree to deposit a copy of this contract with the Supervisory Authority if it so requests or if such deposit is required under national law.

Termination of the Clauses

The parties agree that the termination of the Clauses at any time, in any circumstances and for whatever reason does not exempt them from the obligations and/or conditions under the Clauses as regards the processing of the data transferred.

Appendix

These data protection principles should be read and interpreted in the light of the provisions (principles and relevant exceptions) of Council Directive 95/46/EC.

They shall apply subject to the mandatory requirements of the national legislation applicable to the [Recipient] which do not go beyond what is necessary in a democratic society on the basis of one of the interests listed in article 13(1) of Council Directive 95/46/EC, that is, if they constitute a necessary measure to safeguard national security, defence, public security, the prevention, investigation, detection and prosecution of criminal offences or of breaches of ethics for the regulated professions, an important economic or financial interest of the state or the protection of the Data Subject or the rights and freedoms of others.

Purpose limitation

Data must be processed and subsequently used or further communicated only for the purposes of performing the obligations and exercising the rights specifically set out in the agreement. Data must not be kept longer than necessary for the purposes for which they are transferred.

Data quality and proportionality

Data must be accurate and, where necessary, kept up to date. The data must be adequate, relevant and not excessive in relation to the purposes for which they are transferred and further processed.

Transparency

Data Subjects must be provided with information as to the purposes of the processing and the identity of the data controller in the third country, and other information in so far as this is necessary to ensure fair processing, unless such information has already been given by the [Business].

Security and confidentiality

Technical and organisational security measures must be taken by the data controller that are appropriate to the risks, such as unauthorised access, presented by the processing. Any person acting under the authority of the data controller, including a processor, must not process the data except on instructions from the controller.

Rights of access, rectification, erasure and blocking of data

As provided for in article 12 of Council Directive 95/46/EC, the Data Subject must have a right of access to all data relating to him that are processed and, as appropriate, the right to the rectification, erasure or blocking of data the processing of which does not comply with the principles set out in this Appendix, in particular because the data are incomplete or inaccurate.

He should also be able to object to the processing of the data relating to him on compelling legitimate grounds relating to his particular situation.

Restrictions on onward transfers

Further transfers of personal data from the [Recipient] to another controller established in a third country not providing adequate protection or not covered by a Decision adopted by the European Commission pursuant to article 25(6) of Council Directive 95/46/EC (onward transfer) may take place only if either:

(a) Data Subjects have, in the case of special categories of data, given their unambiguous consent to the onward transfer or, in other cases, have been given the opportunity to object.

The minimum information to be provided to Data Subjects must contain in a language understandable to them:

- the purposes of the onward transfer,

- the identification of the [Business] established in the European Community,

- the categories of further recipients of the data and the countries of destination, and

- an explanation that, after the onward transfer, the data may be processed by a controller established in a country where there is not an adequate level of protection of the privacy of individuals,

or

(b) the [Business] and the [Recipient] agree to the adherence to the Clauses of another controller which thereby becomes a party to the Clauses and assumes the same obligations as the [Recipient].

Special categories of data

Where data revealing racial or ethnic origin, political opinions, religious or philosophical beliefs or trades union memberships and data concerning health or sex life and data relating to offences, criminal convictions or security measures are processed, additional safeguards should be in place within the meaning of Council Directive 95/46/EC, in particular, appropriate security measures such as strong encryption for transmission or such as keeping a record of access to sensitive data.

Direct marketing

Where data are processed for the purposes of direct marketing, effective procedures should exist allowing the Data Subject at any time to 'opt-out' from having his data used for such purposes.

Automated individual decisions

Data Subjects are entitled not to be subject to a decision which is based solely on automated processing of data, unless other measures are taken to safeguard the individual's legitimate interests as provided for in article 15(2) of Council Directive 95/46/EC. Where the purpose of the transfer is the taking of an automated decision as referred to in article 15 of Council Directive 95/46/EC, which produces legal effects concerning the individual or significantly affects him and which is based solely on automated processing of data intended to evaluate certain personal aspects relating to him, such as his performance at work, creditworthiness, reliability, conduct, etc, the individual should have the right to know the reasoning for this Decision.

Explanatory notes

On 15 June 2001, the European Commission adopted a Decision setting out standard contractual clauses ensuring adequate safeguards for personal data transferred from the European Union to countries outside the European Union. This Decision obliges member states to recognise that companies or organisations using these standard clauses in contracts concerning personal data transfers to countries outside the European Union are offering 'adequate protection' to the data.

This precedent mirrors the standard clauses approved by the European Commission and can be used as part of a suitable agreement drawn up in accordance with English law.

Precedent 8

Standard contractual clauses for transfers of personal data to a signatory of the United States 'Safe Harbor' programme

Definitions

Safe Harbor Principles means the set of principles and frequently asked questions and answers issued by the United States Department of Commerce on 21 July 2000 as approved by the European Commission in exercise of the powers conferred on it by article 25.6 of the Data Protection Directive (95/46/EC) regarding the transfer of personal data to countries outside the European Economic Area[1] as may be varied from time to time.

Transferred Data means any personal data (as defined by the Data Protection Act 1998) transferred by the [Name of the business] to [Name of the recipient].

Warranty of the data exporter

[Name of the business] warrants and undertakes that the processing (as defined by the Data Protection Act 1998), including the transfer itself, of the Transferred Data by it has been, and will continue to be, carried out in accordance with all the relevant provisions of the data protection laws applicable in the United Kingdom.

---

1   Ie the member states of the European Union plus Norway, Iceland and Liechtenstein.

Warranty of the recipient

[Name of the recipient] warrants and undertakes that it has, and will continue to have, full legal authority to process the Transferred Data and that it will only process the Transferred Data strictly in accordance with the Safe Harbor Principles.

Indemnity

[Name of the recipient] will indemnify [Name of the business] against all losses, liabilities, damages, claims, costs (including legal and other professional costs) and expenses which [Name of the business] may suffer or incur arising out of, or in connection with, the failure of [Name of the recipient] to comply with the warranty set out in [Safe Harbor warranty clause].

Explanatory notes

On 26 July 2000, the European Commission adopted a Decision on the adequacy of the protection provided by the Safe Harbor principles issued by the United States Department of Commerce on 21 July 2000 regarding the international transfer of personal data to organisations established in the United States.

This precedent includes specific clauses (ie mutual warranties and an indemnity by the recipient in the event of breach of its warranty) for use in contracts involving the transfer of personal data to signatories of the so-called Safe Harbor programme.

Precedent 9

Notice and disclaimer for e-mail footer

This e-mail and the information it contains are confidential. If you have received this e-mail in error please notify the sender immediately. You should not copy it for any purpose, or disclose its contents to any other person.

[Name of the business] cannot accept any responsibility for the accuracy or completeness of the contents of this e-mail as it has been transmitted over a public network and Internet communications are not secure.

All statements made in this e-mail are subject to contract. The contents are not to be regarded as a contractual offer or acceptance. The sender is not authorised to bind [Name of the business] contractually.

[Name of the business] is a limited company registered in England under company number [Company Registration No] whose registered office is at [Registered address of the business].

Explanatory notes

The aim of this precedent is threefold:

- To minimise the potential liability arising from the accidental or unauthorised destruction, loss, alteration or disclosure of information (including personal data) included in or attached to an e-mail.

- To avoid a situation where a business becomes contractually bound as a result of statements made by the person sending the e-mail.

- Bearing in mind that a corporate e-mail amounts to a written business communication, to include the same information that companies are required to provide in their notepaper and faxes under the Business Names Act 1985 and the Companies Act 1985 (ie place of registration, company registration number and registered address).

Precedent 10

Employee code of conduct for the use of communications

1 **Introduction**

1.1 E-mail facilities, Internet access and the telephone are provided by [Name of the business] for business use to enable you to perform efficiently and communicate effectively.

1.2 You may have the opportunity to use the Internet not only for sending and receiving electronic mail externally, but also for accessing the World Wide Web, newsgroups and other facilities on the Internet. This code of conduct explains how these facilities should be used. These rules should be observed at all times and any breach of them will be regarded as a disciplinary matter. This code of conduct also deals with permitted use of [Name of the business]'s telephones and informs you of any permitted monitoring that may be carried out.

1.3 The reasons for introducing this code of conduct are to ensure that:

1.3.1 you make efficient and proper use of the facilities;

1.3.2 you do not put [Name of the business]'s computer systems at risk;

1.3.3 [Name of the business] is protected from external intrusion;

1.3.4 the image and reputation of [Name of the business] is properly protected;

1.3.5 you are aware of what constitutes abuse of these facilities.

1.4 This code of conduct will be reviewed and updated.

2 **Electronic mail**

2.1 Where you have access to Internet e-mail facilities, these should be used by you to send and receive messages and attached documents related to work.

2.2 [The policy on personal e-mail is that e-mail facilities may only be used for a reasonable level of personal use, which should never interfere with your work.] [The policy on personal e-mail is that e-mail facilities may only be used by you out of work hours (for example, prior to commencing work, after work or during a lunch break), so long as this does not effect your ability to carry out your work.] [The policy on personal e-mail is that e-mail facilities may only be used for the occasional e-mail of an urgent nature.] [Personal e-mails are not permitted.]

2.3 You should also be aware that the Internet is not a secure network and so it is possible for others to read e-mails as they pass through it.

2.4 E-mail messages are an increasing source of viruses, particularly viruses sitting within attached documents. If you think that you have been sent a document that contains a virus, you should contact the IT department <u>immediately</u>. You must not open any suspect mail or attachments.

2.5 E-mail messages are classified as legal documents. If you are sending e-mail (the content of which may at some time be used as evidence), you should ensure that you have saved a copy of the e-mail, electronically or on paper.

2.6 As with any document, when composing and sending e-mail, you must consider whether you are likely to cause offence, to enter into a contract (intentionally or otherwise), or to commit to any action. With e-mail messages often being drafted and sent more quickly than letters and faxes, these considerations become more vital. E-mail correspondence should be drafted with the same care and attention as all other normal correspondence.

2.7 Inappropriate use of e-mail may lead to legal action against [Name of the business] and to personal liability for you. In communicating with anyone via e-mail you should not make or forward any statement which could be construed as:

    2.7.1 defamatory;

    2.7.2 sexist or racist in nature;

    2.7.3 a derogatory remark or comment, whether about an individual or a generalisation, relating to disability, religious or cultural beliefs of others;

    2.7.4 for criminal purposes; or

    2.7.5 being of an offensive or obscene nature.

2.8 Client or customer information may only be sent with the express approval of the client or customer. Information which is sensitive to [Name of the business] or its clients or customers may not be sent by e-mail.

3 **The Internet**

3.1 If you have access to the Internet this is to be used in a manner which is consistent with and appropriate to professional business conduct. In particular, accessing or importing any of the following material is strictly forbidden and doing so will be regarded as a disciplinary matter and may lead to dismissal.

3.2 Prohibited material:

    3.2.1 games;

    3.2.2 pornographic, obscene or other sexually explicit material;

    3.2.3 information which is or could reasonably be construed as indecent or offensive;

    3.2.4 illegal material or material for a criminal purpose;

    3.2.5 material intended or likely to incite racial hatred;

    3.2.6 material to gain unauthorised access to or for the corruption of the systems, data, networks or computer equipment of [Name of the business] or other individuals and organisations; and

    3.2.7 gambling or soliciting for personal gain or profit.

3.3 [Personal use of the Internet is permitted but only within reason, so long as this does not effect your ability to carry out your work.] [Personal use of the Internet is permitted but only outside of work hours (for example, prior to commencing work, after work or during a lunch break).] [The Internet must only be used for legitimate business purposes and, therefore, personal use of the Internet is not permitted.]

3.4 The Internet must not be used for downloading software without documented authorisation from the IT department.

3.5 These guidelines apply at all times, not only during working hours.

4 **Telephones**

4.1 [Name of the business]'s provides telephones for its business. You may use [Name of the business]'s telephones for a reasonable level of short personal calls. The following may result in disciplinary action and you being charged for:

    4.1.1 long telephone conversations (over [5] minutes) except in exceptional circumstances. If you think you may need to make an urgent long telephone call you should seek permission first;

    4.1.2 continued excessive use of the [Name of the business]'s telephones even for short calls;

    4.1.3 overseas calls, other than for [Name of the business]'s business;

    4.1.4 calls to premium rate numbers.

4.2 Customers, suppliers and other contacts expect to be able to contact [Name of the business] easily and so the telephone lines should be kept clear for business calls. Personal calls should therefore be kept to a minimum.

5 **Security**

5.1 You are responsible for the security of your terminal and must not allow the terminal to be used by an unauthorised person.

5.2 You should keep your passwords confidential and change them regularly. When leaving your terminal unattended or on leaving the office, you should ensure that you log off the system to prevent unauthorised users using your terminal in your absence.

6   **Monitoring**

6.1   [Name of the business] may monitor your use of e-mail facilities, the Internet and telephone calls to:

6.1.1   ensure that you comply with [Name of the business]'s practices and procedures (including but not limited to this code of conduct);

6.1.2   ensure that you achieve acceptable standards in relation to the performance of your duties and observance of [Name of the business]'s code of conduct;

6.1.3   prevent or detect crime,

6.1.4   investigate or detect the unauthorised use of [Name of the business]'s Internet and e-mail system (as set out in this code of conduct or as prescribed by law);

6.1.5   ensure the effective operation of the Internet and e-mail systems (for example, virus checking).

6.2   [Name of the business] uses web 'traffic monitoring' software which tracks the sites and pages visited, the time of day sites are visited and the length of stay at sites. This system is used to analyse the sites people use to assist in planning for providing additional services. The system will also be used to identify or detect unauthorised or excessive use of the Internet.

6.3   E-mail traffic will also be randomly monitored. However, if it appears to [Name of the business] that e-mail facilities are being abused or used inappropriately it may monitor e-mail traffic more specifically, which may include opening any e-mails sent or received to assess their content.

7   **General**

7.1   You are bound by this code of conduct and breaches of the code of conduct will be treated as misconduct, and will be dealt with within the framework of [Name of the business]'s disciplinary policy. The level of misconduct will be dependent upon the severity or persistence of the breach. For the avoidance of doubt, any activities, which are identified in this code of conduct as prohibited, will be treated as misconduct. If you have a grievance associated with the use of the Internet or e-mail you should refer to the [Name of the business]'s grievance policy for guidance on how to handle your grievance.

7.2   If you have any questions about this code of conduct or do not understand any part of it, you should contact the IT department.

Explanatory notes

Since the early 1990s, employment tribunals and courts have found themselves dealing with many new types of claims relating to the increased use of technology in the workplace. A number of decisions have made it clear that the monitoring of communications will only be lawful where employees are made aware of:

- the fact that their employers monitor their communications;

- the reasons for such monitoring; and

- the extent of the monitoring.

Unless such steps are taken, employees may be able to claim constructive dismissal by arguing that their employer's surveillance systems are a breach of their right to privacy. If an employer dismisses an employee for unauthorised or inappropriate use of a telecommunications system, the dismissal is likely to be unfair, unless the above guidance has been followed.

This precedent is aimed at setting out the authorised and restricted uses of all means of communications available to employees, such as e-mail, the Internet and the telephone. Needless to say, employers adopting a code of conduct for the use of communications must ensure that all employees are at least aware of its content. Employers are also advised to insert a clause requiring informed consent to the code of conduct in all contracts of employment.

Precedent 11

Variation to employment contract regarding the code of conduct for the use of communications

[Name of the business] provides you with e-mail facilities, Internet access and the telephone for business use. The attached document is a code of conduct that explains how these facilities should be used.

The attached document forms part of your conditions of employment. Please ensure that you read the code thoroughly and understand your responsibilities in relation to the use of telephone and e-mail facilities and Internet access provided by [Name of the business].

Would you please sign and date this note and return it to [the Human Resources Department] to show your agreement to the code of conduct for the use of communications. If you have any queries about the code, please contact [the Human Resources Department].

I confirm that I have read [Name of the business]'s code of conduct for the use of communications and agree to abide by it.

Signed: . . . .

Name: . . . .

Date: . . . .

Explanatory notes

This precedent should be used as a covering note when disseminating the code of conduct for the use of communications. By obtaining employees' informed and explicit consent to be contractually bound by the code of conduct for the use of communications, businesses will be in a stronger position to enforce the provisions of the code.

Precedent 12

Communication regarding updates to the Privacy Policy

Subject: Your privacy matters to us

We take your privacy rights very seriously and as a current user of our services, we are writing to remind you of our data processing practices.

Our Privacy Policy explains in detail how we use your information. We have recently made some changes to our Privacy Policy and as part of our commitment to protect your privacy we would like you to be fully informed of those changes.

Our Privacy Policy is available at: [Link to Privacy Policy URL]

We also want to ensure that we can send you promotional e-mails if you want to receive them. From [Date] we will only be able to do that if you specifically say so. Therefore, if you are happy to receive promotional e-mails from us, simply click on the link below and tick the appropriate box.

[Link to opt-in URL]

If you prefer not to receive any such e-mails or have already told us that, then you do not need to do anything.

If you have any queries or comments about this e-mail or our Privacy Policy, please e-mail them to us at [E-mail link].

Explanatory notes

In order to comply with the fair processing obligation set out in Principle 1 of the Data Protection Act 1998, it is important that data controllers keep individuals informed of any changes affecting the way in which those individuals' personal data are used. This precedent is aimed at alerting website users to those changes.

If the data controller relies on the individual's consent to process his or her data and the changes to the data processing practices are substantial enough to consider that the individual's previous consent will not reasonably cover the new processing, data controllers must not only inform, but also renew the consent. However, unless the processing involves sensitive personal data and explicit consent is required, data controllers will be able to imply consent from the individual's actions (for example, an individual who has been notified of the changes continues to use the website).

In any event, once the Electronic Communications Data Protection Directive[1] is implemented, the use of e-mail and SMS for direct marketing purposes will only be allowed on an opt-in basis (ie with the recipient's permission), except for promotional e-mails or SMS messages concerning a business' own products and services which are similar to those purchased by the recipient in the past. Given that this provision will apply retrospectively, data controllers should also be seeking to obtain positive consent from existing customers and contacts in order to e-mail or text promotional information to them.

This precedent is also aimed at seeking consent to send unsolicited promotional communications by e-mail in accordance with the Electronic Communications Data Protection Directive.

---

1   Directive on the Processing of Personal Data and the Protection of Privacy in the Electronic Communications Sector, Council Directive 2002/58/EC.

Precedent 13

Standard data protection warranties for corporate transactions

Seller warrants that:

1   [Seller] is fully compliant with all applicable data protection laws and has taken all necessary steps to achieve compliance with the Data Protection Act 1998, including (without limitation):

    1.1   informing data subjects of the identity of the data controller, its nominated representative, the uses made of the data and any potential disclosures and obtaining their consent (if necessary) in connection with the processing of personal data;

    1.2   having in place appropriate technical and organisational measures against the accidental or unauthorised destruction, loss, alteration or disclosure of personal data and procedures to ensure that unauthorised persons do not have access to any equipment used to process such data; and

    1.3   having in place appropriate systems to identify which individuals have instructed [Seller] that they do not wish to receive marketing information and comply with such instructions.

2   No individual has claimed, and no grounds exist for any individual to claim compensation from [Seller] under the applicable data protection legislation for loss or unauthorised disclosure of data or for any contravention of any of the requirements of the Data Protection Act 1998.

3   [Seller] has not received a notice or allegation from either the Information Commissioner or a data subject alleging non-compliance with the data protection principles or any other provisions of the applicable data protection legislation, or prohibiting the transfer of data to a country or territory outside the United Kingdom or the European Economic Area.[1]

1   Ie the member states of the European Union plus Norway, Iceland and Liechtenstein.

Explanatory notes

Corporate transactions, such as mergers or acquisitions, are common among on-line businesses. This precedent is aimed at protecting the buyer of an on-line business from any liabilities which may arise as a result of a breach of the Data Protection Act by that business ('the Target').

The first clause focuses on three key aspects of data protection compliance as follows:

1   The provision of information by the data controller to the individual concerning the uses made of the data and to whom they may be disclosed is one of the key obligations of the Data Protection Act 1998. It is therefore important for the buyer to know whether the seller has taken any steps to comply with this obligation.

2   From a practical point of view, one of the main obligations under the Data Protection Act 1998 concerns protecting the confidentiality of the data, and therefore the adoption of appropriate technical and organisational security measures is key.

3   Given that the Data Protection Act 1998 puts great emphasis on giving rights to individuals, in particular the right to opt out of receiving direct marketing communications, it is essential to ensure that there are appropriate systems in place to respect the individuals' right not to receive such communications.

This second clause is important because a compensation claim could have a material effect on the overall value of the transaction.

Finally, when acting for the buyer, it is obviously important that the due diligence process investigates fully the data processing activities of the Target and, in particular, whether it has received any notice or allegation of non-compliance with the Data Protection Act 1998, either from an individual or from the Information Commissioner. If the Target has received notice of a breach, it may expose the buyer to a liability in the form of a fine, as well as possible bad publicity and the unenviable task of overhauling its data protection activities in order to satisfy the Information Commissioner, which may involve considerable time and expense.

Index